TO PASS ON A GOOD EARTH

TO PASS ON A GOOD EARTH

The Life and Work of Carl O. Sauer

MICHAEL WILLIAMS

With David Lowenthal and William M. Denevan

University of Virginia Press | Charlottesville and London

University of Virginia Press
© 2014 by the Rector and Visitors of the University of Virginia
All rights reserved
Printed in the United States of America on acid-free paper

First published 2014
1 3 5 7 9 8 6 4 2

Library of Congress Cataloging-in-Publication Data
Williams, Michael, 1935–2009
To pass on a good earth : the life and work of Carl O. Sauer /
Michael Williams with David Lowenthal
and William M. Denevan.
pages   cm
Includes bibliographical references and index.
ISBN 978-0-8139-3566-9 (cloth : alk. paper)
ISBN 978-0-8139-3577-5 (e-book)
1. Sauer, Carl Ortwin, 1889–1975. 2. Geographers—
United States—Biography. 3. Geography.
4. Human geography. I. Title.
G69.S29W55 2014
910.92 — dc23
[B]
2013035018

[CONTENTS]

Carl Sauer was my charismatic teacher. Michael Williams, steeped in the Sauer tradition, was my longtime friend and colleague.[1] Much of this biography came into being during Michael and Eleanore's several tenures in my Berkeley home, a scant stone's throw from Sauer's, and an easy walk from the University of California campus, where Sauer was for more than half a century a guiding beacon.

To introduce this substantive life of America's most eminent geographer, crafted by a scholar of great distinction, is a task alike painful and chastening. Painful because both subject and author are no longer with us, and compeers are nowhere in sight. Chastening because Sauer's mental universe, never confined by disciplinary boundaries, is already hard to convey to an audience today, just two generations beyond his seminal work and influence. The very existence of a polymath like Sauer, whose intellectual curiosity and drive embraced every epoch and every aspect of the ever-changing interplay between humans and their earthly home, is now almost impossible to imagine and virtually inconceivable in modern academe.[2]

In this book, Michael Williams shows how a midwestern son of German immigrants married New World pragmatic know-how with Old World historical and scientific insights to become the acknowledged champion of a humanistic synthesis, in his own and in his disciples' work, that illuminated myriad mysteries of human occupance, conquest, cultivation, and often ruination of the fruitful earth. Building on profoundly ecological insights, Sauer and his students explored the domestication of plants and animals; the transformation of prairie, rainforest, and savanna into cropland and pasture; and the traditional legends and cultural dreams that fueled settlement and prosperity but also triggered the abandonment and degradation of much of the globe. In so doing, Sauerians uniquely brought to bear insights from anthropology and history, geology and soil science, and agriculture and architecture, thereby promoting collaborative inquiry among scholars and sojourners of every stripe.

Yet the success of Sauer's approach, along with its continuing vitality for many, was far from unalloyed. Indeed, Sauer's life history was as much intellectual tragedy as victory, since many of the views he espoused were increasingly rejected in the postwar climate of culture-blind pontifical do-goodism. Sauer's devotion to research untrammeled by social engineering; his growing dismay at the ahistorical scientistic assumptions of social scientists, coupled with their ignorance of the fundamentals of natural science; his continued insistence that ideas were best fostered by investment in individual scholars and personal partnership, rather than in lavish mammoth projects; his prescient yet still unfashionable alarm at the ecological devastation wrought by modern technology, all left him increasingly marginalized and discouraged. Finally, Sauer lived long and wisely enough to become aware that many of the conundrums that had engaged him, many of his bold excursions into arcane realms, needed to be explored with newly developed scientific techniques beyond his own training and expertise.

To Pass On a Good Earth illumines Sauer's extraordinary intellectual career in full understanding of his doubts along with his certitudes, his weaknesses as well as his strengths, his failures along with his successes. Often dyspeptic, Sauer could be famously cantankerous. Intensely devoted to family and colleagues, he could be overbearing or forgetful. Michael Williams gives us a picture of the whole man, and shows how his family background and his personal traits intermesh with the singular qualities that made him one of America's most treasured as well as troubled intellectual pioneers of the twentieth century.

Sauer's magnetic enthusiasms mesmerized not only sober professors but visionary poets and won him the devotion of all those drawn to learn from him, as my own experience will illustrate. Like many other youngsters in the aftermath of the Second World War who had never studied geography before, I was intrigued by the eclectic and innovative work, ranging from the history of plant and animal domestication to the environmental and ecological attitudes of societies past and present the world over, carried on at Berkeley under Sauer's aegis. An added attraction was his active encouragement of students from backgrounds other than geography; indeed, only two of the twenty graduate students in my cohort had majored in that field. Uniquely among American geography departments at the time, Berkeley embraced both scientific and humanistic insights and stressed geography as a bridging perspective rather than a field with some core terrain uniquely its own. While geography elsewhere dwelt chiefly on contemporary issues of economic development, regional planning, urban structure, and social systems, Berkeley's affinities under Sauer were with history, anthropology, and natural science. Sauer took all knowledge as his province, and he propelled his students into every imaginable realm of thought and terrain.

To broaden our intellectual horizons was the first imperative. "Oh, Lowenthal, I see you did history; you'd better get some understanding of soils and plants and animals." So I was shoved into Hans Jenny's marvelous soil science course, and into another on the ecology of flora and fauna. Similarly, students whose background was in natural science would be pitchforked into anthropology and history. All came together for Sauer's own courses and seminars, and for the Thursday afternoon departmental teas where some visitor from an exotic land or scholarly calling, other Berkeley faculty, or a graduate student back from the field would perform and compel critique from each of us.

Sauer's historical geography graduate seminars were famed treats, notorious for scintillating but unpredictable twists and turns. Each week's discussion of some casually chosen topic would lead by uncharted paths to the next, guided only by Sauer's omnivorous curiosity and the ensuing discourse. There were no planned excursions into standard topics, no set assignments, only offhand suggestions of sources to search. But woe betide the student who failed to follow up on those suggestions. On an early occasion, Sauer proposed that we look into Greek and Roman urban morphology, to discern origins and rationales that led to the imperial Roman grid pattern. The following week Sauer filled his pipe, tamped down the tobacco, and asked one of us what he had found. Having read nothing, the student was struck dumb. So too was the hapless next one quizzed. Sauer was silent.

He emptied his pipe, looked at us sweetly, and said, "Well, I guess we'd all better go home." None of us ever forgot that ten-minute dismissal, or failed thereafter to find something of potential interest however seemingly off the mark. For Sauer could shape any quirky knowledge to some provocative and illuminating end.

Let me instance my own experience. One afternoon I came to ask Sauer's advice on my proposed master's thesis, comparing the diverse careers of British, Dutch, French, and Portuguese colonists, and their African slaves and Asian indentured laborers, on South America's Guyanese coast. On that occasion I never got to begin to ask, for Sauer was thinking of something else. He looked at me and said, "You've lived in Connecticut and Massachusetts. What can you tell me about feral deer in New England?" I had never heard of feral deer in New England, but two hours' quizzing yielded an amazing amount of data, folk legend, mental landscaping, and speculative hypotheses dredged from my subconscious and not useless to Sauer. (I also wrote the Guiana thesis, approved by him.)

Graduate research topics were self-generated. Advice was seldom proffered, suggestions seldom made; dissertations were entirely individual. Students were not permitted to embark on the doctorate until adjudged sufficiently mature. For this there were no written criteria; it was a matter of judgment on the say-so of Sauer and his colleagues, John Leighly and James Parsons. Some were found in need of further "seasoning" and sent away for a year or two to another university, or given leave of absence to travel or teach. There was no reason to rush. Completing a dissertation might well require twenty-five years. Indeed, more than one Berkeley geography Ph.D. award nearly coincided with the successful candidate's retirement from academe.

Objections, if felt, were seldom voiced, for all of us were under Sauer's charismatic spell, combining encyclopedic wisdom with questing curiosity and total absorption in speculative inquiry. If we did not share his judgment, if his arbitrary decisions about our worthiness rankled, so be it; the cost was acceptable. The ardent general hope was to come back to paradise at some future date. For those still laboring toward completion, there were teaching posts all around the Bay Area, up the coast to Mendocino or down to Santa Cruz, or in the Central Valley, at Davis or Sacramento or Fresno, while never severing the Berkeley umbilical cord.

In sum, this biography is a testament to a scholarly humanist whose rare qualities of mind and heart made him a cynosure for a host of contemporaries and disciples. Michael Williams has penned a candid and compelling account of the life of Carl Ortwin Sauer, whose own unflinching candor punctured trendy academe in prizing quirky humanity.

David Lowenthal
Berkeley, June 2013

[ACKNOWLEDGMENTS]

Our acknowledgments complement those in Michael Williams's introduction. Among Sauer's many students and disciples, Diana Liverman and Paul Starrs have been particularly helpful and supportive. Diana discussed aspects of the manuscript with Michael when he was writing it. Paul provided penetrating insights on the continuing Sauerian tradition. Ellen FitzSimmons Porzig provided a large file of Sauer family photographs. John Gillis's reading of Williams's text from an environmental historian's purview has been immensely beneficial throughout the whole editorial process.

Staff members at the University of Virginia Press have been uniformly zealous, efficient, prompt, and kindly in shepherding through a book sorely lamed by the death of its author. Press director Penny Kaiserlian was a guardian angel in achieving the publication of the book. The original manuscript, while essentially completed, was more than 650 pages. Through the kind offices especially of Roger Kain, a British Academy grant made possible Kenneth Marotta's astute and empathetic trimming. Mary Alice Lowenthal prepared the manuscript for further work, flagged queries, and assisted with checking the copyediting. With funding from the University of Virginia Press, typist Sharon Ruch in Madison, Wisconsin, assisted with preparation of drafts of the revised manuscript, a considerable task for which we are especially grateful.

David Lowenthal negotiated the University of Virginia publication. He and William Denevan edited the main text, made structural revisions, further condensations, additions where required, and revised and updated the text and endnotes for clarity and accuracy. Denevan compiled the bibliography. We have striven as far as possible to hew to Michael's voice. For the sake of readability, the many quotations from Sauer's boyhood diary and his unpublished correspondence have been edited and are given without ellipses. A copy of Michael's unedited, original manuscript has been placed in the Sauer Papers, Bancroft Library, University of California, Berkeley.

Most of all, we are indebted to Eleanore Williams for far beyond spousal encouragement. She played a vital role in locating and utilizing source materials, translating correspondence from German, and, with Michael, contacting and interviewing scores of Sauer's friends, family, students, and disciples. She has supported our editorial work, helping ensure that this book achieved the appropriate treatment it richly deserved.

David Lowenthal and
William M. Denevan

[INTRODUCTION]

During the summer of 1978 my family and I exchanged houses with an academic family from San Rafael, California, who came to Oxford for Summer School. Early on in our Bay Area sojourn I visited an old friend and fellow Welshman, David Hooson, who was then dean of the Faculty of Arts and Sciences at Berkeley after having been a professor of geography there for nearly two decades. As we reminisced over lunch on the terrace of the Faculty Club the conversation got around to Carl Sauer, who had died some three years earlier, and whom I had never met. "You know," David said, "I've had his professional correspondence cataloged and placed in the Bancroft Library. You should look at it. As a historical geographer you would very probably find it interesting."

Some days later I obtained my reader's card and serendipitously selected Sauer's correspondence with people whom I had known, such as Andrew Clark, Glenn Trewartha, Richard Hartshorne, and H. C. Darby. It was a revelation. Here was a true polymath with ideas on many topics that seemed to jump off the pages, written in a prose that was pithy and memorable. Here was the unmistakable stamp of a remarkable man. I was fascinated, excited, and from that moment on completely hooked on what I read. I warmed to the man and the breadth and intensity of his intellectual concerns, which ranged from pre-Columbian population numbers and the entry of early Americans into the continent to plant domestication, the place of deep time in geography, the question of what was "culture," the exploitation of poorer societies, destruction of the environment, and the role of the individual scholar and scholarship in an increasingly academically bureaucratic age. Most of these topics are live issues, the last three particularly, that have engaged the efforts of environmentalists, development experts, and those with a general concern about the quality of life in an ever-accelerating and complex modern world.

Of the thousands of letters, I decided to concentrate on those that threw light on Sauer's ideas on the role of time in geographical studies, and on the making and implementation of one of the first overtly environmental gatherings—the symposium "Man's Role in Changing the Face of the Earth," held at Princeton in 1955 (subsequently published under the same name).[1] Two articles soon ensued.[2] And there Carl Sauer lay while I pursued other research interests. Then, twenty years after my first encounter with Sauer, I received an invitation to write a biographical entry on him for the *International Encyclopedia of the Social & Behavioral Sciences*.[3] The biographical volume, which comprises 149 entries, ranges from Aristotle to Adorno, Montesquieu to Marx, and Descartes to Darwin, but includes only one geographer—Carl Sauer. My interest in his work was rekindled and widened, and since I was retiring in a few years, the time seemed ripe to think about a full biography of this remarkable man.

In 2000 I went to see Sauer's son, Jonathan, in Los Angeles and spent a pleasant couple of afternoons with him and his wife, Hilda, as they reminisced. Then in 2002, 2003, and 2009 the opportunity came to spend many months in Berkeley working in the Bancroft again and talking with Carl Sauer's daughter, Elizabeth Sauer FitzSimmons. I am grateful to her and her daughters, Margaret Irene FitzSimmons, Ellen Elizabeth FitzSimmons Porzig, and Laura Wightman FitzSimmons, for their hospitality and many kindnesses, especially their generosity in giving me access to Sauer's family correspondence and other material on which so much of this book is based. To have their backing and encouragement meant a lot to me. Others who made the Berkeley visits memorable and pleasant were David Lowenthal and Mary Alice Lowenthal for the loan of their house; David Hooson and Margaret Mackenzie for sustenance, intellectual and otherwise; Betty Parsons and Peggy Woodring; and Winifred (Westher) Hess, Sauer's former student and department secretary, who was a valuable source concerning his working habits. Bill Denevan, a real Sauer buff, provided much information.

It would be invidious to pick out any of the staff of the manuscript room in the Bancroft, since all, without exception, were superlatively helpful. Elsewhere, and at different times, Norman Thrower in Los Angeles was a source of information and hospitality, Donald Meinig at Syracuse the same, and very early on Peter Haggett at Bristol. Ronald Grim, then at the Library of Congress, gave me some fascinating leads.

In the writing of the book others have been most helpful. Judith May-Sapko in the Special Collections department of the Pickler Memorial Library, Truman State University, Kirksville, Missouri, patiently abstracted material on the history of Central Wesleyan College and early editions of its publications, the *Pulse* and the *College Star*. Bill Mayer of Colgate University alerted me to correspondence in archives at Harvard. Douglas Helms, historian at the USDA Natural Resources Conservation Service, guided me through the complexities of the National Archives in Washington, D.C. The staff at the National Science Foundation, Washington, D.C., received me on that fateful morning of September 11, 2001, as they were about to leave the building, and then they subsequently labored to find documents on my behalf. Roxie Schroeder, secretary of the Warren County Historical Society, made available material on the Schowengerdt family. Anna Skeels showed me her fascinating 1993 master's thesis on Sauer's fieldwork[4], which I had been completely unaware of. The British Academy once more generously assisted my journeys through its incomparable Small Grants Scheme, with two grants-in-aid.

My greatest debt, as ever, is to Loré (Eleanore Williams), who not only supplied the support and sustenance that made it all possible but very directly participated in the research with her expert knowledge of German language and literature. She translated and transcribed over 160 letters from Carl to his parents, many in old German script, and retained, I believe, the authentic voice of Sauer in her renditions. These letters and their interpretation supplied endless topics of discussion between us as to what Sauer was "really like," which helped us distinguish between the man and the legend, until he sometimes became a very alive, vivid person.

The question could be asked, why is someone who was never a pupil of Sauer, never a colleague of his, never wrote on topics directly associated with his interests, never even met him, and lives in a different country, writing a biography of this American? The simple answer is, who better to get an independent, balanced view, especially someone who has invested much time in American academic life and writing. Sauer has been a highly contested scholar with a large and stalwart band of supporters. There have been hundreds of academic statements in multiple languages, overwhelmingly laudatory of his intellect and ideas in their tenor, with only a small group of detractors who deride him as out of touch and even reactionary. Clearly, I started from a perspective of sympathy for him, but I did not want to write a hagiography, nor did I want to do a hatchet job. I wanted to try to engage in "truth telling" and give an independent view of his ideas, accomplishments, and life in all its complexity. And complex and contradictory he was at times. He retained an incurably romantic view of his country-bred origins but lived in cities nearly all his life. He made weighty pronouncements that he later disavowed. He was both a rock-ribbed conservative and a congenital nonconformist. He was profoundly concerned with the ethic of conservation, but he mistrusted the political solutions of the New Deal and the fervor of the new environmentalists. He was always a wide-ranging speculative scholar but could be a very effective operator in getting what he wanted. He distrusted intellectuals and most institutions, and he valued individualism. One could go on listing these paradoxes, but suffice it to say that it is my hope that in attempting this biography, with all its intimacies, revelations, and daily routine, a more nuanced and multilayered portrait of Sauer will emerge than is commonly presented.

In short, I am attempting to engage in what Hermione Lee calls "life-writing," which draws attention to its subject's peculiarities and achievements in order to produce an idea of what he or she was "like."[5] Such life-writing will hopefully bring the dead and living closer together. In many places I have let this incomparable stylist and thinker speak for himself, and following his example the book is purposely jargon free and written both for the academic geographer and for others who will find the story of this self-styled "wholly unofficial, and somewhat off-beat American," as interesting as I have.[6]

Michael Williams

Oxford, September 5, 2009

TO PASS ON A GOOD EARTH

Prologue

In the late afternoon, at the end of a gloomy, windy, rainy day at the beginning of March 1907, Carl Sauer, just seventeen, sat at the work table by the window of his room at home, thinking about his life. Home was Warrenton, Missouri, a reasonably busy and bustling small country town and county seat that served an indifferent farming district just south of Highway 40, some fifty miles west of St. Louis. From his window he looked across the yard to the woodlot. Through the split-rail fence that surrounded it, his view extended away to the open fields and small stands of trees (and across north–south Highway 47) toward the empty town lots that bordered Walton Street, the only built-up street before reaching Main Street.

He was moody and unsure of himself, and worried that he lacked the will power to do things and to get down to his college work. And then his relationship with the local girls troubled him. He decided to start a diary in which he would put down daily happenings "to see if it won't help to wake me up and to try to do enough each day," and "to jog my memory."[1] It had been a "dismal day" as March had come in like the proverbial lion, and it made him feel worse. "I must try to make myself be less dependent on the weather," he wrote. The previous day he had "bummed" the afternoon classes at Central Wesleyan College, and later had gone "down town" to buy some postcards and to try to catch up with some of the college gang. "But there were only the girls there; all listen only halfway to me when I talk. Lost my nerve last night, was [as] afraid of the girls as last year."

He thought that he would find consolation in committing his feelings and behavior to his diary. Perhaps, he mused, he'd be like Samuel Pepys, and his entries would bring an intimate self-realization. But after one and a half years and more than 300 pages filled with fairly prosaic entries, about the weather, his work at the college, the odd journeys out of town, his exploits with his friends, and particularly accounts of his success or otherwise in "sporting" with the girls, he decided to abandon his diary, stop being moody, and try to be more agreeable. Carl Sauer was simply no diarist, no Pepys. The discipline and humdrum routine of making a daily entry did not suit his freewheeling, speculative mind, even at this early age. He wasn't interested enough in the major events of his neighborhood or county to be bothered to record them. Nor could he detach himself enough to be introspective and make his own emotions clear. His literary gifts lay elsewhere. He wrote letters — literally thousands of them. In one sense these letters were a continuation of his diary in that they were often self-judgmental exercises, but they were much more than that. They became the means for conveying issues that touched upon his many interests and feelings. He did not want to keep his thoughts to himself but rather to share them with others. He excelled as a communicator, taking up a topic, discussing and dissecting it, and, if a decision was needed, coming up with a commonsense working course of action. Sometimes in later life, when he saw no solution he became melancholy and despondent. His writing was pungent, punchy, and pithy, and littered with phrases that linger in the mind.

This shift from teenage logger of everyday events to adult analysis and reasoning happened suddenly, and we get a hint of this other self in his very last diary entries during the long summer vacation before going to Northwestern University in 1908. The first few were typical:

June 27th. The other day I played tennis with Lorena [Schowengerdt] and we had a fairly grand time. If I don't get much better treatment I'll quit before the summer's over. I certainly like her, but there doesn't seem to be much the other way.

June 28th. We are going to Charrette [a local scenic spot] Tuesday — and Mrs. Schowengerdt is to be chaperone — pshaw! I am trying to plot Mrs. Schowengerdt out of the way. I might just as well look around for another girl.

After a gap of a month, the final entry shows quite a different level of self-analytic maturity:

> July 25th. Another month gone unrecorded. I shall not put in the details, but only sketch the salient points. This summer if remembered at all in the future, will be remembered for my affair with Lorena. I shouldn't be surprised if I had fallen slightly in love during the past month. The true worth of the girl is becoming plainer to me day by day, and my estimation of her higher. I think she has been very patient with me, as I have often been morose and surly. Wish I could keep it down, but this melancholy seems to be there whenever I get with her. I think I'll get turned down sooner or later, but shall try to postpone the date as long as possible. We have quarreled a lot, I have done most of it and made myself abominable by a lot of complaining. Maybe I'll do better bye-and bye — maybe I will and maybe I won't. Oh the perplexity of it.

The perplexity was resolved, and five and a half years later they married. It was the beginning of an inseparable and happy union of sixty-one years until both died within a month of each other in 1975.

Following his arrival at Northwestern, Sauer wrote to his parents almost every week for nearly eight years, and after his father died in 1918 to his mother nearly every fortnight until her death in 1942. Lorena had a letter nearly every day until they married in December 1913. In later life when he was away in the field or on a trip, his children and even his grandchildren received detailed letters. Carl Sauer's role as dutiful son, devoted husband, and doting father and grandfather goes a long way to explain his seeming indifference to outside opinion, fame, and notoriety. Family was central to him. Once in Berkeley, his academic correspondence was voluminous. Some six thousand letters give a better-rounded view of the man, his life, and accomplishments than do the several hundred more disciplinary commentaries on his work. It is that view of a total life that is attempted here.

> The era of the Middle Border ended with World War I.
> Some of us have lived in its Indian Summer, and almost
> no one was aware how soon and suddenly it was to end.
> —Carl Sauer, "Homestead and Community," 1962

1

Warrenton of the Middle Border, 1889–1908

Warrenton, Missouri, with one important exception, was anything but special. It was the epitome of the small-town Midwest, the Middle Border as Hamlin Garland called it in his 1917 novel.[1] Warrenton was an elongated, east-west trending grid of about ten to twelve blocks, aligned on either side of the commercial core of Boone's Lick Road, the town's Main Street. Its mile or more of sidewalks with overhanging wooden verandas was lined with stores, saloons, banks, a pool hall, a drugstore, livery stables, a dentist, a doctor, a baker, a shoe repairer, attorneys' offices, the office of the local newspaper, the *Banner*, a couple of churches, and some private residences. At the western end stood the county courthouse and jail, situated in traditional fashion on a square.[2] Most of the roads petered out in the few fields that had been cut out of the surrounding forests of pine, hickory, and white oak. Some 840 people lived in the town and its immediate surroundings in 1900.

The Missouri Rhineland

Warrenton was typical of thousands of small towns across Midwest America in the late nineteenth century. However, one big difference set Warrenton apart and made it special. In two large blocks along Main Street were the buildings of Central Wesleyan College. The ensemble of multistoried stone buildings, shaded by avenues of elms and other trees, was a graceful adornment that added a cosmopolitan air to this otherwise prosaic little midwestern town.[3] Here William Albert Sauer, Carl's father, was a professor of music and French from 1866 to his death in 1918.

Carl grew up in Warrenton. The town was the cradle, nursery, and school of this remarkable man, and he frequently and nostalgically recalled it as the theater of his youth. Warrenton figured unnamed, in an essay Sauer wrote seventy-four years later entitled, very academically, "Status and Change in the Rural Midwest—a Retrospect." Its working title in manuscript was more evocative and revealing—"Old Haunts Revisited." It was a wistful, melancholy, affectionate glance at an older, simpler, and seemingly pleasanter bygone age during its fading Indian summer, which disintegrated and dissolved after 1918.[4]

Central Wesleyan College was an important element of that memory. The college was one of several small independent institutions created in the United States to cater to the spiritual and cultural needs of immigrant German Protestants. Next to the English, the Germans were the largest European immigrant group in the United States. From a few thousand mainly peasant migrants escaping poverty, even starvation, during the late eighteenth and early nineteenth centuries, the number of German-born migrants rose steadily. Some 952,000 arrived in 1851–61, largely as a result of the failure of what a British historian called "the revolution of the intellectuals" in 1848, which led to the departure of many educated Germans. About five million Germans then made the journey across the Atlantic.[5] Large sections of New York, Philadelphia, Chicago, Milwaukee, St. Louis, Cincinnati, and Buffalo became almost wholly German speaking, as did much of rural Wisconsin, Minnesota, Illinois, Missouri, and eastern Kansas.[6]

Missouri, particularly along the Missouri River and the west bank of the Mississippi, was a favorite destination of rural migrants,[7] attracted to the area by boosterish pamphlets and books. Widely disseminated in Germany was Gottfried Duden's *Report on a Journey to the Western States*. Duden had settled near Dutzow, about ten miles southeast of Warrenton, which he extolled as a veritable Canaan, a paradise to farm, and free from the social and religious restrictions of early nineteenth-century Germany.[8] Known as "the Missouri Rhineland" since most of the immigrants were from Westphalia, Warren County and adjacent St. Charles and Montgomery Counties had towns with names like Hamburg, Bernheimer, Holstein, and Herman.[9]

This great reservoir of German origin made Missouri an obvious location for a college to educate the children of immigrant families and to train ministers. Since instruction in local schools was via the German Bible, the German hymnbook, and German preaching, there was a need for German-speaking ministers. A German American college had been proposed in 1852 by a group of ministers in Winchester, Illinois. Lacking funds, they instead joined with English-speaking Methodists to found a "German and English College" at Quincy in southwest Illinois. In 1864 German ministers launched a more ambitious educational venture, to include a home for children orphaned by the Civil War, and bought 932 acres at Warrenton. The state legislature sanctioned the Western Orphan Asylum and Educational Institute provided it was open to all religious groups. By 1869, now renamed Central Wesleyan College and Orphan Asylum, the institution had expanded physically and intellectually. Its classical and theological curriculum trained teachers for rural schools and the new cadre of ministers. Instruction was bilingual, in German and English.[10]

Two substantial "cottages" housed the orphans, and a primary and later a secondary school taught them and many local residents. Louisa Vosholl, Carl Sauer's aunt, was the main teacher in the primary school for over twenty years, assisted by Carl's mother, Rosetta Johanna Vosholl. The community took its responsibility for the orphans seriously and allowed them to continue their education at the college at no cost.

The faculty members were renowned for conscientious dedication to their educational and religious aims, and Carl's father was no exception. Born in 1844 in Beinstein, Remstal, in the then Kingdom of Württemberg, William Sauer was educated at the local school and a teachers' training college. A gifted musician and an accomplished organist, he began teaching in an orphanage, but in 1865 at the age of twenty-one he resigned because of ill health and emigrated to America, hoping for a curative change of scene. After staying with friends and relatives in Pennsylvania and Michigan, he served for some months as church organist in Bloomington, Illinois. By 1866 he had heard of the Warrenton college, and he turned down a salary of $1,200 at Ann Arbor for one of only $400 to become one of the first teachers •

at Central Wesleyan. However, two years later he returned to Germany to look after his ailing mother, staying for seven years. In 1875 he made the return voyage to America, and in August 1878 he married Rosetta Vosholl, of Freeport, Illinois. Her father was a Methodist minister from the Rhineland, her mother from Brandenburg. Both had come to America in the early 1850s.

For the first few years the Sauers lived in the campus administration building, but with their first child coming they bought a three-bedroom house on College Avenue, adjacent to the college playing fields and tennis courts. Here Henry Albert was born in 1881. Eight years later, on December 24, 1889, Carl Ortwin was born.[11] Henry Vosholl, Rosetta's brother, bought a house next door when, after serving in the state legislature, he returned to Warrenton to teach English literature and ancient and modern history at Central Wesleyan. The family enclave was completed when Rosetta's mother and father retired to Warrenton.

William Sauer was afflicted by recurrent bouts of unexplained ill health, leading to a nervous breakdown and depression. A perfectionist, his "worries" were the constant bane of the household. Sauer's mother, well built even stout, sensible, and mild mannered, subdued her own exasperation and calmed her husband's anxieties. Not only did she help out in the orphan school, but her fine singing voice made her much in demand at local concerts. Thanks to her pastoral activities among the orphans, college students, and townsfolk, she was commonly known as "Mother Sauer."

Despite his health problems, William loomed large in the home, the college, and the community. He was a formidable figure—bearded and bespectacled—and an unabashed evangelizing Christian with the highest personal, academic, and pedagogic standards. He was strict and precise, "punctual, systematic, orderly, and dependable."[12] Although he never hesitated to condemn the bad and uphold the good, he was well liked by the students, over whose life and welfare he took endless time. Carl respected and liked "Papa" and admired his learning and sense of doing a job well, although sometimes, like his mother, he was exasperated by Papa's "worrying."

William's music played a central role in college life. He was resident organist at the chapel and composed tuneful and eminently singable hymns in German with titles like "Longing for God," "Till We Meet Again," "With

Jesus along Life's Way," and "My Bible." He was also the college taxonomist and took Carl on walks around Warrenton, and later in Germany, identifying and discussing the characteristics of local plants. Carl dedicated his doctoral dissertation on the Ozarks to "The gentle memory of my father, at whose side I formed my first appreciation of the things that constitute the living world."[13]

At Calw in Germany

The education of his children was of extreme concern to William. Albert went to the orphanage school and eventually to Central Wesleyan, although he proved only a mediocre student. He eventually learned mechanical skills and then went into farming. Carl was much more academically gifted, and his father, who valued academic excellence above everything, did all that was possible to nurture his talent. William decided the orphanage school was not good enough for Carl, and planned the drastic step of uprooting the family and returning to Germany so that Carl could get a first-class grounding in a wide range of subjects at one of the justly renowned state Gymnasiums, which offered Latin, Greek (essential for entry to a university), and science. For years William saved money carefully, and in July 1899, ostensibly for his health, the family left for Germany.

William had friends and relatives reconnoiter the schools available in Württemberg, which had invested heavily in all levels of education during the later nineteenth century.[14] The Reallyzeum at Calw, about twenty-five miles west of Stuttgart, seemed ideal, providing temporary employment for William. Calw was small enough for a family from Warrenton to find their way around and feel at home. It was pleasantly situated, away from industrial areas, nestling in the hills on the northeastern corner of the Black Forest in the deeply incised valley of the Nagold River, a tributary of the Neckar, which eventually joined the Rhine.[15] Albert attended a technical school in Calw for a year and then found a job in a factory in Orliken near Zurich, Switzerland. But "Karlchen [Little Carl] is our main reason for being here, so that he gets a good schooling, and now he has the opportunity to get this." Normally a pupil went to school for nine years, from about age nine to seventeen. Carl was nearly ten when he arrived, and stayed for two years.

The Gymnasium regimen was strict, even physically harsh. It was run on military lines and wholly directed to German topics. "History is a tool to excite patriotism, and geography, by its great emphasis on Germany, is in some measure her sister." The only relief from the relentless grind was provided by field trips, which Carl loved. As described by a later American visitor:

> In the spring and summer it is a common sight to see long files of school children accompanied by one or two teachers who are taking them down to the river, or to the park to show them the big forest trees, the hay-meadow, the hay-makers, or to the outskirts of the city to see the rye and potato fields, the cherry trees by the roadside, the fruit orchards or factories that they have heard about in geography classes. In vacation these trips are often extended to railroad historical interest days. Objects of historical interest are included, nor is the zoological garden neglected.[16]

Other than these outings, the stay in Calw was not a happy time for Carl, for the strict academic routine took its toll. Many years later he wrote to his mother that he had just seen his own son, Jonathan, and his friends ambling off to Berkeley High School. "It reminds me a little of my boyhood in the *Gymnasium*, only these kids walk off with no fear of what the morning has in store for them. There is no punishment, hardly even the possibility of a reprimand." Jonathan recalled that the only time he ever saw his father seriously depressed was when they revisited Calw in 1954.[17]

William Sauer was aware of the pressures of German "hothouse" education. "The German school at times seems unnecessarily hard, I would prefer that it was achieved through the American principle of 'self-respect,'" he wrote. Hard or not, William's hunch was right—his bright son had been able to handle the situation, and the gamble of moving the family halfway around the world had paid off.

Back in Warrenton

In August 1901 the family returned to Warrenton.[18] William was in better health after long bracing walks in the Black Forest uplands, and he returned to teaching at Central Wesleyan almost immediately. Rosetta would have happily stayed in Calw if she had been able to visit her American relatives once a year, but she easily settled back into the routine of domestic life in Warrenton.

Albert went to Alton, an industrial suburb of St. Louis, to work as a mechanic in an electrical goods factory. There he met Nellie Paul, a bubbly, good-natured girl whom he married in April 1906. After five years in the factory he and Nellie left for Kansas City, where he worked in a variety of jobs. By 1910 he had entered a farming partnership near Jefferson City, Missouri, with a distant relative.

Eventually Albert acquired his own farm, probably with substantial aid from William. "Now they are well established in their new home," Carl wrote his parents. "It must feel really good to see your own land every time you look out of the window. There is something so firm, solid, and pleasurable in owning one's own land that one cannot get from anything else. Poor devils, they have had an awful time for years when they were dependent on the factory." But things never went right for Albert and Nellie. The land was of indifferent quality, and a run of bad seasons, a plague of Hessian fly, plummeting farm prices, and other disasters made their life one of hardship and toil. "Since Albert has been farming I [have] begun to realize how much perseverance is demanded of farmers," wrote Carl.[19]

For Carl, the return to Warrenton was a happier story. In comparison to Calw, life for the teenager in small-town America was liberal and relaxed. Carl was free to come and go as he liked, provided he did his household chores and succeeded academically. Academic achievement, leading a Christian life, and good citizenship were the critical virtues in the Sauer household.[20] He was far in advance of his contemporaries and was rapidly promoted, as at Calw. His superiority marked him out as a bit of an outsider among his classmates. On the way home after school they frequently made him sit on a fence post and fired questions at him on a wide range of school subjects and sports in the hope of stumping him. But they rarely caught him out. He excelled at arithmetical conundrums and had an insatiable appetite and encyclopedic knowledge for baseball personalities, teams, and scores. There seemed to have been no malice in the game, and when they tired of it he joined the gang as one of the boys.

His incredibly wide knowledge never left him and made him a superb impromptu lecturer and assessor for research foundations. Westher Hess recalled that when she took his courses before she became the departmental and Sauer's personal secretary at Berkeley, she and other students would ask obscure and diversionary questions on political personalities and even on tap dancing. But he was never fazed and talked exhaustively on any topic for ten to twenty minutes until the class was more than satisfied. The "Prof-baiting" soon stopped.[21]

Central Wesleyan College

At sixteen, in 1906, Carl began his bachelor of arts studies at Central Wesleyan, the youngest student the college had ever entered. The diary he began a year later shows him obsessed with getting on, flirting—"sporting" was the current phrase—and with an introspective analysis of moods and hopes. "Sometimes I feel like despairing, again like fighting twice as hard for the things lacking or stunting in my make-up. My memory, utter denseness at times, lessening individuality, and originality, lack of energy and cheerfulness," were all obstacles "cloud-high" to surmount.[22] He knew that some of his ancestors were strict pietists "enshrouded in perpetual gloom," which he felt coming over him at times, but he realized that to blame one's blues on background was easier than blaming oneself.[23]

> This is Sunday, so I suppose I had better preach to myself a little bit. This sort of self-contemplation to find out what you're growling about and if you can't find something more to whine about, is going to put me to the bad. I am too much self-conscious and looking chronically for dissatisfaction, and that, I think, keeps me from enjoying myself as I might and should. I don't believe that I know my case, but there's too much of myself in the way for me.[24]

"Too much of myself in the way for me" was an apt self-depiction that held true for the rest of his life. His strong convictions, his determination to succeed, and his sense of the importance of the individual over the crowd often got in his way and brought him into conflict with those around him, or led to his being misunderstood.

So gloomy did he look that one girl, Lorena Schowengerdt (who was just 16), took pity on his misery and gave him a bunch of violets to cheer him up.

TO PASS ON A GOOD EARTH

By the next spring his relationship with Lorena was blossoming, although his jealousy and her somewhat offhand manner drove him nearly to distraction. But William disapproved. Lorena came from a wealthy local family. Her father, John Franklin Schowengerdt, owned one of the biggest general stores in town, and the family lived in probably the largest and most imposing house in Warrenton. Carl characterized Lorena's elder brother, Erwin, a college student, as a "fat-walleted aristocrat." Lorena's background in trade and town was the very antithesis of Carl's background in academia, and William made no secret of the fact that he thought the divide unbridgeable. For him, learning or the land were the only respectable and acceptable occupations.

With Albert now gone from home, it was Carl's task to keep the yard in good order. Every week or ten days he "worked like a slave for a couple of hours," mowing the front lawn. He carted dozens of barrows of dirt to fill holes and depressions in the lawn, made "war on the weeds" in the back lot, trimmed the hedges with a scythe, and reroofed the chicken shed. His main task was splitting wood for the winter woodpile. This was strenuous but acted as a major release from his pent-up emotions; often after a fit of the "blues" he went out with the ax until his hand and shoulders were sore. Years later he recalled it as "about the only form of manual labor I ever really enjoyed." He was not afraid of hard physical work and, as a member of the tennis team, labored throughout the spring of 1907 helping dig out, level, and spread and roll ashes to make the college tennis courts.[25]

Carl often took his academic work over to "dear little Grossmutter," Rosetta's mother, a chatty eighty-six-year-old. He sat in the kitchen while she prepared and cooked meals, but he studied little because they talked so much. Carl admired his Vosholl grandfather, a retired Methodist minister who had survived "the difficulties of pioneer-dom," rarely being ill and currently "looking for a score or more years." On his ninetieth birthday in early 1908, ten German ministers from Warrenton and surrounding areas came to pay homage to their distinguished colleague. Each minister spoke, and "Grandpa got up and gave a better one than any of them did. He has the stuff of the regular after-dinner orator. He was serious and witty by turns, and always to the point."[26]

th intense religiosity at home, compulsory daily attendance at service llege, and constant churchgoing on Sunday, Carl accepted religion as orm of family life, yet his religious skepticism mounted over time. When a red-hot Methodist minister visited the college in December 1907 and January 1908, Carl noted wryly: "Revival services are in progress. According to good Methodist custom, our sins will be preached to us for three weeks and the boys will get a chance yet have their souls saved and see the girls home each night."

Capable and trusted, Carl undertook many tasks for college staff. He wrote articles in German for the college newspaper, the *Star*, and essays on primary school education for his Aunt Lou (Louisa Vosholl) at the orphan school. During his senior year he taught for the college, first French, "trying to pound some of those nasal twangs into 8 American and Dutch heads," then geology and analytical geometry; and when Uncle Henry was away, his classes on U.S. and modern history. The latter required "a lot of reading," but he got "along splendidly," finding that much more interesting than French, especially modern history because Lorena was in the class.[27]

In the November 1907 preliminary exams, he got 98 percent in political economy, 100 percent in geology, and averaged 98.25 percent overall, goading him to "study even harder to deserve these grades." In April of his final year, he "wrote and wrote, and wrote myself dry" in ethics, astronomy, international law, and geology. The class yearbook, the *Pulse*, quipped, "My native village produced at least one great man." Many years later, Sauer's friend Carl Bader wrote him, "You were the brightest star in the not inconsiderable galaxy that emanated from little old C.W.C."[28] As the best student the college had ever had, the board got him a $300-a-year fellowship at Northwestern University, where he opted to major in geology. A new chapter was to open in his life.

Childhood Years Remembered

For all the tensions of his teenage years, Carl's memories of his youth with his close-knit family in Warrenton were of unalloyed happiness and affection. The experience of a small-town community remained a source of strength and provided standards of diligence, thrift, and rectitude. In

Chicago, he found most of his contemporaries similarly "country-bred of prairie and woodland soil, and kept that knowledge and quality when we went to the cities to live."[29] He hoped that his own children would experience the Warrenton flavor on their infrequent visits to their grandmother. As he wrote his mother in 1928:

> When they get to Warrenton the flowers will be at their best, and the children will think Missouri a wonderful country. In a short while the cherries will be ripe and they can climb about in the cherry trees and gorge themselves, especially that one next to Grossmutter's kitchen window, which I always believe has the best cherries in the world. And the old mulberry tree with robins feasting above and children below! Or you remember the time when I fell out of a cherry tree and got the wind knocked out of me. You saw me there unable to move and thought I was seriously hurt and began to cry? I hope the old pear trees still have a few of those sweet pears—you'll think my childhood memories are mostly of the things I ate! They are not a small part and somehow it seems to me that the fruit on Grandpa's place is still the most excellent fruit that ever grew, I can still tell you how the black raspberries and blackberries tasted and can see Grossmutter lovingly tying up the vines and smiling to see us children stuffing on them. I am happy that the children can play with their grandmother and Aunt Lou and get acquainted with their Uncle Henry whom they hardly know as yet. They will be delighted to find out what a lovely old gentleman he is and I hope they behave themselves reasonably well. My immediate expectations of them in this respect are not set too high and I hope yours won't be either.[30]

More than ten years later his memories remained undimmed; on Memorial Day 1939 his thoughts turned once more to his childhood years and family:

> And it has been such a good family to have, I can see them all as if they had been with us only yesterday, Grandma saying "Junge, Junge" [Boy, boy] and Papa playing improvisations on Der Liebe lange Tag [The dear

long day]. There are a thousand memories that come of themselves. And not one that I'd like to forget, not an ugly or a bitter or unpleasant thing [was] ever associated with any of them, only gentleness and kindness and understanding and good nature. It is a sweet and beautiful thing to look back upon those years when we all had each other.[31]

Carl Sauer was a lucky man to have had such memories.

> The study here submitted is the outgrowth of long
> acquaintance with the area and of a deep affection for it.
> —Carl Sauer, *Geography of the Ozark Highland*, 1920

2

Graduate Studies and New Places, 1908–1915

In October 1908 Sauer arrived in Evanston, Illinois, about thirteen miles north of Chicago, the suburban seat of Northwestern University. He came in some trepidation. Although a smart pupil with a fellowship, he saw himself as a small-town boy in a far more demanding big-city academic environment. After cozy, comfortable Warrenton with its extended family cocoon, where everything was slow and easy, Chicago and Northwestern were more than a bit of a shock. "Brash and bustling" was how he described the busy, noisy metropolis, the commercial and industrial hub of the Midwest. "I often sigh and pine," he wrote Lorena, "for good old Missouri where the-people-go-like-this,-gently-gently-gently."[1]

Cousin Mary: A Home from Home

The sharpness of the break from Warrenton, the materialistic and impersonal nature of Chicago, and his loneliness living in a rented room were partly alleviated by the bell ringing of local German churches and familiar hymns and tunes like "Lorelei," "Stille Nacht," and "Sah ein Knab' ein Röslein stehen." What most ameliorated his solitude was finding a refuge in the home of one of William Sauer's cousins, Mary Deininger Werweke, whom he visited almost every Sunday and holiday. Cousin Mary knew little about the Warrenton Sauers, nor they of her.[2] Mary's husband, Frederick Werweke, was something of a drifter, moving from job to job, delivering goods, working on public transport, and finally running a small shop selling fruit, confectionaries, and tobacco.

Mary, probably in her early forties and childless, took Carl under her wing as a surrogate mother. A great chatterer, she enjoyed including him in her Sunday lunches, taking him to visit her friends, to church, even to the circumcision ceremony of the son of Jewish friends. She showed him around Chicago and accompanied him to talks, the theater, and exhibitions. She pressed and mended his clothes and served him hearty fare. Nearly twenty years later he recalled how Mary had given him "a second home" when he most needed it: "wherever she lives will always be somewhat like home to me. And I owe her an everlasting debt of kindness."[3]

One senses that Carl's enthusiasm for Sundays at his cousin's was slightly resented by his parents, who urged him to find company in church, where he went only occasionally. To please them, he tried to take up churchgoing seriously, eclectically sampling several over a few months. But he confessed, "I cannot go regularly to the same church; my church home like my other home is in Warrenton. As a result I do not feel myself pulled to any one particular church. Last Sunday I had to work, and I worked till midday and then went to Werweke's. The work had to be done, and to rest in the afternoon and evening [at] Werweke's was more refreshing for me than if I had gone to church in the morning."[4]

Northwestern

His parents eagerly absorbed all he could tell them about the geology (dear to his father's heart) course work at Northwestern. He reported that he was coping well, though he told Lorena he had developed lazy intellectual habits since returning from Germany to easygoing Central Wesleyan. But at Northwestern the teachers were "springing quizzes every other week." The "good old days of easy living at C.W.C." were replaced by "quiz-haunted nights at N'Wsn."[5]

His wide-ranging geology courses included chemistry, petrology, mineralogy, and assaying, which he found too technical and practical to be interesting. However, another component, physiography, appealed so much that "I've almost made up my mind to make geography my main study. It is the all-embracing part of Geology which alone demands a wider, broader education and at least passes over the pure technical things." He instanced courses dealing with "the relationship of physical surroundings [to] the development of the human race, etc.," and "real" (i.e., visible) geology on the land's surface.[6]

A geology field-mapping exercise provided a welcome break from his course work. Sauer and a fellow student undertook a survey around the little town of Rockefeller, about forty miles northwest of Chicago. It was "good to get out of sight of Chicago smoke and noise, and smell the plowed ground and hear the black-birds and meadow-larks, and see some ruries [rural people]." The greatest pleasure was "to walk down a real board-walk on the main street of a small town, once more, see the dinky electric lights swing out over the street, the farmers' wagons hitched before the general store," all so familiar that he could imagine he could turn into a "small house in a large yard and find myself at home."[7]

Encouraged by the "pleasant and helpful" Professor Ulysses Grant at Northwestern, Sauer decided to transfer to the University of Chicago. At Chicago his work would be recognized "by a German School, and eventually would make it possible for me to visit the AA of colleges," Heidelberg, Tübingen, Freiberg, or Vienna. His father was more than pleased at the prospect of his son studying at one of the prestigious German universities.[8]

But Sauer initially lacked the confidence to apply to Chicago. His father suggested that he give up geology and do an easier subject, like philology. Carl's answer was an emphatic "NO thank you." Philology was

> by far the most boring subject. I would slowly have atrophied. I would rather spend my time on something which gives the opportunity to achieve something. That I am not totally unskilled with my pen is also an advantage. I will not be held back because I can not express myself verbally. Also my knowledge of languages is a big advantage.[9]

He concluded that he was not "suited for geology, but I don't know what else." In the reading room he was far more likely to browse through *Revue des Deux Mondes* or *Atlantic Monthly* than the *Zeitschrift für Geologie*. He would like to study "a little of a lot of subjects." "Geography would interest me, I think, because it is not narrowing yourself down; it is comprehensive." He would apply to Chicago for a fellowship in geography, and if he didn't get it, he'd quit the university after the year was out.[10] After only two semesters at Northwestern, Sauer began graduate study in geography at the University of Chicago in September of 1909.[11]

University of Chicago: The Golden Age

The attraction of the University of Chicago, which had opened in October 1892 with a remarkable array of scholars, was enormous. It was, Carl wrote his parents, the "premier university in the country in Geography as in Geology," adding what would appeal to his father: "They use a lot of German books in Geography." (Letters home were written in German, as his father demanded; Carl would apologize if he slipped into English.) He later extolled Chicago as an academic community of "rarely equalled quality [and] I was there in its golden age."

However, excellence was expensive; costs of some $200 to $300 a year exceeded his fellowship and could only be met by his father's financial help, "a sacrifice" on the part of his parents. He lived frugally, often ashamed of his down-at-heels boots and shoddy clothing. His weekly letters home minutely accounted his expenditures, down to the last cent. Near the end of his first year he asked that any money given him thereafter be regarded as a loan. "I do not want to live next year [as] I have been living this year, and what I need above that I will borrow. I would feel a lot better if I knew it was my debt and not yours."[12]

Sauer's Chicago teachers held him in their spell. The department head, Rollin Salisbury, was a towering figure in American geology, and "a hard-headed man" whom Sauer both admired and was terrified by. Harlan Barrows was a scholarly and helpful "giant of a man." Ellen Churchill Semple, whose lectures on historical geography were "more gripping than any that I have had," stirred his imagination with her fervor and eloquence. John Paul Goode, though fussy, self-important, and unsure of himself, had "skill, taste, and inventiveness in making maps" and was a good teacher. Sauer became friendly with fellow student and instructor Wellington "Duke" Jones and his family. Henry Cowles, a genial and perceptive plant ecologist, introduced Sauer to the "manner and meaning of ecological seeing in the outdoor classroom" on excursions to the dunes of Indiana and the marshes of Chicago. Salisbury, Semple, Cowles, and Barrows bequeathed an intellectual legacy that provided many of the influences that molded Sauer's scholarly character.[13]

The geologist Salisbury had founded Chicago's Department of Geography in 1903, the first in America to offer graduate studies. Like many in the expanding university systems at the turn of the century, he was a farm boy, from Spring Prairie, Wisconsin. At Beloit College in 1878 he came under the influence of Thomas Chamberlin,[14] renowned for his analyses of Wisconsin landforms created by Pleistocene glaciers. Salisbury became his star pupil and his collaborator on a celebrated paper on the driftless (unglaciated) area of Iowa and Wisconsin. After five years as president of the University of Wisconsin, Chamberlin left in 1892 to found the geology department at the new University of Chicago, taking Salisbury along. Salisbury's Higher Geography course embraced not only the study of the earth's features but the relevance of physical geography to human affairs. His energy was prodigious. Long-serving dean of the Ogden Graduate School of Science, he produced with Chamberlin the definitive three-volume work *Geology* (1904–6) and his own *Physiography* (1907).[15]

Not for nothing was Salisbury known to junior staff and students as "the Czar." Sauer described him as "a big man in stature and otherwise. You feel it as soon as he looks at you from under his bushy eye-brows. Greatest living teacher of Geology." In the field he would point to a tiny, insignificant thing—a scratch on a rock, the shape of a stone, an indentation—and use it as an entrée to geological processes in general. In addition, reminisced Sauer later, he was a "superb editor" and "the most sharp witted man with whom I have ever been in contact." His teaching method was an extended Socratic dialogue. Persistent questions were directed at individual students, sometimes for a whole hour. Carl's admiration was tinged with trepidation; by the Thursday of the first week he contemplated quitting. "I go weak at the knees because in class he is totally without mercy. When he begins to question one he follows up with 'how' and 'why' until he has you in a corner." On Friday "he had me on the carpet again but this time I managed better." Salisbury never failed to "make it clear how very stupid one is." But while he made Sauer feel "like a miserable model of impenetrable stupidity" in class, afterward he frequently sat down beside him, put his arm across his shoulder, and talked to him "in a most fatherly way." Salisbury cared passionately about his good students.[16]

As the course went on, things improved for Sauer, though Salisbury was still prone to devastating offhand remarks. He could not stand sloppy thinking. To some students' answers he would retort, "Perfectly true, perfectly general, and perfect[ly] meaningless." But he seemed less critical of Sauer. "He doesn't worry me any more, I don't shake at all now when 2 o'clock approaches." Sauer was entranced by the man and his methods.[17] But he also pitied this "cranky old bachelor," likening him to a "monadnock," a mass of resistant hard rock, a solitary peak above an eroded surface. Salisbury was "splendid and unbroken, but you feel sorry for him in his isolation, and you imagine that he would like to come down on the common level, on the plain."[18] Within a few months Salisbury was inviting Sauer to special lectures and dinners, which he enjoyed immensely. "He is behaving very respectably these days," he wrote Lorena. "I think that he just wears a harder outer shell for show, and that under he is a very attractive person"—a reasonably apt description of Sauer himself in later life.[19]

Harlan Barrows was a workaholic, at his desk at eight every morning, never stopping even for lunch and often staying as late as midnight. Sauer found him "quick-witted and exceptionally clear and exact in everything he says" but a little "rough" (rauh). Barrows was always encouraging and devoted many hours to reading and correcting drafts of Carl's written work. He supervised Sauer's research on the past and present development of Missouri, even offering to go "knocking around the state" with him. By spring or fall of 1910 Sauer became Barrows's research assistant, finding materials for a new course Barrows was to give on conservation.[20] He later credited Barrows with "great industry and within certain limits a strong critical faculty," but also recalled him as "a man of narrow horizons, lacking in originality and a drill master who squelched any talk from the ranks."[21]

John Paul Goode moved in and out of Sauer's life as a teacher and later as a compiler of wall maps for Rand McNally while Carl was working there. Goode had pioneered the use of wall maps in schools. He invented several new projections that depicted the landmasses of the world on a flat page far more accurately than the commonly used but misleading Mercator projection. Goode's attractive *School Atlas* (later *World Atlas*) (1923–), now in its twenty-second edition, has sold over 1.25 million copies.[22]

Of all his teachers Sauer most admired "excellent, entertaining and stimulating" Ellen Churchill Semple, a Vassar College graduate from Louisville, Kentucky, who had subsequently studied in Leipzig with the German geographer Friedrich Ratzel,[23] the sole woman among his five hundred students.[24] The influential first volume of Ratzel's *Anthropogeographie* (1882) showed how the environment shaped — and limited — human activity. More deterministic than Ratzel, Semple applied his approach persuasively in her own influential American and Mediterranean texts.[25]

Although Sauer had serious reservations about Semple's environmentalism, he was bowled over by her lectures. "She expresses herself in a masterly style. Many public speakers would envy her." She had "poetic sensibilities as well as learning, which is a comparative rarity." Later he recalled how she "stirred the imagination and feeling with her fervor and eloquence [and] made the past live as she took us across the Appalachians and to the templed promontories of the Mediterranean."[26]

Semple took a personal interest in Sauer, bringing him to visit and dine with Chicago friends and relatives, and giving him her publications, the works of Ratzel and the economic historian Wilhelm Roscher, and on one occasion a personal note with an extract from Ralph Waldo Emerson's essay "Self-Reliance." "She's been a fine old lady who has staked large horizons for a lot of youngsters for many years," wrote Sauer not long before her death. "She wrote me a nice letter which she closed by saying 'Believe me, Carl, I love you as much as ever.'"[27]

Yet the older Sauer felt that, like so many American geographers, Semple was too prone to attribute well-being or adversity to people's natural surroundings. She had missed the true spirit and meaning of German geography, misconstruing Ratzel by not having read the second volume of his *Anthropogeographie* (1891) on the geographical distribution of mankind and cultural diffusion. While still only twenty, Sauer expressed his fear that environmentalist geographers "cannot avoid the crassest materialism. [They] think that these forces alone control the fate of humanity. If it is true, then perhaps it is better that one lives in ignorance than that one should believe that people have no control over their own destiny and are merely a product of [environmental] forces beyond themselves."[28]

Academic Doubts

Although his parents and teachers had marked him out for a bright future in academia, Sauer had other ideas. He envied fellow students who seemed to know what they wanted to do after college. "It's not that I don't like Geography well enough but I do not know if I care to teach." He had long harbored a vague ambition to edit a small-town newspaper. The call of the country editor "is strong upon me again," he wrote, "the very smell of a printing office lures me."[29]

Within a month of his start at Chicago, Salisbury and Barrows realized what a potential scholar they had with Sauer and had laid plans for him to do a doctorate. "I wonder what they'd say if I told them that there wasn't going to be any Ph.D. for me. They'd tell me I was too big a fool to deserve one, for not realizing my opportunities, which is about right. I don't want to be a learned man right now." He feared he might simply become a second-rate teacher. He warned his parents that he was not hopeful of good results and, were the fellowship not renewed, he would quit. In any case, money or not, he wanted "to re-assess whether this profession is right for me, or whether I should follow something not quite so intellectual. If only I could swap my good memory for analytical thinking, it would all be very easy."[30] He disliked the competitiveness of universities and big institutions. "In small communities where competition is at a minimum, life is easiest; it is easy to keep a pseudo-important place." It was a sentiment rooted in the Warrenton of the past, to be repeated many times in his future.[31]

In his indecisive turmoil he approached Salisbury, who didn't take at all kindly to the idea that he might quit. Salisbury told him bluntly that he didn't think he'd make a good high school teacher. He should stay in the department, which would provide some tutoring work for him. The renewal of the fellowship was dangled in front of him, provided he did well in his exams. Carl buckled in and said he'd stay another year if he could be given one or two classes to teach. After that he was determined to break loose. "I'm going south and west where the work opportunity is written large across the map," he told Lorena. "I should like to tramp through Europe and South America, and the weathered moss-grown Orient."

In April 1910 his fellowship was renewed. In addition, Salisbury recommended he do a major study of the upper Illinois River valley for the Illinois Geological Survey. The lower river courses had been done by James Goldthwaite, head of geology at Dartmouth, and by Barrows, leaving "the upper Illinois uncovered [and] a bigger stretch than either — 125 miles long from Joliet to Hennepin." The prospect was exciting; he was to be given $400 plus expenses, which seemed like a fortune, and do fieldwork he enjoyed, with assured publication of a substantial bound volume, the mark of the truly learned man. It was a glittering prize for a second-year graduate student. He was "scared stiff," he admitted to Lorena, about matching the expertise of Goldthwaite and Barrows, given his far bigger area with more large towns, but scared or not, within a month he felt more confident. "I'm pulling easy these days."[32]

His confidence began to wear thin, however, when faced with problems in the field. A month on, Barrows, on behalf of the state survey, came to see how he was getting on. "Here and there he showed me how I had missed an important point" that needed inclusion or correction, and Sauer, discouraged, found Barrows's criticisms hard to take. He had over-optimistically hoped to finish the fieldwork during the summer vacation. With only ten weeks left he had not yet touched three-quarters of the area. "If it continues like this," he told his parents, "it will hurt me having gone so far to have made a fiasco of it. However, I don't intend to give up yet."[33]

Fieldwork in the canyon country around Starved Rock near North Utica occupied much of the rest of the summer and required a few return forays in October and November.[34] Writing it up also proved much more difficult than he had anticipated. His first draft in March 1911 was twice too long. Not until August 1913 did he send the finished report to the state geologist, Frank De Wolf; it was finally published in 1916.[35] Part of the long delay stemmed from Sauer's diversion to an additional task. The Chicago Geographic Society wanted a book to accompany the 1911 designation of Starved Rock as a state park. This took still longer because Sauer had to await chapters on geology, plant life, and birds from other contributors.[36]

During the summer of 1910 fieldwork, long evenings alone without distraction, living, Sauer said, like "a hermit," gave him plenty of time to ponder his future, and isolation and fear of failure led him to a discouraging conclusion about academic life. He warned his parents, as he had before, that he was going to give up geography and university life and apply for a job with a small-town newspaper. "I've had the call to journalism ever since I could write, and I want to find out if it's a false claim." He felt that he had no realistic prospect of promotion in a university:

> I have just drifted. When I graduated you wanted me to go on with school and I went. Then I had the offer at Chicago—and you urged me to take it. I have just drifted on. I am perfectly happy with geology and geography. It is the academic life as compared to the practical life. My upbringing has been for the first but my inclination has always been for the second. I do not have the fiber of a specialist. Now I also lack the wish to specialize; it is a narrow life. When I observe the teachers in the university and I put myself in their shoes, I do not find it attractive.[37]

The university was an isolating ivory tower; he wanted to be of more use to people:

> When someone has asked me about my work they have nearly always after my explanation asked "What good does it do?" The same question has often come into my mind. I do not believe that a human being has the right to spend their life determining how old a river is, whether the ice covered the Mississippi twice or three times, and so on, at least I do not believe I have the right. I believe that there is more to life, or there should be, than unconformities of pre-glacial valleys, and interglacial periods.[38]

Now Salisbury intervened again. Duke Jones's impending year at Heidelberg left a gap in the department's teaching, and Salisbury appealed to Sauer's sense of loyalty to fill the gap. Carl accepted, but in writing to his parents he made it clear that it was out of commitment to the university, not because he wanted to go on in academe. "This does not, emphatically not, mean that I will be a teacher!" Anyhow, he rationalized, it would give him time to finish his Illinois River report. He then added something he

would most clearly contradict in later life: "I have never wanted to learn for •
learning's sake; I have realized some subjects are interesting and could be
useful as providing change or as pastimes, but they do not seem to me worth
the effort as a life time's occupation when the practical world holds endless
challenges which give us all outlets for our best endeavors."[39]

Before the year was out Salisbury tried to involve him in teaching again,
to no avail. Teaching was not something he wanted to do forever: "the chapter is closed," he said with finality.[40]

Drifting

Life in Chicago held few attractions. "I don't see what I'm doing up here,"
Sauer wrote Lorena, hoping eventually to find a kinder and less thrusting
workplace. He left campus only on Sunday visits to Cousin Mary and a few
forays back to colleagues at Northwestern. Churchgoing held no attraction
as he grew increasingly skeptical of religion, much to his parents' dismay.
By now Carl felt confident enough to discuss with his father diverse geological theories of the earth, but they parted company on Darwinian evolution. Carl had no doubts: "The men of science," like Grant at Northwestern
and Salisbury and Chamberlin at Chicago "do not understand much about
theological theories; their religion is simple, and I believe biblical; they
cannot understand why evolution should be considered unchristian, or why
there should be any conflict."[41]

Emotionally, he was focused on home, Central Wesleyan publications
keeping him in touch with Warrenton, and he couldn't get back soon
enough. "Every thud of the car tracks will say 'home' to me," he wrote, an-
ticipating his return for Christmas. Just happening to come across a topo-
graphical map of Warrenton sent him off, "every line thereon eloquent of
sights that are never equalled because they are the scenes of home."

The chronicle of deaths, marriages, and daily events in the Warrenton
newspaper, the *Banner*, engrossed him until one day in late February 1910
he came across the item "Carl Sauer spent the Christmas vacation with his
parents." "That's it," he exploded. "When I come to Warrenton now it makes
me feel like I am coming as a guest." The absence of two years had estranged
him: "old faces [were] disappearing, faces the like of which you'll never see
again for they're the partners of your boyhood—your boyhood which you

were so eager to outgrow." Yet, when one noticed it slipping away, "oh, how you would like to hold it." He knew life did not stand still and that things changed via the "wonderful law of progress," but he would like to "hold the calendar at today." He concluded that he must be a conservative. Since scholars everywhere were invoking heredity and environment to explain every human characteristic, "I guess I must shift the blame for these unprogressive sentiments of mine on my early environment and my hill-dwelling ancestors."[42] A romantic yearning for Warrenton never left him, and his sympathetic identification with rural people who had struggled close to the land had a strong influence on his later work.

Back in Chicago, Sauer's journalistic aspirations were rewarded by an offer from the Art Institute, the Field Museum, and the State Library to compile a dossier of the city's museums, libraries, and other cultural institutions. He was promised expenses and between $100 and $150 for the production of a handbook, a welcome — even essential — addition to his income.[43] Based in the Art Institute on Michigan Avenue, he began to collect information as the newly appointed secretary of the Municipal Art League. His informative and well-illustrated eighty-page book was published in 1911 as *Educational Opportunities in Chicago*.[44] Backed by the banker (and U.S. treasury secretary) Franklin MacVeagh, Sauer tried but failed to enliven the league.[45] In the end he was bitterly disappointed by this venture with the great and the good of Chicago. His unflagging energy had produced his first publication, but no further opening emerged. The experience would be repeated many times again — people liked him and admired his energy and ability to think clearly and write easily, but they often remained unresponsive to his urgings.

Seeing out his teaching commitment, Sauer was turned down by Salisbury for doing a doctorate in Heidelberg. He was now determined to leave academe. Believing experience in publishing a necessary prerequisite to journalism, in July 1912 he secured, through Goode, a position with Rand McNally, Chicago's largest publishing house, at a starting salary of $1,040 a year. His eighteen-month tenure in the job proved a disappointment far more severe than the Municipal Art League secretaryship. His manifold tasks included compiling and editing an Asian atlas, an elementary geography, a library atlas, children's books on Robin Hood and Grimm's fairy tales, and a manual on farming, to mention only a few. By mid-August he wrote that "the last five weeks have been simple drudgery."

Lorena's father would not let her marry him without a reasonable income. Sauer thought there was a tacit agreement that he would advance fairly quickly up the firm's ladder, but the promised promotion never came.[46] "I am a fool to be piddling along on $20 a week." So it went on, month after month, drudgery interspersed with rows, blowups, and broken promises. "I've had almost nothing but knocks and kicks," he complained, feeling more and more bitterly exploited.[47] September passed with no advancement. But in October Sauer was offered a bigger salary organizing the distribution of school texts in Wisconsin. This was the last straw for his father. William accused his son of squandering his education and ability, becoming a salesman, a "drummer" (i.e., a drummer up of business), lowest of the low in the despised world of commerce. As he wrote Lorena, Father thinks "selling is disgraceful"; a dignified lifelong academic position is "the best sort of thing."[48]

In fact, Sauer had been pinning his hopes on academe all along, for the trustees of the Chicago Academy of Sciences were seeking a new curator and were favorably impressed by him. But their president, the industrialist LaVerne Noyes, who ran the academy like his own business, refused to give him a salary higher than his present one and warned that any appointment would be provisional. Salvation was at hand, however, from another academic quarter. Thanks to Barrows, the State Normal School at Salem, Massachusetts, offered Sauer an assistant instructor position in geography for the remainder of the academic year from January 1914 at a salary of $2,000. Providential at a critical moment, this offer helped resolve his earlier doubts.

Sauer realized he would have been "miserable" as a salesman, since he was not "enough of a rough-neck to be enthusiastic about the road work." He felt immense relief at giving in to the inevitable and becoming a teacher. In a rare moment of self-analysis, Sauer admitted that his objection to teaching "was largely obstinacy, I guess everyone expected me to do [it] and so I felt as though I ought to do something else."[49] He now thought a teaching job infinitely preferable to other uncertainties: "I've experimented all I am going to experiment."[50] And Salisbury insisted that he return to the department after June and over the summer complete his doctoral fieldwork in the Ozarks, ideally to be subsidized and published by the Missouri State Geological Survey.

Marriage and Salem: A New Beginning

The promised salary at Salem would make possible, after several years of separation, what Sauer and Lorena had long been passionately hoping for. Some time early in 1913 neither could stand the waiting any longer, and they actively planned marriage. Lorena's father decided that Sauer had prospects after all, and he abandoned his opposition. With newfound confidence, Lorena told Sauer's parents of their plans. William was bowled over by her maturity. Her visit, Carl wrote Lorena, "pleased Papa especially much. He's quite enthusiastic about you." William's prejudices against the moneyed town merchants had evaporated, and Lorena had shown herself to be not only an accomplished pianist but a good, practical homemaker. In addition, William and Rosetta had had enough of Carl's "drifting." He needed stabilizing and settling, and Lorena had the determination and mettle to do it.[51] "Now that I have a position in the East with a good income the next thing to do is to take Lorena with me," he wrote his parents soon afterward. "There is no point in waiting any longer." In December 1913 they were married in Warrenton. The service was conducted by the president of Central Wesleyan, Otto Kriege, in Lorena's family home.[52]

Sauer's reaction to the East Coast was stereotypically midwestern. It was "effete," with "different country and different people than we are used to," though everyone was open and welcoming. "We are both delighted with our new surroundings," he wrote the Harvard geographer Wallace Atwood. "Salem's the prettiest town I believe in which I've ever been."[53] Above all, after the newness of Warrenton, its antiquity fascinated him, with "old houses built right by the road, and the old cemeteries right in the middle of town." He and Lorena took lodgings in a 120-year-old colonial building, opposite "the oldest house in Salem, built in 1648, and once the home of Roger Williams. On the border of our house is the old Shattuck house, famous because of the Salem witches."[54]

The Salem State Normal (two-year teacher training) School had about four hundred students, all top-notch high school graduates. Sauer found the department chairman, Sumner Cushing, particularly congenial, though he doubted that he knew much about the "science" of the subject. There were hardly any geography books in the school library and little money to buy new ones. Sauer drew on his childhood experience in the *Gymnasium* in Germany, whenever possible taking pupils "burdened by pedagogy" out into the immediate school surroundings — granite hills, moraines, an estuary, the seashore, and offshore reefs.[55] Joseph Pitman, the school principal, also got Sauer to devise a course in the practical sciences, rather like the "German idea of a general introduction to *Wissenschaften* [science]."[56]

On weekends, Carl and Lorena hiked into the surrounding countryside, with keen eyes for the lay of the land and potential field-trip locations. He was fascinated by New England's poor soils, which made the indifferent soils around Warrenton seem a farmers' paradise. "Everywhere the light-colored stone sticks out of the ground; the borders are stone walls put together from the fields. In the pastures you see more stone than earth." It was even poorer ground than in the Black Forest. Westward out of Salem they were almost immediately "in wilderness and rocks. We must have walked 2 or 3 miles and seen about 20 acres of good land. Everything else was wild meadow and forest land." The coast had little open land between the "mass of towns. It would be too cramped for me in such a built-up area," but from Blue Hills, southeast of Boston, "the view is really amazing. The land seems totally covered with forest and one can hardly believe that one is looking over one of the most populated areas of America, where there are almost 2 million people."[57]

The street next to theirs in Salem was shaded by elm trees and flanked by colonial-style houses with beautiful lawns. However, by May "the large elms are badly damaged by moth and look as if they are in the process of dying," he noted. The gypsy moth infestation was a harbinger of the lethal onset of Dutch elm disease a half century later. Not only were the street trees passing away but so were the inhabitants: "The old New Englanders are disappearing. The old houses and gardens give way to flats, and the simple Congregational churches are replaced by impressive Catholic churches. Now more than two thirds of the inhabitants of Massachusetts are of foreign extraction."[58]

But in June 1914 their stay in Salem came to an end. After a few weeks back in Warrenton, they left for the University of Michigan in Ann Arbor, where, thanks to Atwood, Sauer had been asked by Professor William Hobbs, the head of the Department of Geology, to run their two-month summer school. Sauer accepted the position, which included leading excursions to Lake Erie and to Niagara.

Hobbs had discussed the job with Sauer at the meeting of the Association of American Geographers at the American Geographical Society in New York in April 1914. As ever, Carl had mixed easily with the older generation of scholars. Isaiah Bowman and Ellsworth Huntington particularly impressed him, and he them. The highlight of the conference was a guest lecture by the celebrated historian of the frontier Frederick Jackson Turner, of Harvard, entitled "Geographic Influences in American Political History." This lecture may well have been the germ of Sauer's 1918 essay "Geography and the Gerrymander" (see chap. 3).[59]

The Ozarks

Immediately after the summer session, in early September 1914, Sauer set off for three months of doctoral fieldwork in the southern Missouri Ozarks. His choice of the Ozarks was greeted with sarcasm and derision by fellow students, who considered it a backwater too primitive and undeveloped to be of interest.[60] But the Ozarks, on his home doorstep, comprised a highly distinctive physical and cultural region, inhabited by enduring ethnic enclaves. The rugged, deeply incised, and heavily forested Ozark Plateau is the only significant high land between the Appalachians and the Rockies. "Ozarks" had become a byword for rural backwardness. Its inhabitants lived "a still lustily viable frontier life, relying on rifle and axe." Isolation and poor soils meant poverty for most farmers, living in log cabins or rude shacks. Wild game supplemented a meager livelihood of corn grown in valley bottoms; hogs and free-range cattle were kept out of cultivated patches by zigzag timber fences. A few roads, most just rough tracks churned up by passing herds of cattle or hogs, linked small populated pockets. Most transport was by river. Physical isolation bred fierce independence (even lawlessness) and a suspicion of strangers. The Ozarks were and still are famed for the survival of customs, folk tales, ballads, and dialect speech that trace back to seventeenth-century English and Scottish settlers who migrated there from the southern Appalachians.[61]

German and French settlers provided two other distinctive cultural enclaves. The Germans, outliers of the "Missouri Rhineland" south of the Missouri River, farmed the flatter northern fringes of the Ozarks. Ste. Genevieve, Missouri's first European settlement and initially French, was now inhabited predominantly by Germans "from Baden and they speak a south German dialect which I know would be music to Papa's ear." The remaining French were descendants of Louisiana Creoles who had moved up the Mississippi to the eastern fringes of the Ozarks. They spoke "old French," a patois akin to that of Quebec, and could not read modern French. Nor was their spelling standard French: "*Rouleau*, for instance has become *Rulo*."[62]

Sauer crisscrossed the Ozarks by train, hitched lifts with horse and wagon carriers, and often walked up to twenty-five or thirty miles a day, but at other times was slowed down by mud. "It took me four hours to walk 9½ miles," he said when he reached Moselle, northeast of St. Clair. He started at Union, just south of the Missouri River and Warrenton, crossed the heart of the Ozarks to Forsyth, and about three weeks later came back again to Ste. Genevieve on the Mississippi. For the next two months he wound his way through the northern and central Ozarks, then down once more to the heart of the hill country to Houston, Pomona, Gainesville, and Forsyth, eventually turning north through the western fringe of the Springfield Plain. He arrived home on November 22.

Day after day he clambered up and down the steep sides of the deeply incised valleys that cut into the plateau to reach the "hollors" or "shut-ins" of cultivable bottomland: "All they've done has been to clear away the timber for a space wide enough to let a wagon through. When a road climbs a hill a good heavy rain will wash it out to bed rock. Then another track is opened up and in some places you can see four or five abandoned roads by the side of the present one."

Yet no matter how far you were from a house, there was never silence; one always heard the tinkling of bells. "There are bells on cows, horses and sheep, and if hogs' necks were built differently, I'm sure they would have them on hogs." Life was hard. "Everyone is skinny and looks kinda collapsible. Looks like they ought to fatten up on this easy going existence. But they don't, they're just like their hogs." He traveled a short distance with a man "who was tramping 50 miles to save paying the $1.00 [bus] fare! Think of what his time is worth."[63]

Most of those he met were curious about what he was doing, but despite their fierce reputation they were never hostile. On the contrary, they were polite, hospitable, and generous. His Ste. Genevieve landlady saved pieces of pie from the main meal so that he would have something warm when he came in late, "and today she fixed *Bayerisch Kraut* just because I happened to say I liked it." Warming to the Ozark people and admiring "their plain ways and broad hospitality," he thought them "the salt of the earth," and contrasted easygoing life in the Ozarks with that in Salem:

> I'd like to get some of those over-civilized New Englanders out here and turn them loose where they could tramp, fish, or do most anything all over these miles of expansive hills and hollows. Turn them loose where a man can wear a blue shirt and old khaki pants and receive a welcome from every stranger he meets. And yet it would be too bad to corrupt the country with tourists, and turn these good honest folks into scheming resort keepers.

Carl's admiration for their self-contained independence, informality in dress, and enjoyment of outdoor life stayed with him all his life. He never lost his "deep affection" for the place and its people, "homefolks one and all . . . all worth knowing." It was a scene of a time mostly past. Recalling the Ozarks fifty years later, he thought rural life then was more like that of the Civil War era than that of America in the 1960s.[64]

While in the Ozarks, Carl spent several days on the Sauer family property at Whitewater, on the Caston River, a Mississippi tributary in southeastern Missouri. Proximity to the mighty river meant that the farm's forested bottomlands were recurrently flooded. There was also family land in Oklahoma, Kansas, and Illinois. William Sauer was transferring property management to his son, who had to draw up leases, select fencing, and advise on crop rotations and fertilizer needed to maintain soil fertility. The Whitewater house having recently burned down, the tenant lived with his family in a one-room smokehouse. Timber was needed for a new house and more land for crops beyond the thirty-five acres already cleared. Sauer marked some eighty-five trees and with two hired woodsmen cleared about twenty acres in the rich bottomland. This produced the needed wood and augmented his father's income, but the effort chastened him. "I am certainly a tenderfoot. My hands are so blistered that I can scarcely close them."[65] Selling the remaining woodland later provided welcome revenue for Sauer's purchase of a house in Berkeley.

Doctoral Dissertation

The Sauers returned to Chicago during the first week of January 1915 and found accommodation near the university. But after small-town Warrenton, Salem, and the Ozarks, Carl had lost all remaining fondness for Chicago: "The whole emphasis of the big city is on making and spending money, and in my opinion the people in a small town have a much more real inner life, and a more solid basis for external enjoyment."

During the final weeks of the spring term, he worked feverishly on a plan for his dissertation, which was approved by Barrows. With that decided, Carl and Lorena went back to Warrenton. Ambitiously, he hoped he could complete and submit the study by the end of the year, even abandoning plans to spend another month in the Ozarks. By the end of summer vacation he had part 1 in draft form.

Meanwhile, in July Hobbs at Michigan confirmed Carl's appointment to the newly expanded Department of Geology and Geography, pending the completion of his doctorate. It must have been an enormous spur, and he worked even harder to finish writing the dissertation.[66]

He returned to Chicago alone, since their money had run out and he was going to have to be pretty single-minded to get the manuscript in by the end of the year. Lorena stayed in her parents' home, typing up the pages as Carl mailed them and checking references in the St. Louis public library. By mid-November, Salisbury gave back part 1 "without comment or criticism," and Barrows pronounced himself "well satisfied."

In early December Salisbury said it "reads very well," a few days later declaring it "in pretty good shape," though it would need further work if Carl decided to submit it to Bowman, now director of the American Geographical Society, with an eye to publication. At his doctoral examination on December 15, 1915, Salisbury, Barrows, Goode, Tower, and Williston (a geologist) quizzed him all morning about the physiography, meteorology, soils, and settlement and historical geography of the Ozarks.[67] "Everything was all right," Salisbury told him, "and I should go to Ann Arbor and have a good time." In the mixture of euphoria and anticlimax that followed, it slowly sank in that what he had been doing all his life so far was over: "I will never have to sit on the school bench again. No one will ever quiz me any more. I've come as far as the academic line runs." Sauer felt "like I owned the earth with that dreadful degree out of the way."[68]

3

Michigan, 1916–1923

Sauer's euphoria on leaving Chicago and attaining his doctorate was soon tempered by the realities of academic life in Ann Arbor. Pressures of work, the blastingly cold winters, and an anti-German wartime campaign to oust *tidbit* him from the department because of his German parentage got him down. Although at first warmly welcomed, after two years he confessed, "I'm not the least bit enthusiastic about this place."[1] A difficult pregnancy sent Lorena home to Warrenton. During the separation she worried that he would be called up for military service. He consoled her by saying that rumors of the length of the war were probably exaggerated and that any medical examination would pick up his "unreliable heart," which would probably debar him, since "no doctor ever looked at me without saying something about it."[2] He was never even asked to undergo a medical exam and was never drafted.

Their son Jonathan was born on July 6, 1918. A few months later Sauer's father died. For all his father's worrying nature and religious strictness, Carl *in tense* had loved him dearly, and deeply appreciated the sacrifices and encouragement he had bestowed on him. Beyond that, William's steadfastness and love of learning had left an indelible mark on his son. Just over three years later, Carl and Lorena's daughter Elizabeth was born, on January 3, 1921.

The Michigan venue to which Sauer came in early 1916 was essentially a geology department, in which he was the sole geographer. His courses were immediately popular. His freshman Introduction to Geography class attracted 130 students and his Commercial Geography had 93, "more students than all the other men in the department, though the youngest member with the lowest salary."[3] His reputation as a good and interesting lecturer spread rapidly, with many business administration students directed to his commercial geography class. He led departmental summer schools, usually to Niagara and Put-in-Bay Island on Lake Erie, as he had during the summer appointment the year before. After three years at Michigan he created a departmental field center at Mill Springs in south-central Kentucky. It would prove popular with students and some staff, soon becoming a pivotal training ground for geographers from all over the country.[4]

climb

The Mill Springs Field Station, Kentucky

To provide students with comprehensive fieldwork experience embracing all elements of terrain and habitat, Sauer sought a locale that would offer considerable diversity of landforms and habitats within a relatively small area. Michigan was a poor place to experience geographical diversity. Since the entire state was covered by a fairly featureless mantle of glacially derived clays, silts, and sands, it lacked striking physiographic, structural, and geological variety. Scouring U.S. Geological Survey maps for a suitable field site elsewhere, Sauer settled on the Monticello Quadrangle in Kentucky, which promised a wide range of geology, landforms, soils, and economic conditions. Nearby were other distinctive regions—such as the Cumberland Plateau, the Pine Mountains, the Nashville Basin (the Pennyroyal), the Blue Grass Country, the Lexington Plain, the deeply incised Cumberland River Valley (with Cumberland Gap, the gateway to early westward expansion), and many oil wells and coal mines. Mill Springs provided an excellent microcosm. "Within a small compass the region represents conditions that are characteristic of a number of large areas," he wrote in the Michigan summer school catalog of 1920.

Exploring the Monticello area during the summer of 1919, he found an ideal spot near the Cumberland River and negotiated with a local builder and owner of an unused lumber mill to renovate it for student quarters. The station was virtually inaccessible by road, other than a rough eleven-mile track to Burnside, a halt on the Cincinnati–New Orleans railroad.[5] Transport along the valley-bottom flats was normally by river steamer. There was a landing stage below the mill and at every valley mouth. Most local produce went to Nashville, about a hundred miles as the crow flies along the sinuously winding Cumberland River.

Sauer's letters to Lorena from the field station describe the practical problems of renovating the mill, waterproofing the roof, getting a kitchen going, establishing a water supply, building latrines, and arranging for regular supplies of milk, butter, and meat from local farmers. Students picked pounds of blackberries daily. Hygiene was strictly observed because typhoid, hookworm, and trachoma were common in the district. With the "unspeakable" damp heat of the summer, swarms of mosquitoes and flies made malaria and amoebic dysentery ever-present dangers. There was no electricity (that was 25 years off), and one kerosene lamp sufficed for all initially. An ex-navy cook provided meals of corn and pork on a woodstove.

Academic activities included map reading, land-use surveying, digging soil pits, and mapping soil distributions. Excursions were made into the Great Smokies, around the Blue Grass country, the Pennyroyal Plateau, and coal mining districts. On one of these trips Willard Jillson, a couple of years behind Sauer at Chicago and now director of the Kentucky Geological Survey, proposed that Sauer write a regional geography of the Pennyroyal. Sauer could build upon his Ozarks study, demonstrating the prime formative agency of human culture as a geographical force.[6]

Of the field trips at Mills Springs little is known, but Sauer recounted one adventure of going down the Cumberland in a leaky old steamboat that gradually sank one night because the crew had "become lickered up on moonshine" and neglected to turn on the pumps. Unable to scramble up the steep sides of the gorge in which they were stranded, Sauer and his thirty students drifted downstream like Huckleberry Finn on a commandeered barge for some thirty miles. Eventually they reached a landing and hiked back, camping overnight in

a tough little district in the hills with a most villainous looking lot of people by no means friendly in their demeanor. That district is known as the Panhandle. Rough hills and a three counties corner is there with the result that the lawless element of the surrounding country had drifted into this place where it is easy to slip away from a pursuing sheriff. Also said to be a number of army deserters in hiding there and it is full of stills. Before we left they were offering us moonshine, but we have seen plenty of that. It flows freely in this county.[7]

Mill Springs is no more. The station disappeared under a massive artificial lake (Lake Cumberland, 101 miles long and the ninth largest in the United States) that slowly filled the deep river channel when the mile-wide Wolf Creek Dam was built in 1952 as part of the Tennessee Valley Authority's river control and hydroelectricity scheme.

"This Hounding of Hyphens"

Latent anti-German feeling, fermenting since the outbreak of war in Europe in 1914, erupted into outright discrimination and persecution when America declared war on Germany in April 1917. As early as 1915, President Woodrow Wilson had expressed his disquiet about, and hostility to, "the hyphenates," a thinly veiled attack on German Americans.[8] Sauer had long been on his guard, but he was taken aback by a campaign to oust him from the department because of his German background and supposed pro-German sympathies.

Sauer was proud of his German ancestry, and particularly admired German learning, scholarship, and intellectual achievements. He had been brought up in Missouri's "Rhineland" where German was the language of the Bible and the hymnbook and, for many, of everyday life. He took German American cultural pluralism for granted and resented the hysteria, suspicion, slander, and propaganda about German atrocities, spies, and plots, and the demonizing of German culture.[9] Almost overnight, it seemed, German Americans had gone from being the repository of all virtues of "good" settlers to pariahs and "brutal Huns." Work in the Ozarks had reinforced his admiration for the distinctive cultural traits and ways of life of the varied ethnic groups that made up the rich American mosaic. Being American had to do with citizenship, not ethnicity. Yet he was also proudly American, for, as he wrote his mother, "It's a great country we've got."[10]

Mounting vilification from the start of the war in Europe had stung him. During fieldwork in the Ozarks he came across a copy of Harper's Weekly with "an article ridiculing the Iron Cross that got my goat, the most dastardly thing I have seen. It's absolutely unbridled in its fury, somewhat insane, almost. I sat down and wrote them as hot a letter as I could think of."[11]

Back in Chicago, Cousin Mary and her husband were very pro-German and had even hung a portrait of the kaiser in their front room.[12] At church one Sunday the pastor asked the congregation to join him in a rally denouncing American export of armaments to the Allies: "About 1200 people gathered there. They were mostly Germans, Irish, and Hungarian. When one of the speakers named the name of [U.S. Secretary of State and peace advocate] William Jennings Bryan, such a roar rose from the crowd. Some began to play 'Die Wacht am Rhein' [The Watch on the Rhine]."[13]

Carl, however, was never politically active in the German cause, even as a spectator. But his father took the war seriously and personally. That his adopted country condemned his native country as the villain bewildered and deeply depressed William Sauer. Carl picked up pamphlets and newspapers at German bookshops, read Allied and German newspaper accounts in the university library, and sent literature to his family or distilled what he had read into evenly balanced appraisals of the war, hoping to soothe his father's concerns.

Sauer had an impartial grasp of the geopolitics of the war, particularly on the eastern front against Russia and in the Middle East. While he sympathized with Germany's desire for cultural unification, unlike some of his friends in Chicago he opposed German territorial aggression. The "Prussian pin-prick policy" for regaining part of Schleswig-Holstein and expelling the French from Alsace-Lorraine seemed to him obsessive. Of one thing he was sure: "Whatever the political frontiers, no war machine can ensure the unity of the German people."[14]

The departmental campaign against Sauer was spearheaded by the physiographer Irving Scott, who circulated an open letter about his alleged misdemeanors.[15] The details are lost, but it is not hard to imagine what they might have been, given the virulent anti-German feeling during one of America's periodic un-American activities witch hunts. The use of the German language was banned in twenty-six states; Congress introduced a resolution to eliminate German names from cities; German books were burned, and suspects (including ministers) were tarred, feathered, whipped, made to kneel and kiss the flag, and some were lynched.[16] At Ann Arbor four of the five professors of German were dismissed for disseminating German "culture" (which, after all, was their job!); the fifth, to save his own skin, joined Scott's campaign against Sauer. Sauer remained wearied and worried by "this hounding of hyphens."[17]

Despite department head Hobbs's anti-German sympathies and his chairmanship of the Ann Arbor branch of the xenophobic militaristic National Security League, neither he nor the university authorities were impressed by the charges against Sauer. They were without substance. Sauer had given no cause for suspicion, and he was an invaluable addition to the department. Rather than sacking him, Hobbs recommended him for promotion in 1918 and 1920.[18] However, even when the war was over, the threat remained. Discriminatory legislation against German language and instruction lay on the statute books for a further three years until declared unconstitutional by the Supreme Court in 1921.

Sauer's standing within the university was confirmed that very year. Added to his successful teaching were his outstanding publication record and his involvement with state agencies investigating the cutover lands in the northern part of the state. Although severe economizing had hit most academic staff, he was promoted to full professor. He was only thirty-three years old. Compared with those at Chicago, like "Duke" Jones and Charles Colby, who had started teaching long before him and were still assistant professors, he thought himself "unusually fortunate" to pass in six years from instructor to full professor.

> I took a bigger chance in coming to Michigan when [my] work was not established and no one knew whether it would find favorable reception. But the bigger chance of failure has worked out into the bigger chance of growth. I now have a position in geography that is better than any other in the country with the sole exception of Harlan Barrows's position [at Chicago]. And for this success I am truly grateful.[19]

The only way further salary increases would come would be through becoming chairman of the department or moving elsewhere, which "will lie some distance in the future." The star pupil was now the star geographer in a rapidly growing discipline.

Things had begun to look better in other ways, too. At the 1922 annual meeting of the Association of American Geographers in New York, he saw "a big steamer in the Hudson labeled Hansa-Bremen and a mighty fine looking boat it was. And nobody gnashed his teeth while looking at it!"[20] Perhaps German-American harassment was finally over.

Early Writing

Sauer's seven years at Michigan were unusually productive in terms of publications. Some of this work foreshadowed his intellectual repertoire in years to come, especially his distinctive cultural geography and his concern with destructive exploitation of the environment.

His work fell into four distinct topical arenas. Primary was the completion of the three regional studies that he had begun at Chicago: *Geography of the Upper Illinois Valley* (1916), *Starved Rock State Park* (1918; with Cady and Cowles), and *Geography of the Ozark Highland* (1920), based on his 1915 dissertation. These, notably the Ozarks study, were historically based syntheses of people and place the like of which had not been attempted before in American geography. Sauer felt the historical approach essential to understanding present human activities and their relations with the physical environment.

A second topic of concern was revealed in a brief but seminal review of the geologist Ernst Fischer's 1915 essay on human modification of the earth's surface. Noting that man's influence through "voluntary or involuntary meddling" was "dominantly degradational," Sauer warned that "consciousness of this geologic role of man is necessary for the continued well-being of future generations." The topic of human environmental impacts would mostly lie dormant until the 1930s but eventually became a hallmark of Sauer's oeuvre.[21]

Third was an idiosyncratic essay on political geography, "Geography and the Gerrymander" (1918). Fourth and more substantial were half a dozen papers on land use, soils, land classification, and survey methods (1915–24), developed from work done with Wellington Jones and subsequent experience in the Mill Springs Field Station. This culminated in Sauer's foundational role in the renowned Michigan Land Economic Survey (1922), set up to cope with problems of deforestation, soil degradation, and settlement in the state's northern abandoned cutover forestlands.

The Regional Studies

Sauer's first major publication, based on his 1910 fieldwork, was the 208-page *Geography of the Upper Illinois Valley* in 1916, three-fourths physiography and geology, one-fourth geography. The survey covered an area surrounding seventy miles of the river and the adjacent Illinois and Michigan Canal, from Hennepin through La Salle, Peru, Ottawa, and Morris, and nearly up to Joliet. A remarkably mature and accomplished study, it was couched in non-technical language for local inhabitants. Sauer's success in this accessible approach owed much to Salisbury, who spent days dissecting and correcting the work: "I never learned so much about writing as from the queries (as to content) and revisions (as to diction) that he gave me. Moreover, he did not eviscerate my style or idiosyncrasies—he insisted only on clarity."[22]

Sauer skillfully depicted the area's physical geography in terms of its economic activity. For example, on climatic constraints:

As in all similar latitudes, the need of growing a sufficient surplus to tide over the non-productive winter season has stimulated progress. The big barns which liberally dot the prairie landscape and dominate the cluster of buildings around the farm houses speak not only of a sturdy race of farmers and of fertile soils, but as well of the long winters which have taught the farmer providence.

Again, in describing the stepped topography of the terraces near the river valley gouged out by glacial meltwaters:

The hill farmer [on the valley-side terraces] must work harder than his neighbor of the prairie for smaller returns. Prosperity thus avoids the timbered fringe of the valleys and keeps to the open prairie. The uneven surface imposes a handicap upon the hill farmer in the marketing of his products as well as in their production; he begins with a harder row to hoe, and ends with a harder road to travel to market.[23]

Sauer experienced the country in painstaking depth:

Mother thinks I save money but waste energy by going on foot. It is harder and takes more time but when I go by horse I can only look around. When I'm on foot I do more thorough work, following up, connecting points, whereas if I'm on a horse I am held to the road and cannot do detailed work.[24]

The *Starved Rock* report in 1918 was written with Gilbert Cady and Henry Cowles to further the creation of a state park. Sauer's physical geography section was a severe compression of the Illinois River material, the human geography section a more detailed exposition of Indian and French settlement antecedents. His discussion of Indian settlement was one of the first comprehensive accounts of Native American occupance anywhere in the United States. It was a sympathetic portrayal of the intricate complexity of Indian culture when most Americans still tended to dismiss them as savages.[25]

Sauer's *Ozark Highland* doctoral dissertation, based on three months of fieldwork during late 1914 and many library forays with Lorena in Chicago and St. Louis, was published in 1920. He aimed to follow European models in regional geography the preparation of which "has hardly commenced in America."[26] In scale and depth it matched any work in France or Germany at the time.

Together with an exemplary use of English, German, and French historical sources, Sauer deployed census and county data in innovative ways, such as correlating assessed land values with soil types. The chronology of land-use entries indicated areas initially perceived as most favorable for settlement. Distance from roads was mapped as a measure of isolation.

While early accounts of exploration and observation provided abundant material on which to base an understanding of a place, Sauer bemoaned the fact that such observations were almost nonexistent for the early twentieth century. "As facilities for observation increased[,] their number was reduced, until at present there is almost no contemporary [regional] geographic literature."

Six years' absence from the Ozarks gave him "a more objective viewpoint without destroying the old familiarity." His many months of living in and tramping over the region had made it impossible for him to think of it like an outsider—it was part of "home," its scenes "forever green":

The old white church, astride its rocky point, overtopped by cedars that grow on the warm rock ledges, forever looks forth upon the fairest valley. The lower slopes are abloom with red clover, or golden with wheat. Wide fields of blue-green corn border the shaded stream, where the bass lurk in transparent pools. In the distance forests of oak mantle the hillsides, up which, past spacious farmhouses, the country roads wind. The people who move upon the scene of this account are homefolks one and all. Some have succeeded better than others, some give greater promise than others, but they are all well worth knowing, and in all cases an understanding of their various problems of making a living goes far to explain their contrasted conditions. In this spirit the study is undertaken . . . of the old home with its many and vivid associations.[27]

He foresaw the future prosperity of the Ozarks as a recreation ground, water collection area, and scenic state park, although he never envisaged the collapse of traditional hill farming that was to come.

Sauer's insight into how Ozark people lived derived from knowing how that living had been fashioned. It was his first eloquent evocation of the importance of the temporal dynamics of people and place—of the qualities expressed in particular habits and habitats. It was the inception of his distinctive form of historical cultural geography.

A fourth regional monograph, *Geography of the Pennyroyal*, dealt with the eastern region of the upper Cumberland Valley of Kentucky. Fieldwork began in the summer of 1920, with the assistance of Kenneth McMurry and Michigan graduate students John Leighly and Clarence Newman. "The dominant theme . . . is the expression of the individuality of the region, as the site of a particular group of people and of their works." Publication was delayed until 1927 by which time Sauer was at Berkeley.[28]

The Gerrymander

Sauer's 1918 "Geography and the Gerrymander" was one of the earliest academic analyses of a widespread type of political chicanery. The term *gerrymander* came from Elbridge Gerry, the governor of Massachusetts, and at the time of his death James Madison's vice-president. In Massachusetts his administration had consolidated the opposition Federalist Party voters into a few electoral districts, thereby disproportionately favoring Gerry's Jeffersonian Republican candidates. Myth has it that an elongated and strangely shaped new district northeast of Boston was seen in a newspaper office by the painter Gilbert Stuart, who added a head, wings, and claws to make it resemble a lizard-like amphibian. "That will do for a salamander," he reputedly said. "No," said a bystander, "it is a Gerrymander." The gerrymander violates two basic principles of electoral apportionment—compactness and equality of constituency numbers. It maximizes the effectiveness of supporters' votes and minimizes those of opponents. The latter are massed in a single district to reduce their influence in surrounding districts.[29]

Sauer examined how this widely practiced and generally tolerated political abuse operated in Missouri, Kentucky, and Tennessee. All three states exhibited damning boundary manipulations favoring one party or the other. In Missouri, such manipulation enabled the Democrats to stretch "an exceedingly slight majority to a control of seven-eighths of the seats in Congress." Sauer contrasted the eight "geographical divisions" of Missouri identified in his fieldwork to the fourteen congressional districts that cut across them. Thus in the "atrociously gerrymandered" Seventh District, the solid Republican area of German farmers along the Missouri River was outnumbered by Democrats from poorer farming areas of the Ozarks. This violated both electoral fairness and geographic unity. "No argument of common origin or economic interest can be advanced to justify placing the voter of Howard in the Boonslick [German] area in the same district with the citizen from Greene in the Ozarks." Similarly, the Fourteenth District paired the prosperous cotton farmers of the Mississippi valley lowlands with the poorest inhabitants of the uplands, the "most Ozarkian of the Ozarks. A more ill-matched group would be hard to find. There is not even direct communication between extremities of this district." Sauer recommended radical reform: "compact districts with maximum accessibility and due regard to economic and historic bonds."[30] Gerrymandering remains a major political abuse.[31]

Forests, Soils, and Settlement

Sauer's arrival in Michigan coincided with a heated debate about the future economic viability of cutover (logged) areas in the northern part of the state. Michigan's problem had been looming for years. Timber production had peaked in 1889, the year of Sauer's birth, when more than 5.4 billion board feet (b.f.) of timber were cut, of which more than three-quarters was highly prized white pine, a strong, straight-grained, white wood.[32] A decade before, Harvard's Arnold Arboretum director, Charles Sargent, had sounded a warning:

> Michigan once possessed a tree covering of great density, richness and variety but . . . [s]erious inroads have already been made upon the forests of Michigan. The hard wood has been generally cleared from the southern counties, now largely occupied by farms. . . . The merchantable white pine has been cut from the banks of the principal streams and the shores of the lakes, and what now remains is remote from water transportation or scattered in isolated bodies of comparatively small extent.[33]

Sargent had not reckoned on the ability of the lumber companies to prolong the boom and completely scalp the land by laying light railways, easily moved to isolated stands to take away the last remaining logs. With each decade, diminishing, though still enormous, amounts were shipped out. In 1899 it was 3 billion b.f.; in 1909, 1.8 billion b.f. The year Sauer came to Michigan, 1916, was the last when production hit 1 billion b.f. Thereafter it dwindled to around half a billion b.f., almost none of it white pine, mostly hemlock and other inferior species.

To wring the last penny out of the land the lumber companies indulged in boosterish and misleading advertising, selling the stump-strewn acres to prospective farmers, usually unsuspecting immigrants from northern Europe. Unlike southern Michigan, the northern counties had predominantly poor, sandy soils and a short growing season. Failure was common. Land was abandoned by the struggling farmers or never taken up. No taxes were paid, and so state revenues suffered. Moreover, decades of "cut out and get out" logging had left a thick carpet of trash on the forest floor, fueling destructive fires that engulfed many communities nearly every year. The legacy of the cutover was a major economic, social, and geographical problem, not only in Michigan but also in the other Great Lakes states, Wisconsin and Minnesota, and in southern lumbering states.

Soon after arriving in Ann Arbor, Sauer proposed a geographical survey as a basis for possible rehabilitation of the once-forested lands. Soil-type mapping was essential for understanding "the agricultural conditions and possibilities of the region." Still more important, as his experience in the Ozarks had shown, were slope, degree of erosion, vegetation, and proximity to markets. Farmers' experience should be recorded. Survey results could be displayed on county maps as "a complete panorama" of rural conditions and a tool to plan rehabilitation or retreat from marginal farming areas, as well as a beneficial guide to the "progressive resident, the home seeker, and the student of rural affairs."[34]

Sauer stressed the urgent need to evaluate Michigan's soils, for "heavy cropping, deforestation and other acts of exploitation have brought us hard up against the fact that the resource of the land is fast diminishing."[35] By 1921 he had combined all these strands of soil, land use, and agricultural potential into a proposed national land classification system.[36] Ultimately a national survey of land values was required to short-circuit the painstaking analysis of individual county courthouse records such as he had done in the Ozarks.

Sauer wrote against the background of postwar agricultural distress. Farming was soon to be toppled from its preeminence in the economic life of the nation, becoming subordinate to manufacturing. Some 300 million acres of cutovers in the south and 40 million acres in the Great Lakes states could possibly be settled, but this would not be easy. In the northern states "pine stumps, especially white pine, remain a most serious obstacle to land clearing for many more years. There is known as yet no generally profitable way for the removal of the stumps [because] their resinous qualities make them proof against decay." Pioneer farmers were still coming forward to settle the land, but they were less experienced than their precursors. Consequently, the settlement process was "painfully slow and wasteful of human energies, and the correction of mistaken judgments is very costly." Identifying the poorest land would, he hoped, avoid the "alarmingly high rate" of failure. Moreover, while the once-forested land was rarely suitable for farming, it also cost too much to get it reforested. Hence the country faced "a forest famine of appalling proportions."[37]

Through these reports Sauer played a major role in the creation and operation of Michigan's Economic Land Survey. Sauer was no crusader for state action, however, and was careful to lie low after the moves against him as a German American only a few years before. The public campaign was left to the conservationist Parrish Storrs Lovejoy, whom Sauer admired for his punchy, outspoken appraisal of the situation.

Five years older than Sauer, Lovejoy had been a U.S. Forest Service supervisor in Wyoming. In 1912 he was invited to the University of Michigan as an instructor. But he was a maverick. With "splenetic tongue and pen" he railed against the academic "temple," alienating many in the university and state administration. Denouncing the lack of control of logging and fire suppression, he wrote pseudonymous, fanciful stories under the title "Chronicle of Mr. Paul Bunyan" in the *American Lumberman* and *Country Gentleman* throughout 1916 and 1917, castigating land boosters who were trying to sell farms in the cutovers.[38]

"One third of Michigan today is bankrupt," Lovejoy began in his 1919 speech to the Michigan Academy of Science. He exposed the fallacy of the received wisdom that "farms follow forests," directing his venom at landboom frauds in the northern cutovers by colonization companies (often subsidiaries of the loggers and the railroads), aided and abetted by politicians and local boosters "insisting before the world that theirs is truly the garden spot of the world." Agricultural advisers too had misled settlers with unrealistic hopes of fruit growing, grazing, and clover production in the cutovers. The cutovers could only grow "timber or nothing."[39]

Inspired by Lovejoy, Sauer started "dabbling along on some legislative measures concerning Michigan Land development."[40] Ever the consummate summarizer, he converted Lovejoy's diatribe into a carefully worded research proposal "that an economic survey be established."[41] Thus Sauer sold the survey proposal to the state. Work began in September 1922 in Charlevoix County, Lower Peninsula, with a mix of farms, forests, and recreational resources. This became the template for the subsequent sixteen county surveys.[42]

Following initial fieldwork in Michigan's Upper Peninsula, Sauer carried out a pilot survey in Charlevoix County with two students, John Leighly and Warren Thornthwaite, both of whom later went with him to Berkeley. He sympathized with the farmers' poverty and extreme isolation, compounded by the absence of English among most first-generation Finns, Swedes, and

Poles. Many were so poor that they worked barefooted in the fields. But conditions in the Upper Peninsula were still worse. Around Marquette he had to use sign language to communicate with the Finnish farmers, though the team also compiled a basic Finnish/English vocabulary.[43]

Although Sauer had led in the survey's establishment, his status in it remained ambivalent and insecure. He found himself "just a tolerated outsider. The plans are too sketchy and ill-considered for there to be any well-defined job waiting a person."[44] However, the question of his ultimate role in the survey never arose. In May 1921 the University of California had put out feelers to get him to come to Berkeley. A year later he was visited by a Berkeley dean, but "doubt anyway if California will make me an offer that would take me away from Michigan." Michigan had just offered him a professorship in the Department of Economics, and he and Duke Jones had just organized the first of what became a successful series of conferences on field-survey procedures and objectives in agricultural areas.[45]

Earlier that year, after an impromptu talk with the federal secretary of agriculture Henry Wallace and with the head of the Department of the Interior's Land Classification Board, Sauer was appointed to a USDA advisory committee, along with the American Geographical Society's director Isaiah Bowman, and Professor Richard Dodge of Columbia University.[46] At one level all was going well, but his position in the survey was not resolved, and he was committed to endless summer fieldwork with the survey and the Mill Springs summer camp. Many years later he reminisced that he realized he would be "tied down for an indefinite time in the future and I wanted to get out on my own and roam new areas." And so he did. Sauer negotiated a favorable financial arrangement with the University of California, and by July 1923 he and his family were moving across the continent to his new post as chairman of the Department of Geography at Berkeley. The cutovers, land use, surveys, Mill Springs, and Michigan were now things of the past.[47]

> We still suffer badly from an oversupply of men who learn
> their stuff from books and an undersupply of men who
> are building up a science based on observation.
> — Carl Sauer to Arthur Trowbridge, 1935

4

Berkeley

AN INSIDER, 1923–1941

When Carl Sauer and his family arrived in Berkeley in 1923 they left behind nearly everything that was familiar. Warrenton, their birthplace and beloved sanctuary from busy urban life, was far away and time-consuming to visit. The extreme heat and cold of the Midwest gave way to the equable climate of California's Bay Area. He was glad to leave Ann Arbor, of which he "did not ever grow fond":

> I never went back to Ann Arbor and its raw fall weather without the feeling of a man going to a prison sentence, that creeping drabness that precedes the Michigan winters. I must have had some ancestors that lived in Mediterranean climes or perhaps this nostalgia with me was just the European's "Drang nach Süden." Perhaps then it's a long pent-up northern blood which makes me content in California or the desert with a greater contentment than I have known elsewhere.[1]

Also left behind was all the research Sauer had been doing. The Michigan Economic Land Survey, in which he had invested so much, was abandoned, and from then on only two of his publications harked back to his pre-Berkeley time—a short essay on surveys and field studies and the Pennyroyal monograph.[2] He was determined not to be tied down either by summer school teaching or by a permanent field center, as he had been at Michigan.

Settling in was not easy; his growing young children, search for a suitable house in Berkeley, and money worries took much of his time and energy, and he was laden with duties that came with running a department. Sauer was in debt to his mother, his aunt Tilly, and others to the tune of at least $20,000, four times his $5,000 starting salary.

He had been buying and improving farmland to add to what he had inherited. But his faith in agricultural investment, likewise inherited from his father, took a battering after the First World War as prices for land and farm produce plummeted.[3] Farm production and rental provided almost no profit. Desperate for money, he decided to market the timber on his Canalou and Whitewater properties, whose ash, cypress, and tupelo were in great demand, and then sell the land, but low land prices during the 1920s farming depression stymied his sale plans.[4] The farms remained a drain on his finances. He paid dearly for his almost irrational faith in the virtues of the rural life, making his early years in Berkeley one long worry. "I certainly was the prize sucker of all when I took hold of that land" in Canalou, he wrote his mother. "Financially my only hope is to live to see that day when I shall own no more land than will make room for a house." But he did not get rid of the farms until much later.[5]

From the vantage point of Berkeley everything Midwest began to feel distant and irrelevant. Not only was he disenchanted with owning land, even his beloved Warrenton seemed less significant, with few of his boyhood neighbors left. He heard periodically of the deaths of those he had known there, and the premature demise at forty-two of Paul Wipperman, "the friend of my boyhood," struck him forcibly. In 1926 he discontinued his subscription to the *Banner*. "The population has been replaced by newcomers since we left," and "the town appears to have grown almost a stranger, as though we had never lived there." Warrenton was no longer "home," although he missed seeing his nearest relatives. He hoped they would come to him in Berkeley, since "I don't get anything out of these trips back to Missouri anyway and I want a good visit with all of you."[6]

And then there was his cousin Mary Werweke, whose unbounded kindness had provided him with a "home from home" during those early years in

Chicago, and whom he cared for most after his immediate family. She was now widowed and suffering from acute anemia. The thought of an ailing, elderly lady alone in very modest circumstances in Chicago was "nothing less than ghastly. . . . It gives me shivers to think that we might be living in that city—but to Cousin Mary it is the world she knows and no doubt she still likes it as she always did. I can think of no more awful place in which to live unless it be Detroit or Cleveland or fifty smaller cities in that general section—or Los Angeles. But evidently I'm in an unpopular minority since millions have decided in their favor."[7]

As for Central Wesleyan College, he had early become critical of its academic worth. In 1924 he turned down a request for contributions. "I think of it in the past and not in the future. The old faculty is gone or will soon be gone."[8] A few years later the college faced a crisis over finances and insufficient students. It was not attracting the region's German-origin settlers; in the aftermath of the wartime animus against them, they were no longer eager to preserve their heritage. The college finally closed its doors in 1941, its students' records and library transferred to Northeast Missouri State Teachers College, now Truman State University in Kirksville. In Warrenton only the college church has survived.[9]

Geography at Berkeley

Geography had been taught at Berkeley since 1898 but only gained a strong footing with the appointment of Ruliff Holway in 1904. Holway, like most geographers at that time a geologist by training, was made assistant professor in 1914, and full professor in 1919. He retired in 1923 when Sauer arrived, and died soon afterward. Modest and unambitious, Holway's research was in physical geography, notably on the cold-water belt current that drifted south along the West Coast, giving rise to the region's distinctive fogs, and on glaciation in the coastal ranges.[10] Wanting to add an instructor or associate professor to his department, in 1911 Holway asked Rollin Salisbury at Chicago about likely candidates. Sauer was recommended as an outstanding scholar and a "rising star," and Holway offered him an associate professorship in 1917. Sauer declined because he needed to consolidate his geographical survey and land use work and complete the *Starved Rock* and *Ozarks* monographs.

TO PASS ON A GOOD EARTH

During 1923, with Holway's retirement imminent, advances were again made. "The offer raises most intriguing thoughts of what one might do in cultivating the virgin fields of the far West and the Pacific area," replied Sauer. "I have spent my time in apprenticeship at Michigan. I may transfer elsewhere to practice the trade I've been learning."[11] In April he sent University of California president David Barrows his shopping list. Fieldwork was to be an all-important part of the teaching program. He wanted a small department of three: "One for regional (human) geography, one for commercial geography (economic geography in the narrower sense), and one for physical geography and cartography (including climatology)." The first he would cover; the third would be done by John Leighly, whom he wanted to bring from Michigan, a man of "unusual capacity" whose "intellectual curiosity is insatiable."[12]

Sauer was most eager to start field research in Latin America. But that needed money he did not have. He put in a request to the Rockefeller Foundation, "which is skeptical as to whether our Latin American plans involve enough human betterment." The majority of successful applications bore a strong bias toward educational and social reform. Sauer concluded, "Scholars and *Weltverbesserer* [world improvers/starry-eyed idealists] are in the main two different kinds of creatures. Let someone come along and offer almost anything that includes the name 'labor problem' or 'international relations' and promise to hasten the millennium and he can get almost anything he wants." This was the first articulation of his deep distaste for social science engineering which dominated his outlook in later years.[13]

At first too much of his time was taken up with committees, to which the dean of the Graduate School happily assigned him because, in Sauer's opinion, there were "only about 30 men in the university who are any good in matters of judgment! So I should feel flattered, but I do think a university member should be first and last a scholar. I don't know that regulating other folks' affairs helps much. I'm a Jeffersonian in looking at all government as an evil and wishing that life might be as unconfined as ever possible."

When his mother accused him of harboring "socialist" sentiments, Sauer replied:

You have a deal more patriotism than I possess. I am pretty sure that there is less of wisdom and less of high ideals in the seats of the mighty than history records. We have been blessed with a marvelous country but I confess that there is mighty little in our political history or our present that stirs me. The story of our pioneers contains many things that are fine—in the tenacity of humble folk and the institutions they built, but our recent political history wins praise from no one outside this country. We are *"übermütig"* [arrogant], and we worship the sanctity of government much more than is good for us. I am not a socialistie— I hope I am a very old fashioned individual[ist]—hence my Jeffersonian sentiment about the evils of government. I am quite content therefore to be [a] geographer. It is safe and yields the pleasure of a contemplative life. Perhaps that is why the old monks left so much that is fine and enduring. I shall be quite content if I may add a few pages that people may occasionally read after me and say it was well done.[14]

The work piled up and life became "more complicated all the while." But during the next few years he shed some committees, got down to writing, and was enjoying university life. He had established good working relations with Alfred Kroeber and Robert Lowie in anthropology and Herbert Bolton in history. He described Berkeley as "a nice university" unlike the "almost unbearable ruthlessness" of Michigan:

I feel completely at home here. I belong to what goes on around here. These are my associates in work, and there's a real warm feeling of home coming to getting back on the campus that is all very different from a return to the campus in Michigan. At Michigan I was always an outsider looking in. But there's no loneliness here. It's home—more so than I would have imagined seven years ago an individual could feel towards a great institution. I was an outsider, but here I'm an insider.[15]

Sauer was not intensely political, but questions of right and wrong, of fairness, of justice for the disadvantaged versus privilege for big business, and of the assumed superiority of the East Coast's "old colonial or English stock" elicited frequent outbursts in favor of the "underdog." Some of this stemmed from his midwestern upbringing, some from his pugnacious independence, much from his German-American origins and the persecution he had suffered at Michigan in 1918.

During the presidential campaign of 1924, when the Progressive candidate Robert M. La Follette Sr. was attacked as a "Communist Revolutionary, [pro-] Liquor, Catholic, Jew, Pro German, Jap-lover—every conceivable bogey is trotted out in order to scare people," Sauer feared that "we are in an ugly period of religious and patriotic intolerance."

> I really do not believe much in democracy, but I have no use for plutocracy and I believe that the Republic has sold its soul to the money devil. If money meant a competent aristocracy I should be for it but it means the predominance of the sorriest elements in a citizenship. Until we have an aristocracy that is based on actual superiority, I shall feel that the Jeffersonian principles are best and am unable to find them anywhere except in this little group that stands for greater equality to all citizens.[16]

Calvin Coolidge won by a landslide, with La Follette in third place. In 1928 Coolidge was succeeded by Herbert Hoover, whom Sauer disdained, on the one hand for "cold-blooded shrugging of the shoulders at a crisis that will leave our rural sections with permanent scars and on the other for a disgusting readiness to make the government the defender of business speculations." Agriculture was being bled dry. The administration had less "concern for the American farmer [than] it has for the interests dubious and otherwise of American business in Nicaragua and Mexico."

Moreover, Sauer mistakenly thought Hoover markedly anti-German. Sauer warmed to Al Smith as the champion of the underdog, and was incensed by the anti-Catholic opposition to him. "Fanaticism is abroad in the land, as of another sort it was twelve years ago and I'm against it."[17]

Smith made a good showing in the upper Midwest, thanks in part, Sauer thought, to many Scandinavians there who

> were tired of being Yon Yonsoned by the older Americans and who saw in the son of an Irish immigrant a symbol of equality in American life which had been denied them so far. No one has ever seriously striven for the presidency who is not of old colonial or English stock.

They alone have been "the people." For the first time a champion of the "lesser breeds" has arisen in whose success these people may erase some of the inferiority that has facilely been imposed upon them. I can imagine, not only the lowly negro but Italian, Pole, Swede, and German marching under the banner as a declaration of a larger share for themselves and their children in American citizenship.

He felt that if you did not bear a colonial name you were always regarded as inferior:

Though things are far better [in California] than any place I have lived in since I grew up, the children of Dick Humphrey [a Warrenton neighbor] with a college education would have an easier time of it probably than ours will with their German names. [But] the immigrant stigma is breaking down and many see in Al Smith the champion of equal rights for equal merit [regardless] of birth.[18]

Morphology of Landscape

Beyond vague thoughts of expeditions to Mexico and elsewhere, Sauer seemed to have had no research agenda in mind when he moved to California.[19] One thing he wanted to publish as soon as possible, however, was a reasoned statement of his rejection of the philosophy of environmental determinism then dominant in American geography. Rather than humanity being confined to doing what the environment required or permitted, he believed that ingenuity, learning, and culture were primary agencies. Although he admired the lectures and writing of his mentor and friend Ellen Churchill Semple, he rejected her view that environmental forces controlled human fate. In so doing he expected to "disagree pretty thoroughly with almost all geographers in this country."[20]

He sought to vindicate his position by appealing to the exemplary work of European geographers.[21] In this, "I have the chance to do something pretty important." And important it proved to be. "The Morphology of Landscape" in 1925 was a tour de force that defied previously held American notions of human geography.[22] Yet "Morphology" is a heavily learned essay, verbose, abstruse, and complicated, unlike Sauer's usual pithiness, directness, and simplicity.

Sauer may have borrowed the term *morphology* from Goethe, whose works he knew well. Morphology entails process and organic growth in both humanity and nature. Sauer saw all aspects of landscape, natural and human alike, as dynamically interrelationed over time, and not simply dependent on environmental mechanisms. His phenomenology of landscape stressed the importance of a "symphonic quality in the contemplation of the areal scene" that stemmed from empathetic understanding and intuitive insight, or *Verstehen*—the beliefs, ideas, and customs of diverse cultures.[23]

Place and landscape could not be understood "except in terms of time relations as well as space relations in a continuous process of development or of dissolution and replacement." As he had documented in *Pennyroyal*, successive generations of occupants fashioned the cultural landscape out of the natural landscape. Historical geography studied the "changes cultural landscapes have undergone and therefore involves the reconstruction of past cultural landscapes." History was integral to Sauer's geography.[24] He viewed landscape as a palimpsest of past human presence. For example, on a hill slope near San Jose, California, he described a farm that had been in the same family since 1852, originally a Spanish land grant. "There is still standing an old Mexican adobe house. . . . And beneath the house are the remains of an old Indian settlement," relics from which are in the house walls.[25]

At Berkeley, Sauer sought to demarcate the subject matter of geography from that of geology, as well as to "emancipate" geography from determinist thinking.[26] Much to Sauer's distress, his essay subsequently became a new orthodoxy. "My generation of geographers was weaned on it," Leonard Wilson wrote Sauer twenty-three years later. Some regarded it as an inspired programmatic statement of the nature of geography, others as a prescription to restrict geography to the study of "observable" features, many as an authoritative statement of "what geography should not and should be," what it should exclude and what it should include. This was the opposite of Sauer's purpose. He later observed that "several of the Middle Western geographers apparently had spent more time reading it than he had in writing it."[27]

From today's viewpoint it is difficult to appreciate the hostility with which "Morphology" was received by those wedded to ahistorical environmental determinism. Sauer's subversive ideas were even thought to put careers at stake. "My article is apparently disgusting my fellow geographers and I shall have a row on my hands with them," he wrote the following year.[28] However, he subsequently did almost nothing to bolster the arguments in "Morphology," nor did he produce a substantive study of cultural landscape formation along the lines he had set out.

A further attack on the sterility of Semple's kind of environmental determinism, extolling the superiority of the cultural view of change, came in a lackluster survey of the history of geography in which Sauer emphasized the impact of human action on the earth and the need for historical understanding of cultural evolution.[29] A brief but lucid article four years later for the *Encyclopaedia of the Social Sciences* likewise stressed the role of humans in modifying the earth through destructive exploitation resulting in soil erosion and vegetation change.[30]

Sauer had no stomach for methodological disputation, but was dragged into it again by dismissive reviews of Jacob Früh's *Geographie der Schweiz* and Robert Gradmann's *Süddeutschland* in 1930 and 1931. Clearly environmentalism had not yet been exorcised from the American body geographic. Sauer was stung by what he saw as the reviewers' ignorant bias in complaining that the books contained too much physical geography and paid too little attention to the "life responses to the physical conditions of the regions." He wrote to Gladys Wrigley, editor of the *Geographical Review*:

Geographers who do not care to do physical geography have the right to limit themselves, although it is a bit queer that the environmentalists should care so little about the physical qualities of regions. But whence do they derive the authority to correct or even to read out of the party those who concern themselves also with the origin of land forms? . . . I am at a loss to understand this pernicious anemia that has seized upon some geographers, expressed in a weary shaking of the head at sight of a fellow student happily productive and in the monotonous, sepulchral query: "But is it geography?" Imagine geologists saying about their work: "The work is good but is it geology?," or economists forever saying to themselves: "We must not not look into this matter, for it might turn out to be history or political science!"

Barbed wire fences may be necessary in elementary curricula, but the pursuit of knowledge cannot afford to frustrate itself by building fences about narrow plots of learning.[31]

Geographers spent too much time arguing about what was geography and "churning around in methodology." He later wrote: "I still remember those dreadful seminars at Chicago in which there was no curiosity about what a man found, but only discussions of relevance to a particular definition of geography. One would not find anthropologists or geologists indulging in such introspection."

Wrigley sympathized with Sauer and published his "diatribe" with the title "Correspondence" but said she would far rather have a piece about the kind of geography he wanted. He would not oblige. "I have no interest at all in writing on the nature and objectives of the field of geography." He had done that once with "Morphology of Landscape," and "God helping, I shall never write anything more in methodology: it's a habit forming drug." Nevertheless, he was prepared to pen "an apology" to European colleagues whose work was not appreciated in America. He also sensed (hopefully) that younger geographers were rebelling against the "simplified formulas" established near the turn of the century. William Morris Davis, the "Grand Old Man" of geomorphology, had written a "Decalogue" that closed off physiography from further inquiry, and an even worse dogmatism had gripped human ecologists at the University of Chicago. Younger geographers wanted to return to the "older, more generous traditions of the field," but if an established scholar like himself would not take up the cudgels, insecure beginners dare not for fear of losing their jobs. He contrasted geographers' "painful orthodoxy" with the "unceasing questioning of tenets" by anthropologists, for whom time was not static or cyclic, but directional, close to Sauer's environment–human continuum. He wanted a wider and more ecumenical geography.[32]

True to his word, Sauer said no more about methodology until 1940, when his presidential address to the Association of American Geographers repudiated much of his "Morphology of Landscape." Instead he had already started something completely different: geomorphological investigations in Baja California and Arizona.

"I Should Never Have Tackled That Country"

Since studying geology at Northwestern and physiography at Chicago, Sauer had done little physical geography. On arriving in Berkeley he had been "frightened off the study of landforms, soils, and vegetation" by the physical scientists,[33] notably the blunt and irascible geologist A. C. Lawson, who, according to Sauer, was said "to devour geographers for dessert."[34] Perhaps Sauer simply wished to lay the ghost of Lawson. He was pigheaded enough to rise to the challenge. And ever the unconventional academic, just as he had rejected the conventional orthodoxy of environmental determinism for a cultural interpretation of the human landscape, so he now embarked on a similar exercise in physical geography.

The conventional explanations of geomorphological process were those of Davis, who had, said Sauer,

> formulated a theory of recurrent geographic cycles, of uplift, erosion, and wearing down to a peneplain, passing through stages of youth, maturity, and old age. . . . The cycle might be long or short, its length and position in time were irrelevant. Davis was our first and greatest maker of a system that replaced the complexity of events by a general order. Theory was illustrated by models, the block diagrams which he drew so well to show his concept of how the modeling of the land should pass from stage to stage.[35]

But Davis's work included no examples, and Sauer did not believe that landforms were all the same or erosional processes that uniform. Davis had become so adamant that he would take no criticism of his ideas. Such pontificating was to Sauer like a red rag to a bull.[36] Ever to the fore with the latest geographical literature, he thought that the Austrian geomorphologist Walther Penck provided a viable alternative to the Davisian cycle, enabling Sauer to "plant a little seed of discord." That few other Anglophone geographers could actually read the "peculiarly agonized German" of Penck's 1924 *Die morphologische Analyse*, which was not translated into English until 1953, added to Sauer's sense of leading a revolution. Penck suggested that much erosion involved the mass movement of weathered-down slope material rather than slow attrition by streams. This made sense when one looked at California hillside fence lines, which sagged with the movement of the soil.[37]

During the winters of 1926 to 1929 Sauer made extended visits to Baja California and adjacent Arizona—the very region Lawson had made his own. But Sauer had problems interpreting the landforms. By 1929 he had made little headway on this "hard and not very congenial task." The lesson was clear:

I never should have tackled that country if I had known how elusive its problems are. But having invested the time and money in it I am trying to drive myself to get it out of the way. The physical geography is almost throughout the hardest stuff in the world. Almost no one has dared to tackle any of it. It's primarily a problem of crustal movements, and to interpret those in the topography, soils and drainage features is delicate and dangerous stuff.[38]

His first conclusions, in "Land Forms in the Peninsular Range of California" (1929), were and remain highly contentious, being "fully as *a priori* as any Davisian interpretation." He struggled on with a poor and inconclusive second essay on southern Arizona, "Basin and Range Forms in the Chiricahua Area" (1930). "One has the distinct impression," concludes a later geomorphologist, "that most of his observations were from the railroad car."[39]

In 1931 Kirk Bryan and Gladys Wickson at Harvard criticized the 1929 paper as slipshod and its Penck-derived conclusions as questionable. It was a disastrous verdict for Sauer, who had admired Bryan's work in the past. The critique and ensuing publicity were deeply wounding.[40] It was the end of his futile foray into geomorphology, which showed bad judgment at a time when he should have been concentrating his energies on the things he was best able to do. It was typical of him to react against some handed-down orthodoxy, and to the pomposity of those who set themselves up as infallible intellectual leaders. He admitted, perhaps a little arrogantly, that he had done so. Yet he could not forgive Bryan's public criticism, and added him to his demonology of Davis and other "experts":

The more I see of Bryan the more I think he has the bumptiousness of the half literate. He excommunicated me in the Warner Valley study.

Goodness knows I don't consider that paper as anything more than asking a series of questions. Bryan seems to have undertaken to suppress all observing and thinking which does not follow him or his prophets, and believe me he is a long way from having the skill or the knowledge necessary to the success of such censorship.

Sauer had learned a hard lesson that left him feeling pretty low.[41] However, Bryan was a dangerous enemy, and the spat would have more serious consequences in future years.

The Berkeley Department, 1930s

While Sauer was doing pathbreaking work on the nature of geography, he also had a department to run. That entailed endless meetings, teaching classes, and graduate student supervision. Moreover, this was also when his reputation reached prestigious heights in government, foundation, and academic circles.

On campus Sauer was at ease in his own department, where he was king. The small department had not grown since his arrival in 1923. There were three staff members, himself, Leighly, and a visitor, a position filled by Sauer's Latin Americanist colleague Oscar Schmeier from 1925 to 1929, and various others thereafter, plus a few graduate teaching assistants. "I range after a fashion over the New World as to regional courses, and am sponsor for the work in land forms and partly for historical geography," he wrote in 1932. "Leighly has maps, climate, and a share of Europe. [The German cultural geographer Gottfried] Pfeifer has economic geography and another stake in Europe. We have nothing on the other side of the Pacific because we know nothing about it."

A departmental strong point was the virtual absence of disciplinary boundaries. Staff and graduate students ranged over many academic fields. Sauer's major contacts were with Kroeber in anthropology and Bolton in history: "There are very few geographers with whom I could have as much in common. We three supplement each other in [a] manner that removes all thought of competition and certainly of friction. Bolton says I am a good historian, and I know that Bolton has got his historical geography straight."

They all felt that their strength lay in "joint fields for degrees and also of joint fields in research."[42]

Sauer later worried that the Berkeley campus was becoming too big, more "an assembly of specialists," less and less a place in which individuals could pursue their own interests. His hardening conviction that "smaller is better" began to loom large: the small community limited the degree of specialization. "Perhaps because of my small-town background I have a lingering confidence in such less specialized groups."[43]

Sauer and His Students

Early on Sauer had shared Salisbury's view that the material taught was of "little significance, the value of a teacher is in the influence he has as a teacher," inspiring students to learn for themselves by wide reading. He was a firm believer in self-direction generated by intellectual curiosity. True scholars needed no assignment but merely the leeway to follow their own bent, as he had been fortunate enough to follow his.

Sauer's undergraduate teaching was a fairly consistent routine. A former graduate student, Joe Spencer, recalled that it was his habit "to enter the classroom about one minute prior to the time for the class to begin."

> He usually sat on a stool in the corner, whittling a match with a pen-knife, ignoring everybody and everything. The time for the class to begin passed and he still sat silently. Then perhaps in another minute, he would begin to speak, slowly, almost hesitantly, silences breaking sentences in two. By the time fifteen minutes had passed, however, the tempo had picked up to the point that it was hard to get down a full set of notes. By the end of the hour a listener was aware that, with no notes whatever, Dr. Sauer had quietly given a polished lecture that put new light on an old subject.[44]

Sauer's main concern, however, was with graduate students, whom he taught in evening seminars. With them he sat on a thread-worn swivel chair and puffed away on his pipe, creating clouds of smoke and saying a few words to get the discussion going. He left it to the students themselves to initiate questions: those who did would command his full attention, those who did not were ignored. Ann Marshall, a master's student at Berkeley in 1937–38, and later a colleague of mine [Michael Williams] at the University of Adelaide, recalled Sauer's "ordeal by silence. If you took him a question he would sit and think for minutes—giving you time to go over the question and wonder if it sounded silly."[45] Sauer wanted students to think critically, to search for what lay behind statements. If silence produced the spur, so be it. Once the lead was given, it was up to the student to pursue the topic. Sauer was not going to turn out graduates like those he heard at a conference in Denver: "Most were solemn, perspiring and utterly dull; then there was a breed of youngsters, urbane, well-tailored, with ringing voices and effective delivery, but duller than the others because they had nothing behind the delivery." Unlike those who had not "done anything with their minds," he wanted young people who could "think and will work."[46]

Some found him frightening, others benign; his formidable intellectual scope could catch a student unaware as he pursued a topic brought up in passing. Marvin Mikesell recalls discussions ranging from marine terraces, the Pennsylvania Dutch origin of his unusual name, and California Indians; David Lowenthal, about New England feral deer; and David Hooson, a Welshman appointed to the staff in 1965, about whether the Madoc of Welsh legend had made the first early crossing of the Atlantic to the Americas.[47]

After presenting half a dozen or so seminar papers, and demonstrating a proficiency in German and French, the student was ready to start fieldwork for a dissertation. No one was pressured into any particular topic. Sauer felt passionately about Mexico, plant domestication, and destructive exploitation, but his own students did not have to work on any of these. Nor were his own programmatic statements any guide; indeed, he rarely referred to them. As with Sauer's *Starved Rock* report, "When I asked Professor Salisbury about the range of the observations required, his reply was that this was left to me to determine and defend."[48] So it was left to his students to determine a topic of inquiry and defend it by whatever method they chose.

Once in the field they were left alone. "Carl Sauer would give a graduate student a handful of raisins and a hundred dollars and tell him to go south and come back with his thesis," recalled his botanist colleague Lincoln Constance. "I am a great believer in considerable anguish of spirit in the early part of a field job," Sauer wrote Isaiah Bowman, with reference to Bowı son, Robert, in Puerto Rico; if he heard nothing in about a month thı would write to him. In 1956 he accompanied Mikesell in Morocco for a v "I received no advice from Sauer . . . on what I should do. Nor did he question me on what I was seeing or what I should do." On leaving Morocco, Sauer sensed that some comment was necessary. He hesitated for a moment and then merely said, "You'll be all right."[49]

The resulting dissertations were highly diverse, but Sauer expected his students to recognize a long past (ignored at one's risk), highlight distinctive cultural traits, and show the role of soils, climate, and plants in people's lives.

That Sauer's varied "intellectual children" did so well was a tribute to his ability to develop their critical faculties. When he subsequently tried to place his students, the respect his judiciously worded recommendations carried proved crucial to many prospective employers.

Critics have remarked that there were few women among Sauer's graduate student classes, but the complaint is anachronistic. In the 1920s and 1930s the aims, aspirations, and career expectations of few women extended to higher degrees. Sauer held no bias against women in academe. He adored Ellen Semple as teacher and friend and deeply respected Isabel Kelly, the archaeologist with whom he collaborated in Mexico. Sauer commended Ann Marshall to the University of Adelaide as "not only a talented teacher but she can rouse the latent spirit of inquiry to a rare degree."[50]

The case of Alvena Suhl is instructive. When Sauer came to Berkeley, she had been appointed a teaching fellow. With her M.A. in geography she went on to develop the Department of Geography at San Diego State College. In 1932 Sauer urged her to complete her Ph.D., but she was well established at San Diego and not prepared to give up that position for the hard and uncertain postgraduate grind. Later when Sauer asked her to teach at Berkeley during wartime drafting of staff she declined reluctantly: "I have a 2½[-year-old] son and a husband. I don't see how I can come up as much as I appreciate your asking me and much as I should like to be able to return the many good turns you have done me."[51]

"These Lice Called Nazis"

At the end of 1935 Sauer was asked to recommend someone to teach geography at the University of Iowa. His own excellent graduates—Leighly, Fred Kniffen, Warren Thornthwaite, Sam Dicken, Peveril Meigs, and Donald Brand—were all spoken for, and his current crop of students were not yet "ripe for appointment." He thought no other American graduates worth considering. The only alternative was visiting European scholars and refugees.[52]

Sauer was deeply attached to the land of his forebears. Perhaps the most enduring aspect of his German heritage was intellectual—the beauty of the language and the rich legacy of German geology, geography, history, and literature. For Sauer, these had few equals in America, and were only partly matched by British culture and science. He was incensed by the outburst of ill feeling against German Americans during the First World War, and was scared and scarred when colleagues tried to get him dismissed as pro-German. Enough resentment remained to alienate him from the old East Coast WASP establishment, and he classed himself with other immigrant groups as an underdog and one of the "lesser breeds." His contempt for many things American was nowhere more clearly expressed than in his geographical biases. Simply put, with few exceptions, American geographers were poor unless trained by him, and those trained in continental Europe were usually superior.

Sauer was rueful that Germans had not promoted their intellectual and cultural achievements earlier or with any finesse. Until after the First World War, German attention to the *Ausdeutschtum* (German cultural areas overseas) was only a "patronizing or casual interest. Now they are desperately seeking to make good some of this neglect of their kinsmen."[53] But with the rise of the Nazis in the 1930s, Sauer became increasingly pessimistic and disillusioned. Seizing power in April 1933, the Nazis dismissed Jews from academic posts, including many whom Sauer knew. One was Moritz Bonn of Berlin University, who had lectured at Berkeley several times and done much to dissipate anti-German American prejudices. He was a brilliant economist, defender of capitalism, and a charming person.[54]

It is [the Hitlerites] and not the Jews against whom they have an insane hatred who are the menace to Germany. I can't understand this gibbering fear of the Jews who are likely to show more sense than anyone else. If I thought the Jews would run the world, I for my part should be perfectly willing to entrust its conduct to them. It would be a more sensible world to live in than the one we now have.

Nazi mobs stormed university buildings, sacked libraries, and burned books by Jewish and other "unpatriotic" authors, among them the Columbia University anthropologist Franz Boas, who "has never written a line to which German patriots could take exception," said Sauer. "In fact he has written almost exclusively on American Indians, on whom he is the greatest authority. Yet these lice called Nazis destroy his books with which he honored his [Kiel] University library."[55] Of a refugee professor newly appointed to the University of California and his wife, Sauer remarked that "they are an ornament in any civilization and better representatives of it by far than strutting brownshirts with their childish Heil Hitler nonsense."[56]

Sauer's view of the superiority of European geography, his penchant for welcoming overseas visitors, and his disgust at the "grotesque situation" in Germany became intertwined and, at times, confused. He sought employment for the promising exiles and refugees who came his way, all the more eagerly because he felt the homegrown products lacked ability: "I look on the judicious introduction of some good talent from overseas as a needed process in raising our level. What geography needs most is half a dozen good geographers who can set the pace. If it is going to take us twenty years to generate these out of our resources and we can do it in five by some importations, we should by all means bring in the new blood."[57]

One such "importation" was Leopold Scheidl from Vienna, who had a two-year Rockefeller Fellowship at Berkeley to study the economic and historical geography of the redwood country north of San Francisco. Because he was a non-Nazi, one of his Austrian professors had been dismissed for supporting him, and another intimidated "to the point of incoherence" by Nazi "bully boys." Scheidl had been dismissed from his post in absentia, and feared that if he returned to Austria he would be put in a concentration camp. Sauer's concern about Scheidl reflected his own First World War experience: "I have more than a sneaking suspicion that given a similar amount of tension, we would do as silly things in this country." After several failed efforts, Sauer found him a research position in Japan. However, Germany got the Japanese government to terminate the appointment. Sent back to Austria, Scheidl was immediately drafted into the German army. He survived, largely thanks to being captured at an early stage by the Allies. Eventually Scheidl got a job at the Graz Institute of Geography and with Sauer's help was awarded a Fulbright fellowship to the United States in 1951–52.[58]

EPIC

The German geographer Leo Waibel from Bonn had emigrated to the University of Wisconsin in 1941. Two of his students, Fritz Bartz and Karl Pelzer, had previously come to California to leave a Germany that was changing in a way they did not like. They were also fulfilling an old and sound tradition, said Sauer approvingly, "undertaking work in some distant part of the world. This insistence on the journeyman period has been one of the major strengths of German academic geography." Sauer got Bartz a research post in the geography and economics of Pacific coast fisheries at Stanford's Food Research Institute, and placed Pelzer with Bowman at Johns Hopkins on a population projection project.[59] Among the German and Austrian refugee scholars were holders of exchange chairs in China. Sauer hoped to secure for his own department "a really competent geographer of the Orient." These included Wilhelm Credner at Sun Yat Sen University in Canton, an authority on Siam, and Walter Hacker at Nanking, who later gained a post at San Francisco State.

There were other visitors, some potential refugees, some not. These included Wolfgang Panzer from Berlin University, Herman von Wissmann of Tübingen University, and Sigfried von Ciriacy-Wantrup, with whom Sauer ran a seminar on destructive exploitation and who later joined the Berkeley faculty in agricultural economics.

Keenness to get "new blood" in geography was Sauer's paramount concern, and his disgust at the treatment of Jewish academics in Germany became less prominent during the later 1930s. He seemed almost to be coming to terms with the realpolitik: the Nazis were in total power and pressing Germany's decades-long quest for Germany's "rightful" place in Europe. With a naive conviction that Germany would eventually be rational and fair, he assured Glenn Trewartha in 1937 that it would be safe to offer Credner a visitor position at Wisconsin: "The German government is not simply a

TO PASS ON A GOOD EARTH

band of madmen, and forms and procedures are maintained quite well." Credner's position at Munich was "guaranteed by law and he is not affected by the new [race] laws that have been made," though his Jewish wife and children were. Time and again, Sauer argued that it was only by good grace and some luck that what was happening in Germany was not happening in the United States: "we sometimes see by how narrow a margin we are on the better side."[60]

An example of what could so easily happen came from Victor Wolfgang von Hagen, a famed explorer and anthropologist, whose expedition to the Panamanian rainforests was well under way in 1940. Von Hagen returned to Washington to learn that he was being investigated by the FBI simply because he had a German name. He wrote Sauer, "If we have to go through *Dachshund* killing, Goethe smearing, [Richard] Wagner hissing again, I think I'll 'take a walk.' Of course if our great melting pot is not that but an enlarged colony of English-Irish-Scotch forebears and all that are not are far outside the pale, then I understand the position of those who are of German ancestry." In December von Hagen was imprisoned for twelve days as an enemy alien. "The FBI is so well informed that they could not find out that my people had lived in Missouri since 1834 and that, myself, was born in St Louis." Von Hagen's history was too much like Sauer's own for comfort, and his story must have haunted Sauer; perhaps everybody with German names would be jailed. (After he was released, von Hagen was drafted into the U.S. Army.)[61]

In 1936 Sauer took the prevalent American isolationist view. "I am pretty much a fence sitter in this international show." Perhaps the "bitterly opposing camps are nevertheless about equally concerned with a better world," and there were enough people of good will on both sides to divert the "present turmoil into a renaissance rather than a catastrophe."[62] The Anschluss with Austria in March 1938 and the occupation of the Sudetenland suggested to him that a "dam of repressed energy" had broken, and past wrongs were being righted, but Germany's invasion of Czechoslovakia and Poland in March and September of the following year no longer seemed a "draining off of the impounded forces" but rank aggression. Sauer's optimistic hopes were shattered. He must have been deeply saddened, but not surprised, by the outbreak of a war initiated by Germany once more, and harbored fears of some sort of repeat of the events of 1916.

Sauer's preference for German geographers accompanied his conviction that most American geography was in a pitiful state, basic research almost nonexistent, and practitioners badly trained. "What place have pots and pans in Geography?" asked one geographer, in reference to Sauer's interest in ceramics for working out cultural relationships through time. When Bowman congratulated Sauer on the stimulating and original way he had combined region, method, and result in his Mexican studies, Sauer said he was "unaccustomed to any comment from other American geographer colleagues, with the exception of my ever faithful band of Michigan friends." He rarely found contacts with American geographers satisfying, for he felt they indulged in semiacademic journalism and lightweight theories. Sauer thought anthropology a much more structured and focused discipline. Geographers seldom transcended static description "to explain development or change."[63] "The anthropologists got their most important method from Ratzel, the study of the diffusion of culture traits. On it they have elaborated what is easily the best developed social science in this country. On it the German geographers had established *Siedlungskunde* [settlement history]. We have been little touched as yet by the activity of either group."[64]

Sauer's critique was partly muted when he was sounded out as to whether he would accept being nominated as president of the Association of American Geographers in 1940. "I am sure your first reaction will be to say no," said Bowman, suspecting that Sauer was sore at not being asked before, and assuring him that those who had opposed his nomination previously were now quieted. Sauer was conscious that his absence from AAG meetings for nearly two decades, along with his trenchant criticism of American geography, must have been resented. After deliberating for two weeks he replied, "If the boys are not so peeved at me that they will blackball me, I am willing to stand." As for his absences from the annual meetings, he explained that they came right in the middle of the best five weeks for getting into the field in Mexico, something he was never prepared to forgo.[65] Another influence was the publication in 1939 of Richard Hartshorne's *Nature of Geography*, a seemingly authoritative text that defined the boundaries and content of geography.[66] "When a subject is ruled, not by inquisitiveness, but by definitions of its boundaries, it is likely to face extinction," thundered Sauer against the "pernicious anemia of the 'but-is-this-geography' state." That it marginalized historical geography was especially dismaying. A restriction of geography to the present, he thought, is fundamentally wrong.

His presidential address, "Foreword to Historical Geography," was an impassioned plea to see human geography and history, not as "quite different subjects, [but] different approaches to the same problem of cultural growth and change." As Gavin Stevens, the lawyer in Faulkner's *Requiem for a Nun*, put it, "The past is never dead. It's not even past." Sauer concurred. "From all the earth in all the time of human existence, we build a retrospective science, that out of this experience acquires an ability to look ahead." In an oft-quoted phrase, Sauer declared: "Retrospect and prospect are different ends of the same sequence. Today is therefore but a point on a line, the development of which may be reconstructed from its beginning and the projection of which may be undertaken into the future." After denouncing the prevailing presentist paradigm he detailed a prospectus of themes for investigation, dealing with cultural habitats and habits that ranged from fields and pastures, plants and pets, to diseases and dialects, American bank failures and Mexican straw hats.[67]

Sauer stressed the relevance of the whole span of human time. The archaeologist Cyril Fox's *Personality of Britain* (1932) was "one of the swellest geographic jobs I've ever seen and lies completely in pre-history." As much was to be learned from the archaeology of the Mississippi delta as from its current fields of sugarcane, and "the geography of Basketmaker Man or the Bell-Beaker Folk is as revealing and absorbing as anything in the present-day world."[68]

Only by understanding past origins, conditions, and processes could one learn "how things came to be what they are." Since landscapes and habitations accumulate experience and residues, we need to "see the land with the eyes of its former occupants from the standpoint of their needs and capacities." To achieve this, scholars must master the past's written and pictorial records along with its fossil remains on the ground and in the culture—relics "that document formerly dominant, but now old-fashioned conditions." Sauer instanced classics in historical geography—Philipp Clüver on ancient Germany and Italy, Alexander von Humboldt on Mexico, August

Meitzen on agrarian landscapes, Harold Peake and Herbert Fleure, and Eva Taylor on Britain. He noted how Eduard Hahn had deployed place-names, dialect terms, obsolete skills, and culinary habits to reconstruct past ways of life. Vestigial hearths, structures, technologies, soil impacts, and vegetal remains, escaped household plants like "lilac bushes of the northeast, Cherokee rose of the southeast, pomegranate and quince" in Spanish America, showed "the habitat in terms of former habit." In striving to "relocate forgotten places, to see where the wilderness has repossessed scenes of active life," one comes at length "to that high moment when the past is clear, and the contrasts to the present are understood."[69]

And Sauer extrapolated the past's ineffable differences into the present. Just as he considered environment "a term of cultural appraisal" not subject to natural law, so "there are no general laws of society, but only cultural assents. . . . We deal not with Culture, but with cultures," unless "we delude ourselves into thinking the world made over in our own image." That "there are very few 'common-sense' qualities about living habits, . . . things most sensibly done in one way only," was a truth lamentably ignored by theoretical social science, especially economics. And he chided those who failed to apprehend past masters, like past mores, in fully unique lifetimes. From his treble curricular underpinnings—physical geography, the cognate realm of anthropology, and the history of geography—Sauer nominated four precursors, the Germans Ratzel and Hahn, the English Vaughn Cornish, and the American George Perkins Marsh, "for full biographical inquiry, . . . learning to know these men through the whole range of their work."[70]

Sauer's magisterial advocacy of the shared terrain of history and geography touched provocatively on a score of topics that invited exploration, both in the field and in the archives. But for all his eloquent enticement, his suggestions were taken up by few geographers beyond his own students, and many of his proposed topics still remain terra incognita. Of the four great precursors Sauer felt should be better known, for example, only one, Marsh, has received full biographical inquiry.[71]

5

Larger Horizons of Place and Time

MEXICO AND THE SOUTHWEST,

1923–1935

Sauer's provocative foray into geographical methodology and his abortive
dabbling in geomorphology were mere sidelines to his major research interests during the early Berkeley years. His main focus was on cultural and
historical fieldwork in Mexico and adjacent parts of the American Southwest. He first crossed the border in 1926 and went back again almost every
year until 1950, spending some fifty-six months there in all. His dedication
to fieldwork in a foreign land had few equals.[1]

Fieldwork

Sauer had a dogged faith that fieldwork would reveal problems worth investigating and supply some of the answers. That had guided him in the
Illinois Valley and in the Ozarks. The land itself and the people who worked
on it were the keys to understanding. Yet he spent a lot of time trekking
and retrekking fruitlessly across vast stretches of Mexico for no apparent
yield. In his student days he often talked of his "wanderlust" and expressed
a longing to "tramp through Europe and South America." The opportunity

presented itself in Mexico. No doubt the trips offered respite from administrative grind and campus infighting. But they also had a deeper purpose, enabling him to shed a layer of his cultural skin and see a remote culture from the inside. This was *Verstehen* in action—an empathetic understanding of people and places. He prided himself that unlike other "gringos" in Mexico he could converse easily with and gently handle folk who lived a simple life, close to the land.[2] Joe Spencer, a student who went with him into northern Mexico during the winter of 1930 and spring of 1931, described his mode of operation:

> After dinner we went to . . . a tavern, where Sauer bought drinks and handed out cigarettes to get the locals to talk about things he was interested in. As the evenings went along, he occasionally would look at me and wiggle his fingers when some bit of information impressed him. . . . His lines of questioning in the taverns had to do with everything under the sun, but he kept on coming back, again and again, to the matter of evidences of old settlements, signs of [former] cultivation, irrigation, specific kinds of deforestation, etc.[3]

Coupled with empathetic understanding was slow travel. Walking was the preferred mode, but not always practical given the hundreds even thousands of miles Sauer covered. He disliked riding by horse or mule, so he usually ended up in a car or truck, traversing poor and unmade tracks. For reasons of economy as well as empathy, wherever possible he preferred to camp out, and in towns he tended to pick the cheaper hotels, or better still to lodge with peasants. From Mazatlán he wrote: "We're staying with little Mexican families and being well fed according to the best of their lights. Pigs and chickens mingle in the household and are not disagreeable except early in the morning when the pigs scratch against your bedstead. They are quite clean animals, however, and certainly no less attractive than the dogs." But sometimes there were unpleasant consequences. The archaeologist Isabel Kelly recalled how Sauer had rejected a perfectly clean and reasonably priced hotel for a cheaper one: "In the morning we came upon him, very aggrieved on a bench in the park where he had spent most of the night, owing to *chinches* [bed bugs]."[4] Similarly, he loved Mexican food, the hotter the better. To get the authentic thing he frequented restaurants of questionable cleanliness, and often ended up with severe intestinal ailments, diarrhea, even dysentery. After Lorena's serious bout with bacillary dysentery in the field in 1930, Sauer became choosier about hotels, preferring those run by Germans or Chinese.

His faith in fieldwork never wavered, though after 1931 his enthusiasm for it diminished. Increasingly he came to appreciate the value and richness of the written record, and over time the gloss of roughing it wore off. By 1933, after a particularly hot, grueling summer crossing the mountains and spending weeks in the archives of Chihuahua, Parral, and Durango with severe stomach upsets, he was despondent. Uncharacteristically, he fulminated against mestizos: ??

> I'm rather fed up with the north of Mexico. I thought this interior section might be better to work in summer than the coast. It is almost as hot and quite as dirty. These half-breeds are more like poor white trash in the South than anything else I can think of. They are slovenly, working by fits and starts and never get anywhere. A real Mexican Indian had a certain staidness about him that makes him a respectable person. These people of the north have no such appeal. They have neither the initiative of the white nor the persistence of the Indian.

He looked forward to "getting back to civilization, cleanliness, water you can drink, fruit you can eat, air that doesn't affect your nose. Mexico is alright where there aren't people but where there are it's pretty offensive." Two years later he termed Mexico a country "I shall be glad not to see again for some time."[5]

Given Sauer's enduring reputed affinity for matters Mexican, it comes as a surprise to realize that his publications on the archaeology, historical geography, and linguistics of ancient Mexico were mostly finished by 1935.[6] Of course, the legacy of his Mexico experience did not end there. New questions emerged, such as how and when the rich variety of plants were domesticated and used, how misuse of the land had led to environmental destruction, and how diverse pre-Columbian cultures had proliferated and differentiated in the mere ten thousand years conventionally allotted to human entry into the Americas after the melting of Pleistocene ice. Finally, what had happened to the countless tens of thousands of Indians who had occupied the land in pre-Conquest times? These bigger questions were to become his later life's work. All were underlain by a strong sense of history and evolution.

Sauer initially found contemporary northwest Mexico unintelligible without an understanding of early Spanish settlement. Eventually he felt it necessary to go "back to the origin of man and his cultures."[7] Understanding prehistoric culture required archaeology: locating and describing old Indian settlement sites and analyzing potsherds. By the 1930s he worked increasingly on the rich store of untapped Mexican archival material, augmented by the records copied for him in Spain. These revealed the catastrophic impact of European conquest on native vegetation, Indian culture, and population.

Sauer had at first enjoyed taking the family south to the warmth of the San Diego area to escape the fogs and cold rains of Bay Area winters, but he found Southern California research already well staked out by other university departments. Nearby northwestern Mexico was a virgin field, an attractive exotic locale as yet no one's "stamping ground."[8] On a 1924 visit to San Diego, where the university wanted him to inspect normal (teacher training) schools, he took "a little run down into Mexico," quite far down Baja California. This whetted his appetite for "possible expeditions into western Mexico."[9] He became convinced that Baja California and adjacent Sonora on the Mexican mainland were the hearths from which Californian and southwestern indigenous culture had grown.

Early in 1925 he suggested to his Berkeley student Peveril Meigs that it would "be nice to study Lower California as the mother of California historically," and by 1926 he decided on a "real camping party" to San Fernando de Valicatá, a quarter of the way down the eight-hundred-mile peninsula.[10] While Meigs focused on mission sites, Sauer looked at Indian shell mounds for traces of human habitation, yielding an essay on missionary activity and native economy.[11]

Since Sauer's ability to work in Mexico was hampered by his lack of Spanish, he set about learning it. During the 1927–28 academic year he borrowed a Spanish grammar in German. Knowing German, Sauer was familiar with the concepts of the gender of nouns and verb endings. Thanks also to a thorough grounding in Latin, he had a reasonable command of Spanish within a year.[12]

Kroeber and Lowie

In pursuing his Mexican interests Sauer found kindred spirits in Alfred Kroeber and Robert Lowie in anthropology, Herbert Bolton in history, and, to a lesser degree, Paul Taylor in economics. They met frequently to coordinate research initiatives. Kroeber was the driving force. Dynamic and forceful, a major figure in American anthropology, he created one of the world's greatest research museums and anthropology departments.[13] His interests in antiquity, culture, and Mexico immediately attracted Sauer.

Kroeber

Kroeber and Lowie probably had more influence on Sauer than anyone since Rollin Salisbury. He and Kroeber worked together in the field and taught together. Geography students were required to attend Kroeber's seminars. The two men shared similar backgrounds. Kroeber was born in Hoboken, New Jersey, in 1876. His father was German-born, and his mother the daughter of immigrants from southern Germany, like Sauer's forebears.[14] Like Sauer, Kroeber had been a precocious student, and at the age of sixteen entered Columbia University, where he studied under the renowned anthropologist Franz Boas. And like Sauer, Kroeber displayed interest and sympathy for ordinary folk and put great emphasis on the independence of the individual scholar, expressing distaste for directed research programs. Again like Sauer, he disliked overarching theory and stressed the diversity of humankind and human cultures.[15] Sauer's views were enriched and deepened by close academic association and personal friendship with Kroeber.

Lowie had an even more profound intellectual influence on Sauer. Lowie's Viennese Jewish family had come to the United States when he was ten. *Lowie* He was appointed professor of anthropology at Berkeley in 1923, the same year as Sauer in geography, and they became friends immediately. Gentle and affable, Lowie was immensely widely read and learned. It was he who got Sauer to abandon his prejudice against Ratzel, alerting him to the second volume of Ratzel's *Anthropogeographie*, on cultural diffusion, and to the work of Leo Frobenius and the Austrian *Kulturkreis* school concerned with the diffusion of similar cultural traits from a few centers of innovation.

Lowie later introduced Sauer to the work of Eduard Seler on Mexican high culture and that of the German geographer Eduard Hahn on agricultural origins and diffusion, which became major research interests of Sauer's.[16]

From Geomorphology to Cultural Corridors

Sauer went south thirteen times from 1926 to 1935, largely with the objective of establishing whether "a continuous and coexistent corridor of higher culture extended down the coast of Mexico, joining Pueblan and Mexican cultural realms."[17] During May and June 1928 in Sonora he came across the ruins of pueblos, evidence of an ancient advanced culture. Similar ruins in southern Arizona suggested a connection between the two regions, contrary to the conventional wisdom that Arizona's Pueblo culture hearth petered out toward the border into wild, almost empty no-man's-land.

He planned a follow-up trip into Sonora in the spring of 1929, but "I no sooner get interested in Mexico . . . than a bunch of idiots start a revolution" (the Cristero War of 1926–29). He was disdainful of the revolutionaries' motives: "They haven't any real grievance—they're a bunch of generals and governors not fighting for any ideals or popular issue—they simply want to get control of the government and bigger jobs than they now have. The sooner they get it in the neck the better for Mexico." By early April the revolt was about *"ausgespielt"* [played out], and only scattered bands were left to round up.[18] He finally left with his student Donald Brand to collect pottery shards for Kroeber to identify and classify.[19]

The consuming search for evidence of the higher culture that he felt had once connected Pueblo and western Mexican realms gained a solid boost during his sabbatical leave starting in December 1929. The "bitsy" trips could be replaced by one long stay and concentrated work. With his family he set sail on the SS *El Salvador* rounding the tip of Baja California and landing at Mazatlán on the mainland on Christmas Day. With them were Brand, the Rockefeller Foundation scholar Gottfried Pfeifer, and Pfeifer's wife, Ruth.[20]

Mazatlán became their base camp from which archaeological forays were made by hired car or local bus. True to form, Sauer rejected the only decent modern hotel in town, first for a lesser one and then a boarding house. At one stage in the hills, they shared rooms with Mexican peasants, chickens, and pigs.[21]

Scouring the coastal zone north and south of Mazatlán, Sauer found thirty-two sites in Sinaloa and Nayarit. Each had remnants of high-quality polychrome earthenware, two-edged obsidian knives, decorated pipes, spindle whorls, and terra-cotta figurines in proximity to ruined temple mounds, which bespoke his conjectured advanced ancient culture. Sauer detailed the landforms, soil quality, and water supply of each site to reconstruct the economy of the inhabitants. Most sites were on good alluvial soils on a floodplain, where corn, beans, and squash could be grown without irrigation. There was evidence of fishing and salt making. The "Aztatlán," as he named them, were farmers, fishermen, and manufacturers. Sauer surmised they might be the missing link between the Pueblos of Arizona and Aztec high culture.[22]

Sauer's "excellent companion" Kroeber joined the party for a few weeks at the end of January. He was collecting data on dying native languages, perhaps linguistic remnants of a lost culture. In late February a severe stomach complaint hospitalized Lorena at the United Sugar plantation a hundred miles north. Lorena recovered after a few days, but Sauer realized that he would have to find more congenial habitations. He decided to move to Nogales just across the border in Arizona. At 3,700 feet the air was bracing, and the surrounding peaks were capped with snow; after roughing it in Mexico the children "were all excited" about the idyllic place.

Sauer fretted about losing the opportunity for extended fieldwork along the coast.[23] However, it might still be possible to establish an ancient cross-border archaeological and cultural corridor. Nogales was just northwest of the area in Sonora where he had found numerous pueblo settlements in 1928. He, Brand, and Pfeifer mapped the distinctive *cerros de trincheras*, "hills with entrenchments," on both sides of the border. Nearly all the sites were distinguished by "short rock walls, about six to eight feet high and a dozen feet wide." Clearly not cultivation terraces, these could only be defensive walls, Sauer believed. The conventional view was that the walls had been built by the aggressive Apaches, but the Apaches had been nineteenth-century latecomers, driving out the native Mexican Indians. The walls were probably of pre-Conquest origin. This great culture "at its height must have exceeded in number of people and extent of country that of any, perhaps all other sedentary peoples of the Southwest." The archaeologist Omar Turney estimated that in the Salt River valley of Arizona more than 50,000 people had cultivated over 100,000 acres by canal irrigation. Their disappearance was not due to climatic failure, as was commonly supposed, but to successive waves of warfare.[24]

By the end of May it was time to go home. At the border Sauer had an experience that he never forgot, or forgave. On the American side, he wrote his mother, they encountered trouble:

> First I was rather sharply questioned by one of our immigration officials. Then they hauled out my bag and started pulling it to pieces. Shortly they uncovered the old blue comforter you gave me years ago, slashed it open with a knife, discovered it had cotton batting and confiscated it. Next came one of the dark quilts you made for me. It was slashed open and confiscated. They admitted that the quilts were obviously "American." "But you should have had a permit slip to take them across." My answer "you didn't tell me that when I went across" brought the retort that "ignorance of the law was no excuse." My plea that the intent of the regulation was to prevent the bringing in of boll weevils in raw cotton, that we had not been in any cotton country, that the cotton batting was not raw cotton, that weevils couldn't live in old quilts, and that all that was involved was a technicality of a slip of paper about which I was not informed brought the retort that they had regulations and they were going to enforce them.
>
> By this time I was pretty tart and told them that such enforcement was stupid. I said, "I've got a cotton shirt that you might as well confiscate with more weevil hazard than the quilts." To which one of them answered, "If the regulations covered cotton shirts we'd take it from your back." Another added, "And there are enough of us here to do it!" My answer was, "You fellows make me appreciate that the Mexican officials are gentlemen." With that we drove off, the two quilts lying in the road. There are an awful lot of hard-boiled, mean rough-necks in the border service. I've never been riled by a Mexican trade official, and I've had several run-ins on our side, though none so disastrous as this one. I much suspect that your nice woolen quilt is keeping one of these defenders of the law warm [at] nights. The worst of the lot are

the USDA inspectors and next the Immigration officials. The way the latter bully the Mexicans is a crime. Many a high-class Mexican won't come to the US for a visit anymore because of bullying at the hand of these ignorant hill-billies. Our inspection policy and enforcement, as well as our tariff policy are as insolent and piggish as anything that modern history affords, and are helping to make us the best hated people on earth.[25]

From Field to Archive

In 1931 Sauer received a Guggenheim Fellowship to continue his work in Mexico. Trying to link it to the American Southwest, he extended his search into the heart of Aztec central Mexico. The first destination was Colima, in the mountains off the west-central coast. However, "the tropics don't seem to agree with anyone but me." Both children, Jonathan and Elizabeth, fell ill, and Lorena was not well. So he moved north and inland "to a cool place," Guadalajara, five thousand feet up, even cold at night. Guadalajara had "fine public buildings from the Spanish days" but the rest of it was "pretty dirty." The surrounding open landscape had an "American aspect until you see that they are plowing with one handled plows pulled by oxen."[26]

Unable to get on with his fieldwork, Sauer decided to look at the archives. Not everything could be seen or experienced in the field. Some things could be revealed only by the written record of the past. Kroeber observed, listened, and described people of the present day and projected their culture backward in time. For him the present was often the key to the past. Sauer's research method was more the reverse; the past was the key to the present.

Archaeological evidence in the field suggested larger populations than existed in the 1930s. There were two likely explanations. Once was intense climatic change, as proposed by the Yale geographer Ellsworth Huntington, an idea that Sauer dismissed as lacking evidence and implausible. The other was that disease, warfare, or both had reduced numbers. The key lay in the written record of what the conquistadors first saw just over four hundred years before. The material he found astounded and excited him. Guadalajara's public library held "thousands and thousands of parchment bound volumes of centuries old monastic records. They were 'pure gold.'"

For three hundred years this was the capital of the Viceroyalty of New Galicia. Very many of the documents were destroyed during the late revolutions. Soldiers carried them off to cook their suppers [with], but still there are great quantities left. The Franciscan missionaries had their Headquarters here for the whole west coast and the monks stationed out in the Indian Pueblos made up their reports to the superior at the local seminary.[27]

But in many cases the paper was brown with age or perforated by wormholes, or the ink had faded. Those written before 1600 were in a strange script, at first "entirely unintelligible." There were other problems—lack of good light and his failing eyesight.[28]

What most fired his imagination were the accounts of the missionaries who had

cleared and planted and built their little worlds and how they watched over their Indians, especially against white men. The accounts are full of bitter complaints against Spanish miners who drifted in and gradually debauched the Indians. And the greatest of all traditions is that of the Jesuits; none of the other orders could touch them for the courage and persistence with which they established near-utopian Indian communities and defended them against the encroachment of the Spanish colonists until the very date of their expulsion from Spanish territory [1767] as unpatriotic undesirables! There is no false picture spread throughout the world than that of the Jesuits. If ever a group saw the Kingdom [of Heaven] on Earth and sacrificed themselves for it it was these Jesuits of the 17th and 18th centuries as they fought the battle of liberalism against the Inquisition and bigotry all over catholic Europe. And their thanks is that still most people get a shiver at the mention of the word Jesuit.

Jesuit, Augustinian, and Franciscan missionaries all lived under vows of poverty. They often engaged in bitter battles with the established clergy, who served Spain against native interests: "The Catholic Church was for the white man, the large land owner and the rich mine operators. The missionaries' ideas were for the poor, the Indian — it's the old class antagonism which still runs through Latin American life."[29]

Most intriguing were the reported large numbers of Indians in the pueblos, far greater than census counts for later centuries. Were the missionaries lying or had the indigenous population been drastically reduced? In 1560 Bartolomé de las Casas, a Dominican friar and bishop of Chiapas, estimated that 40 million Indians had died in the Indies (Americas) since ✦ 1492, a figure dismissed as a gross exaggeration by most scholars. What Sauer was unearthing in the archives seemed to support Las Casas's report of massive depopulation.[30]

In July and August 1931 Sauer spent six weeks in Mexico City, mining the archives in the basement of the Palacio Nacional, where the riches of Guadalajara were augmented in abundance. Calculating that he could work there the entire summer and still not finish, he paid a couple of hundred dollars to get some of the larger documents copied by a paleographer.[31]

Motoring down the new highway to Acapulco on the Pacific, Sauer stopped to view Montezuma's palace in Cuernavaca. The interior walls had been adorned with murals by Diego Rivera. They struck him as a gross falsification of historical truth:

The frescos portray the cruelty of the Spaniards, the greed of the priests, the oppression of the Indians, and finally the millennium of the Revolution. Rivera is a tremendous painter and terrific distorter of history. Everywhere he represents the Spaniards as the incarnation of evil, the church as the tool of the rich, the upper classes as gross, cruel, selfish and thus he proceeds to the glorification of the Revolution and its chiefs, against which to my mind, the earlier days of Mexico were for the most part a veritable golden age. Rivera has been the greatest propagandist of the Revolution and has carried hatred into the hearts of the peón and has supplied the politicians with a picturized history that has been of inestimable value to them.

Rivera was then painting other enormous murals in the Palacio Nacional in which all the missionaries, great aristocrats, and liberal radicals of

Mexico were replaced by current "revolutionary" leaders. These were portrayed as

> the redeemers of Mexico and incidentally the new capitalists of the country who have made their fortunes out of the revolution. But of the fact that the old aristocracy is replaced by an infinitely worse plutocracy derived from generals and politicians of revolution, Rivera says not a word. He continues to soft soap the masses with his idealization of the revolution behind which stalks as corrupt and cold-blooded an exploitation as any modern people has suffered.[32]

But no one dared to say that was happening, least of all foreigners who could be given notice to quit the country at once, without a hearing.

After the Mexico City stay, Lorena and the children returned to Berkeley, while Carl went into the field again at Hermosillo, his old stamping ground on Sonora's western coastal edge. Once more he scoured the archives for pueblo records, while awaiting the arrival of Leslie Hewes, a graduate student who accompanied him on a mule trek through the mountains and south almost as far as Culiacán. However, few early Indian settlement sites were found, and Sauer "got kicked in the chest and had a toe stepped on" by a frisky mule, which put him out of action for a few days. He found no clear archaeological link between the cultures of the west coast of Mexico and the Southwest of the United States: "We're through with Sinaloa. This end of the trip has been the most disappointing of all, and there is no use fooling away time here. *Agrarismo* [agrarian reform] has ruined the sections which the revolution did not. Everything is in dissolution in this end of the great Jesuit Province. The Mayo simply live in scattered huts in the brush with ragged little corn patches. The *ranchos* have gone to the devil." Sauer's speculative thesis of a cultural link extending a thousand miles along the west coast of the isthmus was simply not demonstrable.[33] While he had unearthed a unique and previously unknown culture, he could not prove that culture's connections with the American Southwest and central Mexico.

Aztatlán and Cíbola

Back in Berkeley he began writing three "fearfully difficult" essays about historical Mexico. If it was hard to understand the current generation, then "how much chance is there of really knowing how people a century ago—or a thousand years ago—looked at the world? I've been reading some Spanish accounts of three hundred years ago. I can get plain facts contained therein, but views and beliefs as conveyed by words into my brain are probably two entirely different things. Nothing is fixed—nothing that doesn't change its meaning, or lose it with time."[34]

The "*trincheras*" paper, written with Brand, was largely an exercise in field archaeology, more or less completed by this time. But the two other substantive and ultimately more important papers were mainly drawn from extensive archival work that needed careful interpretation.[35]

Kroeber, who had accompanied Sauer in 1929 and 1930, concentrated on the ethnographic and linguistic evidence of this vanished culture and was quite content to leave the archaeological work to Sauer. But when Sauer realized the impossibility of relying on the physical remnants alone to reconstruct the Aztatlán culture, he embarked on an "archaeogeographical" account that combined archaeological, geographical, and archival evidence.

Aztatlán was not an arid region dependent on irrigation culture like the southwestern United States, as was conventionally assumed, but a tropical savanna with a short and sharp summer rainy season. Its floodplain crops had been able to sustain a dense and prosperous population in large villages, as the Spaniards found when they arrived about 1530. Their leaders, Nuño Beltrán de Guzmán—"the Himmler of New Spain"—and Francisco Coronado, had systematically oppressed and plundered the native villages, killing many thousands. Those left were either enslaved or wiped out by measles and smallpox. The conquistadors were about "as hard a gang of killers as Spain let loose anywhere in the New World; there was no stay upon the killing propensities of the conquerors." The truth about Indian numbers was becoming clear. The missionaries had not exaggerated; the once much greater population had been eliminated. The history of Aztatlán was "one of the most distressing chapters in the story of the destruction of the Indies."[36]

With the "loss of his corridor" thesis, Sauer set about rescuing what he could from the time and energy he had expended on the project. He took pride in making some of the "most important additions of the decade to the knowledge of Latin American archaeology."[37] He traced the main artery of prehistoric and early colonial communication from Guadalajara up the coast and inland to present-day Tucson. He called his book *The Road to Cíbola* (1932), since the main reason for Spanish incursion was the search for the legendary golden "Seven Cities of Cíbola."

Sauer had covered virtually all the country between the Gila River in the north and the Río Grande de Santiago in the south, "by car, on horseback, and afoot," and had seen "all but a few miles of the route a number of times and at different seasons of the year." He detailed the mismatch between the routes he had seen firsthand and the customary rendering of their course. Such a revision of accepted knowledge was not without its dangers. He was "taking issue with a lot of accepted history and hence have to watch my steps."[38] *The Road to Cíbola* was well regarded by historians for its painstaking archival work and the link to the Mexican landscape, but it did not satisfy Sauer. Perhaps one more field trip would yield some missing sites or startling new evidence.[39]

Habitat, Habitation, and Population

In 1933 Sauer traveled again to Mexico, staying a week in a German Mennonite colony west of Chihuahua, then striking west and south to Parral, the old capital of the Spanish province of Nueva Vizcaya.[40] There he stumbled on "a very rich and unknown collection of Spanish documents" and amassed much new material on pre-Conquest Indian numbers.[41] Newly energized, Sauer wrote two more papers on early northwest Mexico, one on population and another on languages.

However, the topic he thought the most important, pre-Conquest population numbers, would bring him into direct conflict with Kroeber. Kroeber did not accept the Las Casas estimate, nor those by the German geographer Karl Sapper, the French anthropologist Paul Rivet, and the American archaeologist Herbert Spinden, who put the pre-Columbian New World population between 37 and 50 million.[42] Kroeber argued for only 8.4 million, the anthropologist Julian Steward for 15.6 million.[43] Sauer did not want to offend Kroeber, to whom he was beholden professionally and personally. He'd been badly scarred by the geomorphology incident and could not afford to let that sort of thing happen again. His paper on tribal languages between the Gila River in Arizona and the Río Grande de Santiago near Guadalajara can be regarded as a diplomatic olive branch to Kroeber. Sauer's skillful use of archival material in reconstructing the location of linguistic groups from 1531 to 1768, and his large foldout map, were a masterly summation of complex data. Kroeber liked it and published a complementary critique fitting Sauer's work into his own classification of Uto-Aztecan languages.[44]

Yet Sauer remained convinced that population numbers had been much greater than credited by Kroeber and other accepted authorities. He estimated an Aztatlán population of at least 225,000 (the same as the 1920 census figure for the region), and probably double that if the contemporary accounts were to be believed, far higher than the 100,000 estimated by Kroeber in 1934 for all of northwest Mexico.

Sauer's *Aboriginal Population of Northwestern Mexico* (1935) related the Jesuit records of pueblo numbers to ruined settlements on the ground. He estimated a pre-Columbian population in excess of half a million, vastly depleted over ensuing centuries. The reduction reflected a history of great suffering, caused unintentionally by lack of resistance to common European diseases like measles, influenza, and particularly smallpox, and by deliberate slaughter and enslavement.

Initially, Sauer's estimate of Indian numbers was regarded as sensational and even subversive in maligning the morality of the Spanish settlers and undermining the popular thesis of the conquest of supposedly "empty lands." Kroeber was skeptical and said that the estimate was "revolutionizing."[45] But over time the Berkeley demographic historians Woodrow Borah and Lesley Simpson and the physiologist Sherburne Cook confirmed Sauer's general thesis of large numbers. Most scholars today accept a hemispheric total of between 40 and 80 million, some, like the ethnohistorian Henry Dobyns, much higher.[46] One historian regarded Sauer as "the true founder of the so-called Berkeley school of demographic history."[47] The history of the Americas would never be looked at in the same way again.

6

The Frontiers of Knowledge

"What do you consider your most important publication?" asked geographer
J. Russell Smith in 1939. Sauer wasn't sure. He knew that his work on dis-
parate themes had attracted attention, both favorable and unfavorable. He
seldom referred to his previous methodological writing and lamented that
his field and archive studies in Mexico were well known to archaeologists
and anthropologists but ignored by geographers. What interested him most
at the time were destructive exploitation, settlement, and cultivated plants.[1]

Sauer's easy, attractive, and direct writing style led publishers to badger
him for textbooks. But this highly lucrative activity did not interest him,
and in any case, he had no time for it. Time and again he quoted a line from
 Chaucer, "The lyf so short, the craft so long to lerne."[2]

I'd much rather be doing what I'm doing and helping a good youngster
to pioneer along with me now and then than to do what Barrows and
Atwood and Perkins and Dodge have done and become academically
speaking a plutocrat. I wouldn't trade places with them. They never
had the thrill of turning up an ancient civilization, or discovering a
new type of mountain sculpture or of reconstructing the missions of
a vanished frontier. There's a zest to it that you wouldn't exchange for
 all the reviewing of other people's ideas in a text book.

He toyed with a suggestion from the publisher Alfred Knopf for a book on "sketches of village life" in Mexico of a "somewhat popular character. I'd rather like to try that sort of thing."[3] However, there was no time even for this. He was determined to persevere with his research on the frontiers of knowledge.

Mexico and Cultivated Plants

The work of the German geographer Eduard Hahn had persuaded Sauer that domesticated plants and animals were cultural artifacts just as surely as were buildings, walls, tools, and routes.[4] Sauer had noted how intimately interwoven Mexican peasants were with their cultivated plants. Corn (*Zea mays*), for example, was more than a crop; it had symbolic and spiritual meaning for those who grew it. If crops were cultural artifacts, then their distribution was a key element in cultural diffusion. Where they had originated, where and when they had spread, were vital topics to be addressed.

While studying crops in April 1935 in Guadalajara, Sauer was also pursuing a new cultural corridor hypothesis. Perhaps the Mexican link with the southwestern United States wasn't west of the central plateau, as he had earlier argued, but through the center of the country. The center was richly endowed with varieties of native crops, as well as putative evidence of early metallurgy, as seen in Isabel Kelly's excavations in Sinaloa.[5]

Without his family he followed his usual bent of staying in third-class hotels. The inevitable *chinches* and stomach upsets interrupted archival work in Mexico City. Rains and indifferent health made for "a miserable summer, but the country is lousy politically, anyway." "I believe I can write *finis* under the Mexican fieldwork. I've eaten my share of dirt and flies."[6] Despite this sour farewell after having invested so much time in the country, he did return numerous times.

Cultivated plants and their origins increasingly preoccupied him. A 1936 essay entitled "American Agricultural Origins" was his first speculative foray into that field. The renowned Soviet plant scientist Nikolai Vavilov had suggested that the domestication of crops originated in just a few locales, and Sauer sought discrete centers where slope, soil, altitude, and climate favored agricultural development. Today, Vavilov's hypothesis is discredited in favor of multiple domestications in many parts of the world. Sauer too thought the rich variety of South American starch-laden plants, such as maize and manioc, suggested "many centers of plant domestication." One thing seemed crucial, following Hahn: most seeding was initially done by planting with a dibble or digging stick, difficult to use in heavily matted grasslands. Hence, American agriculture had most likely begun in fields cleared from woodland where trees could easily be killed by ringbarking and then burnt when dry.[7]

Sauer energetically pursued the "possibilities of genetic study" of crops. Seed varieties collected in the field might be propagated in plant-breeding stations and thus contribute to crop development. California's agricultural research stations might concentrate on tomatoes and chili peppers, or maize, beans, and squash.[8]

Carl Alsberg, at Stanford's Food Research Institute, was eager to set up a Pan-American experimental station to preserve crop strains that were fading out, disentangle varietal origins, and relate plants to environmental elements. It was a project worthy of the "greatest corn-growing nation in the world." Why not start with a station serving Indian communities in the Southwest? Recovery of variants of maize might appeal to Secretary of Agriculture Henry Wallace, who had a corn-breeding background.[9] Bureau of American Ethnology agronomists currently favored methods and strains better suited to Nebraska corn farmers than to the Navajo. An Indian experiment station was needed to promote indigenous knowledge. There was something "sound and essential," Sauer felt, in Indian "symbiotic relations" with their homeland.[10]

In Mexico Sauer proposed three specific objectives: the preservation of archaeological finds of plant materials, the collection of early Spanish accounts of native and introduced plants, and the collection of surviving primitive strains of American domesticated plants. Such a collection was essential "raw material for practical plant breeding." He knew just the place to start. In the "forlorn mountain coast country north of the Río Balsas," cotton and corn cultivation had flourished in early Hispanic times, and the area therefore should contain many primitive survivors. This was just where he had been working earlier in the year.[11]

Sauer's enthusiasm gained new impetus from a visit in March 1936 by Vavilov. Russian research had shown the desirability of studying the characteristics of domesticated crops and the practical utility of an exhaustive collection of varietal forms. Since California was the prime bean-growing area in the United States, basic research into the pre-Columbian genus *Phaseolous* would be most useful. Sauer suggested that the University of California establish an institute of applied botany, genetics, and plant breeding. But nothing materialized.[12]

ahead of the curve

Destructive Exploitation of Resources

Although Sauer could not determine where cultivated plants had come from originally, he could certainly document their destruction and disappearance over the past few hundred years. The "destructive exploitation" of resources by modern Western civilization was, he told a friend, an uncomfortable "footnote to civilization."[13]

In the 1890s and early 1900s, following the exploitation and mismanagement of water and forests and the overgrazing of remaining public lands, perceived impending resource shortages had aroused deep concern in America. The ensuing conservation movement pitted long-term national needs against selfish corporate interests. Sauer sympathized with this "Progressive" crusade against malefactors of great wealth.[14] He read vivid descriptions of soil erosion in Charles Van Hise's *Conservation of Natural Resources* (1910),[15] and in the *Proceedings* of a conference of state governors in 1908, headed by U.S. Forest Service chief Gifford Pinchot.[16] Nathaniel Shaler's *Man and the Earth* (1905) and Thomas Chamberlin's "Soil Wastage" (1909) contrasted the slow process of soil formation with speedy agricultural exploitation and soil destruction.

Awareness that humans altered landscapes for ill as well as good shows up in Sauer's earliest publications. His Illinois River valley study of 1916 includes a substantial discussion of the topic "Man as a Factor in Erosion." The landscape had been virtually untouched (he then believed) by its previous Indian inhabitants, but pioneer settlers, "accustomed to think of the resources of this country as inexhaustible," had accelerated erosion by forest clearing and overgrazing: "To-day the scene is much altered. The grassy prairies have been converted into tilled fields, and the soil is bared to the action of wind and water. Much of the timber has been removed from the valley; gullies are cutting back into the prairies in many places, and the streams run murky with their load of sediment washed from plowed field and denuded slopes."[17]

A 1913 essay by the French geographer Jean Brunhes alerted Sauer to the Russian geographer Alexander Woeikof's work on human impacts, based in large part on Élisée Reclus's La Terre (1868), which in turn drew heavily on George Perkins Marsh's Man and Nature (1864), later famously celebrated by Sauer, who has been wrongly faulted as culpably negligent for being unaware of Marsh until the 1930s.[18] According to Woeikof, environmental destruction worsened as humans became factory workers and city dwellers, hence "disassociated from the earth." In a brief review of articles by Woeikof, C. P. Lucas, and Ernest Fischer, Sauer, early in his career in 1916, extended the discussion of human impact from soils and rivers to the organic world:

Man is an important ecological factor, . . . modifying profoundly the paleontological record of the future. The adjustment of plant associations is being disturbed by the introduction of new species, by the clearing and cultivation of the land, by fire, and other means resulting from the voluntary or involuntary meddling of man. Similar revolutionary changes are wrought in the animal world, especially among the larger animals and among numerous parasitic forms.[19]

His years in Michigan had brought Sauer face to face with massive misuse of resources and the malign influence of humans on the earth (see chap. 3). The northern two-thirds of the state exemplified calamitous exploitation.[20] Three of his early publications pointed toward what would become a major element in his thinking: In Geography of the Pennyroyal Sauer noted that farmers had largely been "dissipating the real productivity of the land"; their "contact with nature has been unfortunately destructive." Here, as over most of the American South, ruinous exploitation was aggravated by the ease of moving on, exchanging worn-out land for new land.[21] A 1927 essay expanded on Brunhes's and Ernst Friedrich's work on resource depletion as Raubwirtschaft (destructive exploitation).[22]

Sauer's subsequent work with the federal Soil Conservation Service and observations in the overgrazed dry lands of the Navajo Reservation brought home the stark reality of soil degradation and the urgent necessity of reform. Humans were "aggressive animal[s] of perilous social habits" who heedlessly exploited and destroyed vital elements of the natural environment. As in the historical present, so in the deep past, humans had a severe impact on the earth. But although pervasive and significant, primitive alterations had never been as harmful as "the catastrophic upsets brought by the saw, the plough, and livestock."[23] Judging "the 19th century as a time of doubtful benefit to the human race," he concluded, "We may very well have come to the end of what we have been pleased to call modern history, the expansion of western peoples and civilization over the thinly or weakly peopled spaces of the earth."[24]

Sauer's concern about environmental degradation was furthered by a "swell young German in agricultural economics," Siegfried von Ciriacy-Wantrup from Bonn University, with whom he held a series of seminars in agricultural economics.[25] Fired up about the destruction of the "good earth," Sauer in 1937–40 presented three critical papers on resource exploitation. All bristled with pithy, barbed comments about reckless human disregard for the natural world.

At the 1937 International Geographical Congress in Amsterdam, Sauer sought to "shove under the noses of the Europeans the association of white colonial settlement, commercial production, [and] destruction of resources." The colonizers had "short-sightedly or recklessly" disregarded ecological and human communities. Most damaging was the monoculture of crops that had originated in simpler hoe culture economies but had become "veritable destroyers when shifted to row plow culture." Thus tobacco, cotton, and corn had ruined millions of acres of American farmland.[26]

Then in a 1938 address to the Social Science Research Council, he berated the assembled economists and political scientists for seeking universal behavioral truths about progress while ignoring the natural history of degradation. "To-day's triumph in social theory is tomorrow's footnote to culture history." Social scientists' view of culture history as growing environmental mastery blinded them to the "revenge of outraged nature against man." He detailed the destruction of the natural world during Neolithic and classical times. And since the late eighteenth century, the impact of European exploitation had become ever more marked. "In the space of a century and a half—only two full life times—more damage has been done to the productive capacity of the world than in all human history preceding." He instanced exploitation of forests, fish stocks, and oil fields. Many plant and animal species and varietal forms had become extinct, impoverishing biological diversity. Other useful species had been restricted in their range, and soils destroyed wantonly. "The modern world was built on a progressive using up of its real capital" to the point that the whole Western commercial system "looks like a house of cards."

The talk did not go down well with some of his audience, especially when told that no social science planning could avert the "suicidal [thrust] of our current commercial economy." The prevailing Western ethos was an "optimistic anthropomorphism" that had its origins in the old "north European freebooters [who] overran the world and put it under tribute. We have not yet learned the difference between yield and loot." It was a damning critique of Western imperialism.[27]

At the Eighth American Scientific Congress (AAAS) in 1940, Sauer noted that the global sway of modern agribusiness was making matters worse by wiping out alternative forms of subsistence. "The present spread of scientific agriculture and breeds, strains and varieties from United States breeding stations is rapidly extinguishing in area after area to the south of us [Latin America] the older, more primitive forms, with their greater range of genetic diversity [and potential] . . . long-range breeding value."[28]

With these essays, Sauer became an important voice on conservation issues.

"A Dreadful Lot of Scholastics"

Sauer's conservation concerns were aggravated by many social scientists' denial that any environmental problems existed. For Sauer, environmental destruction was not only a matter of soils and climate or resource economy but also a manifestation of cultural attitudes that fueled his animus against social scientists. They were "universalizing thinkers," while he was a "particularizer."

Sauer's distrust of social science "abstractions" became an obsessive leitmotif. It had not always been so. Like most universities, Berkeley's curriculum distinguished social from natural sciences. Geography, like anthropology, involved both but was principally, Sauer felt, a social science, "fundamental" to other social sciences. Were it grouped with the natural sciences, it would be "peripheral." Thanks to his close relations with the anthropology and history departments at Berkeley, geographers moved freely among these disciplines. Seminars and research programs on Latin American culture and the economies of the West straddled disciplinary boundaries, and as late as 1934 Sauer termed staff and students "social scientists working in common to so large an extent that we no longer feel it incumbent upon ourselves to label the individual as economist, historian, or geographer."[29]

However, Sauer began to change his view with the advent of the New Deal. During the early years of his presidency, Franklin Roosevelt relied heavily on social scientists' reformist zeal for advancing social democracy. At first Sauer was hopeful that the entry of disinterested academics into public policy would lead to a "juster and better order of things." But his optimism waned as the ideological and programmatic blinkers of New Deal social and economic planning became clear. Sauer deplored social scientists' reformist agendas as coercive social engineering premised on antihumanistic materialism. He was by no means alone: Lewis Mumford, Walter Lippmann, Friedrich von Hayek, and Robert Lynd, among others, questioned the goals and methods of social science planners. For them as for Sauer, the example of emerging totalitarianism in Germany was to be avoided.[30]

In 1934 Sauer joined the Social Science Research Council Advisory Committee on Population Redistribution, chaired by Joseph Willits, then head of the Wharton School of Finance and Commerce at the University of Pennsylvania. Sauer sensed a kindred soul in this economist and was delighted that the committee, whose very title implied future planning, had turned instead to studying the origins of the problem:

I am distinctly dismayed by the number of my friends, especially younger ones, in the social sciences, who are espousing economic planning and social planning. I have had sad years of experience with planned control of soil erosion, on the basis of little or no knowledge of the causes or processes of soil erosion. I feel pretty strongly about the fuzziness of the line between science and service. I should hate to be considered opposed to the use of science in prediction and program[ming], but we know pitifully, tragically little about social and economic process. I do resent substituting dynamics of theory for an organized knowledge of our social and economic conditions. There is a dangerous tendency to evade the very difficult business of understanding by facile programming.

He went on to outline a program of research on population movement (including its ethnic and social makeup and living standards) and the destructive impact of rural overpopulation on resource exploitation.

Willits concurred with Sauer's critique of social scientists who wanted to "build the fifth story before they have erected the foundation or the intervening ones." He had been "shocked" by fellow economists' enthusiastic embrace of Rexford Tugwell, flamboyant doyen of New Deal social engineering, who had advocated the compulsory coordination of the nation's manufacturing industry. "To splash into a totality of such a thing merely because it looks nice is the act of an aesthete and seems to me to be very naïve." From here on Sauer and Willits became close confidants.[31]

Sauer refused to review Stuart Chase's *Rich Land, Poor Land* (1936) because he mistrusted "prophets and evangelists who preach sermons." He likened them to religious zealots and theologians: "I really wish the pulpit as a career would again become more attractive. There might be a little more room and encouragement for the poor scholar."[32]

In an antieconomic diatribe written for the Pacific Coast Economic Association, Sauer began with a playful allegory.[33] History and geography, the eldest members of a tribal confederation, were losing power and prestige and being overrun and forgotten by newer tribes (e.g., economics, political science, sociology). These tribes' shamans "were growing in power and wealth, whereas those who fetch things and work goods are poorly regarded." Consequently, many young men in the newer tribes sought to become shamans too, while fewer carried on the crafts of the people. As an older tribesman, Sauer stressed the importance of history and geography in "underpinning" the newer social sciences, which lacked their analytical rigor. Economics had degenerated into the science of money. A "pluralistic" acceptance of social diversity was essential. "This curious world is unendingly fascinating. It is not our business to make it conform to our reason," so as to produce a universally normative globe. He invoked an anthropology devoted to the historical and dynamic diffusion of cultures of multiple origins, skills, attainments, and attitudes.[34] He rejected emphatically the view that history and geography were mere providers of "facts" on which others built theories: "the small bourgeois descriptive sciences and the aristocratic theoretical sciences." This distinction left social science schizophrenic.[35]

There was no "weirder term" to label what his economistic hearers did than "social science":

First of all it turns out to be dominated by philosophy rather than science. Next, the only well-developed and recognized method is the highly limited one of statistical correlation. Finally, a (large) part of the understanding aimed at is not within the reach of [the] scientific approach, but frankly is and must be an art.[36]

To a correspondent he added that "the theorists and dialecticians have their heels on our necks. Social science is going in for soul saving and the pure doctrine. We try to describe and analyze. The boys who set the fashion want first to think straight and then on this basis of illumination to save the world in a generation."[37]

Social scientists' entrenched opinions masqueraded as patent truths. "Those who insist most on their objectivity, are most likely to have a rigid set of values which they take pains to conceal." Diplomats at Versailles who saw themselves as the "arbiters of destiny" had made a mess of carving up Europe because they did no work on the ground.[38] Social science was reductionist, unscientific, and antagonistic to cultural history, Sauer warned Stacy May at the Rockefeller Foundation. There seemed to be "two quite different cosmologies, the conflict between the one god and the pluralistic world. On the one side are the universalizing thinkers, on the other the particularists. The one group deals with formal logic and the workings of the mind, the other is concerned with the logic of events that are forever conditioned by the frame of time and place. It is Milton against Goethe, perhaps St. Paul against the Greeks."[39] Those with a historical bent like himself were out of step with American social scientists.

Geographers at Berkeley represented a lone view, and even in anthropology the historically minded were giving way to the functionalists. Cultural history was weakening in the United States. Economics was embracing the "cult of the Great Number":

> [Those] interested in cultural origins and changes must follow these currents whichever way they go. That does not lend itself well to logical social science, applying theories to the critique of political procedures. Our job is analytic and comparative. Our theology is that all gods are true gods as long as they have authority. I really don't think there is anything to be done about it, except that one should not follow a course that is expedient but takes one away from the goal of understanding what one sees.

Theorists strive to universalize norms and values, collapsing cultural diversity within a single formula; "their *Zeitgeist* discounts the pluralism of culture, reduces and discourages curiosity concerning the ways of men, and invents pedantic unity, to which it then must try to compel assent."[40]

Sauer denounced "two spurious patron saints" who led social scientists into error. One was Saint Bureaucraticus, who sought to create "more and better jobs" to guide "this wobbly world." The other, Saint Scholasticus, was devoted not to the pursuit of knowledge but the working of theory and the production of "five-dollar phrases for commonplaces."

The prevailing trend, which seemed to him endemic in American society, rewarded those who served the expansionist goal to export American norms and values abroad. His fellow social scientists were "a dreadful lot of scholastics. I have found in my contacts with them a lack of curiosity as compared to the natural scientists. It seems to me that we have inherited the people who in earlier days would have become theologians." Perhaps Sauer should drop the label that he had once borne and call himself a humanist.[41]

Henry Vosholl (1818–1908).
Carl Sauer's maternal grand-
father, a Methodist minister.
(Photograph courtesy of
Elizabeth Sauer FitzSimmons
and Ellen FitzSimmons Porzig)

William Albert Sauer (1844–1918).
Carl Sauer's father, a music professor
and plant taxonomist at Central
Wesleyan College, Warrenton,
1890s. (Photograph courtesy of
Elizabeth Sauer FitzSimmons and
Ellen FitzSimmons Porzig)

The Henry Vosholl house,
Warrenton, where Carl Sauer
was born. (Photograph
courtesy of Elizabeth Sauer
FitzSimmons and Ellen
FitzSimmons Porzig)

Carl Sauer, age one to
two, Warrenton, 1890
or 1891. (Photograph
courtesy of Elizabeth Sauer
FitzSimmons and Ellen
FitzSimmons Porzig)

Rosetta, Albert, Carl, and William Sauer, Warrenton, late 1890s.
(Photograph courtesy of Elizabeth Sauer FitzSimmons and
Ellen FitzSimmons Porzig)

Carl Sauer at the *Gymnasium* school
in Calw near Stuttgart, Germany,
ca. 1900. (Photograph courtesy of
Elizabeth Sauer FitzSimmons and
Ellen FitzSimmons Porzig)

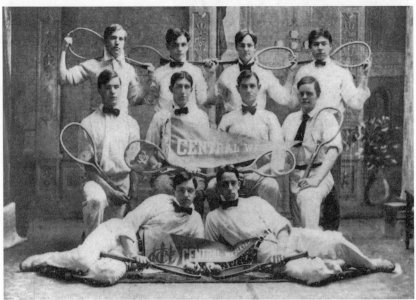

Tennis Club, Central Wesleyan College, 1908.
Carl is in the top row, second from the left.
(Photograph courtesy of Martin Kenzer)

Lorena Schowengerdt, age
seventeen, Warrenton, ca. 1908.
(Photograph courtesy of Elizabeth
Sauer FitzSimmons and Ellen
FitzSimmons Porzig)

Schowengerdt house.
(Photograph, 1970, by Ellen FitzSimmons Porzig)

Carl Sauer, at the University of Chicago, 1911. (Photograph courtesy of Elizabeth Sauer FitzSimmons and Ellen FitzSimmons Porzig)

Wedding of Carl Sauer and Lorena Schowengerdt, Warrenton, December 1913. (Photograph courtesy of Elizabeth Sauer FitzSimmons and Ellen FitzSimmons Porzig)

Carl and Lorena Sauer in Salem, Massachusetts, where he
taught at Salem State Normal School from January to June 1914.
(Photograph courtesy of Elizabeth Sauer FitzSimmons
and Ellen FitzSimmons Porzig.)

Rollin D. Salisbury (1855–1922).
Chairman of the Department of
Geography at Chicago, 1903–19, and
Sauer's dissertation adviser in 1915.
(Courtesy of the University of Chicago
Library Special Collections Research
Center)

Ellen Churchill Semple (1863–1932).
Leipzig, Germany, 1891 or 1892.
Sauer's favorite professor at Chicago.
(Photograph from Geoffrey J. Martin,
2005)

Carl and Lorena with baby Jonathan, Ann Arbor, 1919.
(Photograph courtesy of Elizabeth Sauer FitzSimmons
and Ellen FitzSimmons Porzig)

Carl Sauer in the field, northern
California, 1935. (Photograph
by Karl J. Pelzer; courtesy of
Elizabeth Sauer FitzSimmons
and Ellen FitzSimmons Porzig)

Carl Sauer, 1937.
(Photograph by Robert G.
Bowman; from Preston E. James
and Geoffrey J. Martin, 1978)

Carl Sauer, northern
Mexico, 1940s.
(Photograph courtesy
of William Bowen)

Carl and Jonathan Sauer with unidentified
botanist (with hat) in Peru, 1942.
(Photograph courtesy of Barbara Fredrich)

Carl Sauer at "Man's Role
in Changing the Face of
the Earth" symposium,
Princeton, 1955. (Photograph
courtesy of Paul Starrs)

Elizabeth Sauer FitzSimmons with daughters
Margaret (elder) and Ellen, 1950.
(Photograph courtesy of Elizabeth Sauer
FitzSimmons and Ellen FitzSimmons Porzig)

(*Top left*) Alfred L. Kroeber (1876–1960).
Berkeley anthropologist, and Sauer's
neighbor and colleague. (Photograph by
G. Paul Bishop; from the *American Anthropologist*, 1961)

(*Top right*) John B. Leighly (1895–1986). Carl
Sauer's first Ph.D. (1927), and a close colleague
at Berkeley. (Photograph courtesy of the
Berkeley Department of Geography)

(*Left*) James J. Parsons (1915–1997). Berkeley geography faculty member, 1945–86.
(Photograph by Barry Evans, ca. 1965; from
the *Annals AAG*, 1998)

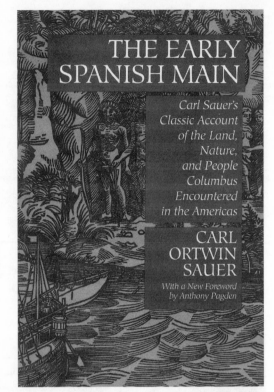

THE EARLY
SPANISH MAIN

*Carl Sauer's
Classic Account
of the Land,
Nature,
and People
Columbus
Encountered
in the Americas*

CARL
ORTWIN
SAUER

*With a New Foreword
by Anthony Pagden*

(*Right*) *The Early Spanish Main*, by Carl Ortwin Sauer, 1966. (Cover photograph from the 1992 edition; with permission from Elizabeth Sauer FitzSimmons)

(*Bottom*) The Sauer house, 1340 Arch Street, Berkeley. (Photograph courtesy of Elizabeth Sauer FitzSimmons and Ellen FitzSimmons Porzig)

Carl Sauer at home, Berkeley, 1972.
(Photograph by Dennis Galloway; courtesy
of the Berkeley Department of Geography)

7

"The Great God West of the Sierras"

Sauer's prestige but also aloofness had become legendary. In 1937 his old
Chicago friend and mentor Wellington Jones urged him to attend the up-
coming Association of American Geographers' annual meeting in Ann
Arbor "and show yourself to a whole generation of younger geographers
who think you are a semi-mythical personage on the Pacific Coast. I cannot
indefinitely convince them that you actually exist."[1] At that meeting, with
Sauer as ever absent, Richard Hartshorne, the distinguished geographer
then at the University of Minnesota, referred to the influence of "this great
god" Sauer.[2]

Sauer's reputation and continued absence from AAG meetings also reflected his multifaceted commitments during the 1930s and 1940s besides
his many academic chores. Service on soil erosion for the Science Advisory
Board of the National Resource Council involved a lengthy expedition in
the southern Piedmont during 1936. He was a prominent consultant for
the Social Science Research Council, the Advisory Council of Fairfield Osborn's Conservation Foundation, the National Resources Planning Board,
the Rockefeller Foundation, and later the Office of Naval Research.

In 1935 he was appointed to the five-member Guggenheim Fellowship
selection board, on which he continued to serve for thirty years. He was

inordinately proud of this position and took great pleasure in it. It was also immensely time-consuming. In 1938 an offer of the presidency of a major eastern university "was buzzing in the air." All the while he continued his Mexican research on Indian economies and population numbers, and embarked on a new inquiry into plant domestication and diffusion in the Americas, while lobbying individuals and foundations to fund an institute of Latin American studies at Berkeley.[3]

In 1948 he joined the Board of Visitors of the newly founded Air Force Academy, pleased that for any meeting of the board a plane would be sent for him. Inclusion in the inner circle of American strategic policy mitigated his long-harbored resentment at nonacceptance as a German American.[4]

The Ruined Land

The physical degradation of American farms particularly needed Sauer's expert attention. In January 1934 Isaiah Bowman, chairman of the National Research Council, asked Sauer to help the new Science Advisory Board formulate an American land-use policy. Within three months Sauer completed a 195-page document, a tour de force of clarity and readability advocating wise use for present and future needs.[5] "Your ears must have burnt yesterday," wrote Bowman after a conference of the Departments of Interior and Agriculture adopted Sauer's proposals, "in view of the number of complimentary things that were said about your report."[6]

Sauer's specific proposal to study the mechanics of soil erosion in critically affected locales was enthusiastically supported by Soil Erosion Service chief Hugh Bennett and assistant chief Walter Lowdermilk. His own immediate task, in late June and July, was a survey of affected Navajo lands. He aimed to gauge the severity of erosion in different landforms under varying intensities of rainfall. The presence or absence of these landforms could then be used as predictors of how erosion might be arrested. The chosen area was the Polacca Wash, a thirty-mile-long channel or arroyo in the Navajo-Hopi Reservation in northeastern Arizona, an area he later termed "a place of evil omen." Personal and professional rivalries turned early promise into an unpleasant experience.[7]

Sauer's team was dismayed at the start by the antagonism of the regional conservator in the Soil Erosion Service, Hugh Calkins, who resented their intrusion. The team also suffered internal dissensions. Sauer put Dick Norman, a geographer with administrative experience, in charge, assisted by the geologists Perry Reiche and Francis Johnson. Johnson was resentful that Norman, who did not have a doctorate, had been made his superior, a resentment exacerbated by late and irregular payments of his salary. A former classmate of Lowdermilk's, Johnson sent him private reports critical of the work and its conceptual plan, which Lowdermilk ignored but retained in administrative files.[8]

Unaware of Johnson's gripe, Sauer reported good progress during the first year. Studies showed that "engineering structures for stemming erosion," revegetating wash beds, and erecting fences to keep out livestock were useless. Ever historically minded, Sauer enlisted Harold Colton, director of the Museum of Northern Arizona at Flagstaff, to gather data on the pregrazing vegetation, and on what changes had taken place when, notably owing to the introduction of alien plants such as Russian thistle, Colorado bee plant, sage bush, and snakeweed.[9] Students gathered Mormon and early Spanish accounts of vegetation and erosion and compiled an annotated bibliography on erosion history in the Southwest.[10] The Navajo project gained further impetus when Warren Thornthwaite, who had followed Sauer from Michigan to Berkeley as one of his first students, was put in charge of climatic and physiographic research.

Just as all seemed to be going well, the whole thing blew up. Johnson had been seeing Sauer's old adversary Kirk Bryan, who resented Sauer's intrusion into his own Arizona preserve, and disagreed fundamentally with Sauer's view that soil erosion and arroyo development stemmed from misconceived land-use practices—rather than climate change, as Bryan believed. Bryan wrote Bowman that the Polacca Wash work was mischievously ill informed. Thornthwaite was incompetent, Lowdermilk was wasting public money, and Sauer's elaborate plan was "ill-advised at best and definitely stupid at the worst. [He] knows very little about erosive processes and nothing about the genesis of land forms." Sauer should be fired before "too many young scientists have been ruined by stupid programs laid out by men of inadequate scientific knowledge, training, and ethics." Bryan assailed Sauer as

<u>Enemies</u>

able with words, [but] his report to the Land-Use Committee is something like his paper on "The Morphology of Landscape" which sounds as if it meant something but is nonsense. Sauer's paper[s] on the "Peninsular Range in Southern California" [and] the Chiricahua mountains in Arizona are full of egregious errors of observation and of analysis. It would be easy to forgive Sauer for a little carelessness or for ignorance but he is wrong-headed and has completely erroneous notions about geomorphology.[11]

Bryan's "worm's-eye view" was thoroughly rebutted by Thornthwaite, who declared that Sauer had "more ideas in a minute than Bryan has in an hour," so Bowman took no action.[12] However, the Polacca Wash incident confirmed Sauer's disenchantment with government work and time-wasting bureaucratic rivalries. Erosion control, important as it was, moreover diverted him from his plant diffusion concerns and from Guggenheim tasks that increasingly absorbed him. Simply put, he was not a research administrator or an experimental field scientist. In December 1936 he concluded that the past year had been a "complete distraction from my field of interest." The main task at hand was to finish his chapter for a Kroeber festschrift on the origins of agriculture.[13]

A Swing into the South

Sauer, however, continued to be involved with soil erosion, which provided a national forum for his views on destructive exploitation. Soil erosion in the southern Piedmont had become a serious issue, and Sauer was duly appointed by the Soil Conservation Service as a senior soil conservationist in geomorphology with a staff of four scientists. In May 1936 he began his "swing into the South" in Missouri and proceeded through Kentucky and Tennessee into the Piedmont, revisiting areas where he had worked years before. His Ozark and Pennyroyal studies had sparked off hunches about the nature of erosion on specific soil types. The limestone country, in particular, might yield interesting results: two promising locales were Cape Girardeau County, Missouri (the location of his farm at Canalou), and Bowling Green in Kentucky.[14] Spartanburg, South Carolina, in the northwestern part of the state, became base headquarters for covering the tobacco country of North Carolina and the cotton country of the Georgia Piedmont to the south.

Cape Girardeau, one of the oldest settled areas west of the Mississippi, its limestone upland free from flooding, had long been planted with wheat and tobacco. It had suffered disastrous erosion since Sauer's visit in 1912–13. Thereafter land use had shifted to livestock farming, and it was important to see if the change had arrested erosion. To the southeast the Nashville basin in the Pennyroyal, where the earliest farming had favored the rich limestone soils, had been surveyed in detail in the Mill Springs camp days and would make another good marker of erosion.[15] Nothing, however, prepared him for the scenes of devastation: enormous gullies scarring the landscape, and whole hillsides of stones where sheetwash erosion had stripped off all the soil and dumped it into the valleys.[16]

Sauer's report to Thornthwaite was a catalog of widespread disaster. Erosion was bad on the Piedmont proper and devastating in the limestone lands, where with a "quickness and finality" it stripped away the shallow soil mantle. He needed to know "the farther agricultural backgrounds" of the region, as past land use was more important than soil type in explaining erosion. "The villains in the southern drama are cotton—omnipotent and omnipresent—and tobacco." The history of cotton was already well known: detailed reports in the censuses of 1880 on cotton and tobacco growing would reveal the intensity of cultivation in the past and the attrition of the soils subsequently. The Soil Conservation Service should now concentrate research on the newly opened up tobacco lands and devise a program of preemptive remedial work. An "agricultural revolution" was underway in the shift from dark tobacco for pipes, cigars, and chewing to the bright, flue-cured, mild tobacco favored by the growing cigarette industry after the First World War. "The tobacco revolution is so young that it has not yet impressed itself as an erosion hazard." This new tobacco belt was a "pioneering zone [with] lots of new settlers, new houses, new communities." Hitherto neglected sandy soils being cleared of their forests would inevitably erode in the future.

Sauer's detailed plan of action comprised (1) an analysis of gully types and depths through various soil horizons, (2) a survey of re-cut valley floors to see what material had been removed from the slopes before and then again after agriculture, (3) slope-soil profiles, (4) an areal history of extremely destructive land use, (5) an erosion history of communities whose protective measures had left soils intact, and histories of (6) terracing, (7) vegetation succession, and (8) slope wash.

At a news conference in Spartanburg, Sauer reported that cotton was misplaced in the humid South. Unless means were devised to halt the ravages of erosion, such as fewer "row crops" and more "broadcast"-type farming, the South faced a "tragic era": "They are waging a slowly losing fight. They've just dissipated the greater part of their soil wealth and they have to keep on wasting it because they can hardly raise anything else but cotton and tobacco. I feel sorry for the people who are caught up in the set of circumstances here. The only crop that never fails is babies, and where all people who are growing up in this area will make a living I don't know." He was utterly despondent about the future of farming in much of the South.[17]

An English visitor, Phyllis Morris, recalled that "in the evenings we [the field staff] sat and talked, mainly about problems of the day's work for Sauer was very friendly and non-professional. To me, his most memorable remark, in a reply to a question on what should be done with a particularly badly eroded tract of land was 'Give it back to the Indians.'"[18]

Sauer and his team turned southwest into Alabama, visiting the Milledgeville gullies famously described by the British geologist Charles Lyell in 1849, which had not been in existence some twenty years before his visit. Sauer found them "both impressive and still active after a hundred years." They then made "a sorrowful inspection" of the Black Belt of Alabama. Its "dramatic erosion history" was the most shocking part of the trip: "Minimum slopes, yet disaster nearly complete. Unless the [Soil Conservation Service] can discover new and better pasture plants, I know nothing that can be done about this area, since the farmers are trying to save themselves by a shift to a livestock grassland economy."[19]

Sauer's overview proved invaluable for years to come, inspiring others to see the land through the eyes of the farmer as well as the soil scientist. Although it was never published in full, some of the results appeared in Sauer's *Handbook for Geomorphologists* for the Soil Conservation Service in 1936, his last formal contribution to the study of landforms.[20] Whatever the lessons learned, war soon intervened, and survey work was suspended. Erosion still lingers as a matter of concern throughout the Piedmont.[21]

The Guggenheim Foundation and "Reasonably Speculative Risks"

Sauer's work for the Science Advisory Board in 1934 had led Henry Moe, head of the Guggenheim Foundation, to solicit his suggestions on a number of issues. The punchy directness of Sauer's responses dazzled Moe, who was used to getting noncommittal, evasive advice. In October 1935 he asked Sauer to join the Guggenheim Fellowship selection committee.[22]

Sauer went to Guggenheim meetings in New York twice a year (a trip at first requiring several days by train), usually stopping to visit his mother in Warrenton. After the first meeting he came back laden with a "case full of books" to be read before the next meeting.[23]

The taxing Guggenheim duties contributed to his sense of "rushing through life." "The old man is slowing down badly," he wrote when he was not yet fifty, "he is an overburdened camel."[24] But the work was extremely stimulating: "I have a boy scoutish glow as to our good deeds." His remit for adjudication was widened from earth sciences and anthropology to Latin America and American regional fiction, the latter, in particular, enormously adding to his load.[25] But his zeal never wilted, and he gave the Guggenheim all the attention he could. When Moe congratulated his penetrating judgment in favor of some unusual candidate, Sauer expressed his disdain for the compilers of facts and his preference for the "variant individual" or "maverick":

I like to encourage reasonable speculative risks. I have guessed right several times on heretics who made good. I am descended from darned near every type of protestant non-conformist which found refuge in central Europe. The difficult thing is to draw the line between the fellow who is driven to say "here I stand, the esteem of my fellows notwithstanding," and witch doctors.

We professors are likely to make it hard for the queer bird unless he saves himself by urbanity of manner. The memory of [Thorstein] Veblen is too fresh with us not to serve as caution. I should even be willing to encourage the support of the brilliant, but ill-balanced mentality, as, for instance, a person of the stripe of [Oswald] Spengler or of my colleague Griffith Taylor of the University of Toronto. Such men, though they go seriously astray, however, have an extraordinary insight into certain factual matters. But there is another type of persons, especially bothersome in geography and anthropology, who have a large smattering of information that they have taken over from superficial contacts with the real workers. They don't actually control any line of evidence but are quick at making constructions. Among well-known illustrations in geography are Ellsworth Huntington in this country [at Yale] and Lionel Lyde in England [University College London]. This combination of lively imagination tending to generalization, and a large collection of partially understood facts borrowed from others, is the most hazardous of all. Such people are tremendously earnest, with great driving force, and likely to be quite persuasive as one first meets them. That's the difficulty, to draw the line between the false prophet and the true one, or at least the one who finds a new beam of light. Even Veblen's adversaries had to admit the penetrating knowledge of the man. Isn't that perhaps the safest measure by which to judge a maverick: Does he demand respect at least in the mastery of his evidence?[26]

Along with several of his own students, a number of Berkeley colleagues received Guggenheims during Sauer's lengthy tenure, almost all "reasonably speculative risks." They included the historical demographers Sherburne Cook and Woodrow Borah, the ethnologist Alfred Métraux, the agricultural economist Ciriacy-Wantrup, the archaeologist Isabel Kelly, the geologist Adolf Pabst, and Mark Shorer in literature. "My conscience still seems clear," Sauer wrote. Certainly they came to him to ask if they should apply and he encouraged them, but he did not recommend awards from any "mood of campus patriotism," but rather on the basis that they "were the kind of people your foundation wants."[27]

Latin American Ventures

Sauer's ready entrée to government and foundation circles after 1934 lent impetus to his campaign to stimulate Latin American research programs.

Through Moe at the Guggenheim, he came into contact with major figures in the Rockefeller and Carnegie Foundations. Joseph Willits, with whom Sauer had established a warm rapport on a New Deal population agency in 1934, headed social sciences at the Rockefeller Foundation between 1939 and 1954.[28]

Sauer sought to tap these foundations to fund his long dreamed of Latin American institute at Berkeley, building on his collaborative efforts with Alfred Kroeber, Herbert Bolton, and Paul Taylor. The longer he worked in Mexico the more he saw the need for scattered Latin Americanists to come together to discuss overlapping issues: "The field is so vast and the workers so few and insulated that our progress is pitifully slow. Personally, I feel the lack keenly. My contacts as a geographer with geographers are not sufficient to satisfy me, because I have interests and queries regarding [the] culture history of Latin America that do not concern my more intimate professional colleagues." The same might be true of Latin Americanist archaeologists, historians, and anthropologists. They all needed "mobilization."[29]

Following discussions with Stacy May at the Rockefeller Foundation, Sauer wrote a six-page prospectus outlining the history of interest in Latin America at Berkeley, the founding of the Ibero-Americana monograph series in 1932, and the 1936 inception of an undergraduate degree in Spanish American history. An interdepartmental "working association" carried out studies in archaeology, aboriginal material culture, the demographic disaster of the sixteenth century, the impact of the missions, Spanish colonial administration, and current economic patterns.

The Rockefeller Foundation might ask, "Why the preoccupation with Mexico? Why the concern with Indians? Why the emphasis on the past?"

We have worked principally in Mexico because it is the closest to us and least expensive to get into, but also because Mexico as New Spain represents a perfectly valid summary of Hispanic America. It was from here that the structure of the Spanish colonial empire was elaborated and from which it was applied to other parts of the New World. We have found it necessary to concern ourselves with Indian backgrounds because, unlike our own country, Latin America was built on the exploitation and later the integration of Indian blood and institutions.

My first interest in Latin America was in current economic geography. I quickly saw that until I knew the Indian, his attainments, his values, I was incapable of making a critical study of that field. As a geographer I can no more disregard Indian culture than I can disregard climate in interpreting forms of life. We have all become historians of culture because the past is to such an extraordinary extent the living present in Latin America.[30]

Grants-in-aid were desperately needed to enable isolated scholars, North American and Latin American alike, to carry out research and visit the planned new center (or institute) for short periods. But Rockefeller was no more willing to provide support than Berkeley and the Guggenheim had been.

With the onset of the war in Europe, official interest in Latin America suddenly went into high gear. Concerned with its own backyard for strategic and resource reasons, the State Department decided that it should aid modernization in order to bind Latin American countries more closely to the United States—Roosevelt's "Good Neighbors" policy. For Sauer the implications were both good and bad. The provision of roads and sewers could not but be good. But he saw the familiar world of Mexican peasant culture swept away as the price of development with "a big loss of the old fashioned." While the Spanish baroque churches would instantly become tourist attractions, modernization would eliminate the pottery, weaving, and decoration of a "very honest folk art. South of the border, they still think that Colonial art is something that looks like the Escorial or Prado," not the blanket or pot of the village craftsman. At the very least, Sauer sought the preservation of peasant crafts, areas of local culture, and the seventeenth-century Franciscan and Jesuit mission buildings.[31]

By 1940 Sauer's persistent lobbying had persuaded Willits that the Rockefeller Foundation should fund Latin American research. Sauer's prospectus urged the simplest possible institutional structure: "The student should be allowed to do the things he most wants to do. I am against the breaking down of a field into the assignment of projects. The foundations have done a grave disservice to scholarship insofar as they have lured persons to draw up projects because funds might be offered. The fewer conferences the better, for conferences become the *rendezvous* of professional committee-men, rather than of craftsmen." "Professional Committeemen," he later added, "ride back and forth from one meeting to another, becoming expert on platitudes, cocktails, and dinners, all in the name of research, which they don't do, can't do, and which makes it difficult for others to do."[32] Small personal grants would enable American scholars to "go down into the field again and again, for the particular connotations of a foreign culture upon which the individual is engaged are learned and synthesized slowly. This business is one of cumulative dividends, and one isn't much good at it until learning gets to the point where he sees the cultural situation from the inside." As for Latin American colleagues, most lived in poverty: "The men with whom we talk shop down there are likely to own one ancient suit and never to have heard of money for research." Younger local academics could do things more intimately and understandingly than any foreigner. "Their number is not negligible, but their means are nil."[33]

Sauer cajoled Moe to arrange a gathering of Latin Americanists in New York; a little bit of competition between the foundations would do no harm. Following the meeting, an enthusiastic Moe came to Berkeley to discuss aims. Their conversation "ran on most of the night and touched on our dreams of how money might be spent in Latin America." Soon after, en route to New Mexico, Sauer was in an elevated, even sublime mood as he looked out the train window "over the little green valleys and juniper-covered rock which frames them." He typed off three long letters to Moe in four days, "dreaming freely" of his vision of a Guggenheim program on life as lived in Latin America. It should certainly not invite the "experts"; he was "all for the provincials, definitely not for New York, B.A. [Buenos Aires], or the common values of civilization."

> I'm being a geographer; I'm not starting out from any *general* premises, as good social scientists would do. I want to start with the particulars of Latin America, particulars that are localized and dated, and see what we get in the way of cultural patterns and vitalities. This is straight regionalism in which I am interested, call it "personality" of a land, *genre de vie*, *Volk und Raum*, pluralism of cultures. It's the kind of world of limited and varied order that interests me, of groups, not

"society," of localized attitudes and innovations, not social psychology. I think there are many gods and that their authority is restricted to the lands of their nativity. This is important: Jehovah and his prophets (e.g. our theoretically oriented social scientists) deny the reality of a pluralistic world, and we Occidentals have done and are doing our best to reduce the world to one system.

Here, "thank God, is a big part of the world that shows less tendency to march under one ideology or to close its local flavors by learning the same pattern and motions. *Vivan las provincias!*" Grassroots expressions of culture could be aided by support for "Little Magazines"; local historical, geographical, antiquarian, and anthropological societies; provincial museums of culture history; preservation of monuments; and collections of aboriginal and colonial plants. Local crafts needed protection against technical innovations that were destroying their integrity, for example, the use of aniline dyes instead of time-honored natural ones. Finally, he stressed the need to safeguard the Mexican environment against predatory destruction by American business, tourists, and sportsmen. Logging was destroying forests, and hunting was reducing wildlife; he suggested bringing in someone like Aldo Leopold to head a conservation unit. To do nothing was to bequeath a miserable legacy: "We do not leave good will behind us in these lands insofar as we skim their resources and leave them impoverished as to their primary wealth."[34]

The Rockefeller Foundation and the South American Trip

For all Sauer's eloquence and cajoling, Moe did not initiate a program of grants for Mexico.[35] But he got Willits to propose that Sauer spend a year in South America to scout out talented younger people and assess the viability of academic institutions, for the Rockefeller Foundation. As usual, Sauer needed persuading, in view of his teaching and research commitments. Getting further leave from Berkeley might be a problem, since he was even then on sabbatical leave in Mexico. Willits confessed to Berkeley president Robert Gordon Sproul that he had been "playing around a little in your backyard. You may and come and play similarly as often as you like," replied Sproul, appreciating the kudos gained by the university.[36]

Sauer realized that such a trip could greatly further his newfou
est in native crops and agricultural practices. Western South Am
saw as the cultural hearth of the Americas. He left Berkeley on De
17, 1941, with his son, Jonathan, then a graduate assistant in geogr;
the University of Wisconsin–Madison. They stayed nearly two months each
in Chile and Peru, a month each in Ecuador and Colombia, and a week in
Bolivia, returning to Berkeley the following August.

The twenty-four letters to Willits on South American agricultural geography, culture history, and social science scholarship were Sauer at his
reflective and perceptive best, and they had a tremendous impact on Rockefeller personnel. Willits, ecstatic, wrote Walter Steward, chair of the Board
of Trustees: "These Sauer letters . . . have spice, flavor, and discrimination."
He commended "these extraordinary, interesting, and penetrating letters
from Carl Sauer. . . . There is such sagacious wisdom and scholarly awareness in them that I feel many times repaid for the small expense involved in
sending him."[37]

Sauer reciprocated Willits's praise. The Rockefeller Foundation's famed
medical work had been a "password to a universal brotherhood of scholarship. I had a freedom of contact, a reception without reserve, . . . because
they felt that I had no other mission than that of common intellectual interests." But Andean academic conditions sorely hampered such interests.
Except at underdog Catholic universities, Sauer found research heavily po-
liticized, salaries derisory, tenure at the mercy of education ministers, libraries painfully inadequate, travel funding negligible, European contacts
few and dwindling. Scholars lacking independent means were desperately
impoverished and woefully isolated even within their own country. "There
are good men in Lima who have never been to the [Peruvian] highlands,
[geographers] in Santiago who have scarcely gotten out of its valley." After
poverty he faulted privatism. Publications sent to institutes became direc-
tors' personal property, often sold off to second-hand bookshops. Far better
were local learned societies such as Quito's Amazonian Institute, "where
twice a month, oil geologists, friars, doctors, school teachers, aristocrat
and plebians, listen to somebody's paper and follow it with a free and often
lengthy discussion." Sauer thought such centers "the real seed beds of intellectual activity . . . where the scholars meet and sustain each other."[38]

The trip rewarded Sauer with invaluable insights into indigenous American agriculture, which were put to immediate use in his essays and supervising several dissertations on Andean topics. And along with earning him the gratitude of the Rockefeller Foundation, it established Sauer's reputation as the expert on Latin American historical and cultural issues. He was elected to the American Philosophical Society (in the biological sciences) in 1944, a rare honor. If not the revered (and resented) "great god west of the Sierras," he had come to many to seem all-wise and all-knowing, highly respected throughout American academe, even if viewed with some suspicion by social scientists.

Office of Naval Research Contract

The new batch of postwar graduate students needed financial backing for fieldwork. Sauer subsidized some students out of his own research money from Guggenheim. He complained bitterly to the University Research Board and then to President Sproul about the poor backing for his Baja California work, but Sproul felt Sauer had only himself to blame, since he hadn't requested funding through his departmental budget. Sauer had literally pushed aside administration circulars to concentrate on his own research and correspondence.

When Sauer could not get funding from Berkeley for work in Mexico, he tried to get it for other parts of Latin America where Cold War tensions gave the military an interest. The Caribbean was America's "soft underbelly" near its strategic Panama Canal sea link. Early in 1951 he sent a persuasive proposal (as only Sauer could write) to the Office of Naval Research (ONR) to fund a field-studies program on Caribbean geography. Louis Quam, in charge of geographical research at the ONR recognized "the value of investigations into coastal geography," which, given the island nature of much of the Caribbean, covered most places. The contract continued for seventeen years, 1952 to 1969, and supported thirty-five scholars at a cost of less than $120,000. It gave rise to forty-eight articles, five Ph.D. dissertations, and seven master's theses.[39]

8

The Farthest Corridors
of Human Time

During the 1940s Sauer trod a speculative and controversial pathway of research into human origins in the Americas, still a topic of lively debate. What especially engaged Sauer were the domestication of New World crops and the antiquity of initial human entry into the hemisphere. The origins of the first crops and of the first Americans—the "paleogeography of man," as he called it—became a consuming passion throughout his remaining years, leading eventually to a grand synthesis of global agricultural domestication and diffusion.

In the late 1930s Sauer realized that his long-sought cultural corridor, from central Mexico up the west coast to the southwestern United States, was chimerical. While the Mexican work had led to his bombshell conclusions about pre-Columbian population numbers, it had not provided the "missing link" between Mexico and the north, the main rationale for his lengthy fieldwork.[1]

Crop Diversity

Yet the years in the field had left him increasingly impressed by the rich variety of crops in the peasant repertoire. The staples—maize (*Zea mays*), squash (*Cucurbita*), and beans (*Phaseolus*), and to a lesser extent tomatoes

(*Lycopersicum*) and potatoes (*Solanum*) — displayed enormous variation from place to place. Had the different varieties evolved naturally or had the Indians carefully selected and bred types that best suited certain locales? Did some crops, like maize, have social or religious significance, as Eduard Hahn had suggested? In any case, it was clear that cultivated plants were artifacts and cultural traits of great antiquity, just as surely as were pots, weapons, and buildings.

The shift in Sauer's research interests profoundly affected his intellectual life. In his previous work, the help and approbation of anthropologists Kroeber and Lowie had been indispensable. Once Sauer moved into the study of plants these links became less important than those he forged with botanists and geneticists such as Edgar Anderson at Washington University in St. Louis and Paul Mangelsdorf at Harvard, both concerned with the origin of maize.

Sauer saw the genetic and ecological separation of cultivated plants from wild flora as a tremendous realm of "neglected enquiry" for understanding the origins and spread of culture. Domesticated species might yield evidence that contradicted the conventional records of archaeology, linguistics, and ethnology. They might also help to date the diffusion of native peoples in the Americas. Moreover, obscure native strains of common crops could hold the key to the breeding of better-yielding strains that would help solve global food problems, provided they were not extirpated by blundering agricultural modernization. In this he was critical of what became the "Green Revolution" of the 1960s.[2]

The Pursuit of Maize

As Sauer embarked on his 1942 tour of Andean South America for the Rockefeller Foundation, he realized how ill equipped he was for tracing interrelationships among climate, soils, and plants.[3] He had a sharp eye and abundant curiosity, but no genetic training. What, Sauer asked Anderson, should he and Jonathan be looking for in South America? In Sonora he had seen, but ignored, many exotic varieties. He was keen that this should not happen again. "Tell us, what we can do to provide you with corn materials."

Anderson was precise: the Sauers should get as many samples as possible of tasseled corn from specified areas. Because corn was a cross-pollinated crop, one had to see the whole adjacent stand of twenty to thirty plants in order to make sense of what was going on. Anderson needed to know the number "of nodes above the upper ear, number of ears, maximum leaf width, length and width of ear, number of tassel brushes, length of pedicel and pediculate spikelet, and length of spikelet" of each plant.[4]

Sauer also asked Anderson whether genetic analysis of the different types of maize that Isabel Kelly had gathered in western Jalisco could throw any light on cultural differences. Anderson happened to be working on another maize collection from Texas and Cuba and was keen to collaborate. He fully backed an interdisciplinary approach, and regretted that maize geneticists were unaware that "primitive" strains survived in out-of-the-way places. Indeed, he told Sauer, he had recently had a paper rejected for labeling some Papago corn a "real" variety when every right-thinking geneticist knew it was merely "a peculiar mongrel strain."[5]

When Kelly's bundles of maize arrived in Missouri, Anderson planted them to see what the mature stalks would reveal. Back from the Andean trip eight months later, Sauer found Anderson very excited because the period of maximum differentiation, which occurred just as the pollen was shed, revealed even greater variety than he had gauged from examining the cobs alone. There really was something in this idea of primitive types of corn: "I have a bull by the tail," he told Sauer, but to unravel it needed an extended investigation. A Guggenheim Fellowship would be ideal, but would he be too old at forty-five to apply? he asked Sauer apprehensively. If not, would Sauer support him? He could not rely on any backing from fellow geneticists "scandalized by my ungenetic approach."

The plight of the lone academic maverick battling rigid, orthodox thinking immediately appealed to Sauer, and he pulled out all stops to secure a Guggenheim for Anderson as well as funds from the foundation's budget for Latin American diet and nutrition studies. The whole Latin American crop situation cried out for investigation. Cotton was as confused as corn, squash was "an awful mess," and beans were no better. Anthropologists could not help, since they lacked genetic knowledge.[6]

Sauer invited Anderson to Berkeley to "work out a program" for a wider study of native food resources. The geneticists George Stebbins and Ernest Babcock were keen to have Anderson on campus,[7] as was the physiologist

Sherburne Cook, an authority on primitive diets. Sauer organized university-wide seminars on crop domestication, aided by his student Webster McBryde, who had long been collecting maize varieties as cultural indicators in Guatemala. He had helped assemble samples for Paul Mangelsdorf and R. G. Reeves's seminal 1939 paper on the tripartite origin of Indian corn, which in Anderson's opinion had started the "genetic ball" rolling.[8] Mangelsdorf and Reeves believed that the hundreds of types of maize stemmed from three wild grasses.[9] An assumed (but never found) South American pod corn had spread to Guatemala and hybridized naturally with Tripsacum, and a third wild grass, Teosinte.[10] The biological technicalities were beyond Sauer, and he was cautious: "I don't think we are ready to fit the pieces together as yet, and I fear commitment as to origins." But he did support Mangelsdorf and Reeves's hypotheses in his 1950 article "Cultivated Plants of South and Central America."[11] However, subsequent research has indicated that Teosinte is the sole ancestor of maize.[12]

Sauer was enthusiastic about the broader ramifications of the origins of maize. It established "a bridge between biological and social sciences," both in Berkeley and in the wider academic community, while illuminating "the origin and spread of cultural traits." It also had a practical relevance for North American involvement in Latin American agricultural development, then blindly reliant on "scientific agriculture" with its "attendant contempt for native crops and methods."[13]

By July 1943 Anderson's corn was "growing like mad" and had distinctive features. He had never seen anything like it before, and the nearest similar corn was waxy maize from China. Anderson's suggested Asian origin was not exactly what Sauer wanted to hear, since it ran counter to his hypothesis that maize was a cultural indicator in the Americas. Anderson's earlier genetic work had hypothesized two reasonably clear pathways for the diffusion of maize, one up the west coast of Mexico and another up its east coast into the Mississippi valley and then eastward.[14]

So Sauer used his knowledge of Latin, early Spanish, and German to scour the herbals produced during the first flush of printing in early sixteenth-century Europe, with plants drawn in detail. The results were confusing, even at times contradictory. Maize was not known to Chinese scholars in the twelfth century, but it was known by the second half of the sixteenth.

Asian maize could not have come from the Atlantic coast of the Americas, first encountered in 1492 by Columbus, since it was most like maize from the Andes of Peru, not reported by the Spaniards until the 1530s. Maize was not grown in Europe until later. Therefore, Chinese maize could not be an overland transfer eastward from Europe. Sauer began to entertain the almost heretical idea of pre-European Pacific crossings of people and crops. "The more I learn the less I believe in the isolation of materials in the New World from trans-Pacific man." It was to be another seventeen years before Sauer published his ancient herbaria maize research.[15]

Anderson was a far more seminal thinker than most botanists have admitted. His work on corn showed the need for a "common meeting ground for agronomists, geneticists, archaeologists, geographers, anthropologists, and taxonomists, as Professor Sauer had been advocating for some years."[16] Anderson and Sauer later collaborated on the 1955 symposium "Man's Role in Changing the Face of the Earth" (see chap. 11).

Preservation of Crop Variety

Sauer's own interest in plants shifted away from genetics to how plants had been manipulated and modified by early man.[17] His disenchantment with retrospective genetic investigations reflected his discomfort with "improvers" who sought prospective genetic change to increase yields and make plants more disease free. When the director of food supply in the Bureau of Inter-American Affairs asked for samples of his Indian corn, Sauer pointed out that any region would have a basic stock best suited to that region. Superior native stocks should be selected for possible improvement rather than "the introduction of pre-determined foreign blood."[18]

Sauer had not the least interest in flooding Latin America with strains and varieties of seeds from the United States:

> In fact I am very much against it. The Latin American countries hold an enormous reservoir of domesticated plant forms which are the result of thousands of years of plant breeding. I shall not do anything willingly or wittingly to destroy this immeasurable valuable cultural heritage. This is, I think, not a sentimental attitude on my part, but a longer term view of wishing to preserve for full development as much

as possible of the wealth of genes that have been produced in cultivated plants.

Scientists in the United States had contempt for native crops and methods.
In conforming to commercial preferences of the moment, they discarded
plant forms that had developed over countless years to suit foreign physical and cultural environments and that did not make excessive demands
on the earth's resources. Sauer had long sought to encourage grassroots
conservation of cultural diversity. Plants now joined museums, buildings,
anthropological and literary societies, and crafts as the "life as lived" being
destroyed by the American juggernaut of modernization.[19]

This was part of Sauer's wider concern about the diversity of human societies unsullied by industrialization. "I like the world because it does resist
uniformity and still its diversity is not chaotic," he wrote in 1938. Societies,
like organisms, thrive on diversity. The destruction of cultural diversity accelerated after the Second World War, and he judged the Western urge to
improve "the underdeveloped world" one of the tragedies of the age. Such
"progress" was probably irreversible. In a well-worn diatribe he termed
most development "actually exploitation" for the insatiable appetite of the
industrial world. "The prevalent mood of increasing economic expansion is
neither smart nor humane."[20]

June 1943 saw Sauer plunged into an urgent new assignment for the long-
anticipated *Handbook of South American Indians*, edited by the anthropologist
Julian Steward. Within a month Sauer had drafted a masterly survey of Latin
American field crops: "I can't do any more. I am brash enough to undertake
this much because I am becoming steadily more aware of how little I know
and how little is known about crops and agriculture. At least I am perhaps
less ignorant about the subject as a whole than anybody [else] you could get."
He also wrote the "Geography of South America" chapter for the *Handbook*.[21]

In December 1944 Carl and Lorena went down the west coast of Mexico
to Tepic, getting "some fun out of life" while studying local crops and collecting seeds at village markets between there and Guadalajara, their base
for the next six weeks. They were sometimes accompanied by Isabel Kelly
and Chema, a knowledgeable native informant on local crops and agricul-

Radicality?

tural practices. By the end of March they had traveled by bus to Mexico City, Puebla, and Oaxaca, visiting libraries, museums, markets, and archaeological sites. Returning north, they spent three weeks around Lake Chapala, southeast of Guadalajara, with Kelly and Chema, ending with a side trip to Zacatecas.[22] Sauer was particularly taken by Lake Chapala: "I lost my heart to San Juan Cosalá and am already dreaming of my own bit of land on the lake shore and my own garden and fig trees and luscious papayas. What a spot that is and as yet an unspoiled lot of fisher folk. I think it's my chosen spot to retreat from the world if it doesn't get overwhelmed by civilization."[23]

The First Americans

Sauer's work on the *Handbook* made him ponder how so many plants had been domesticated. Genetics provided important evidence, but he could not personally contribute to knowledge in that field. For primitive humans to have brought about such great changes in the continent's biota required more time, he believed, than archaeologists were prepared to allot. Hence the "calendar of man's record in the New World must be lengthened."[24]

"A Geographic Sketch of Early Man in America" reached Gladys Wrigley, editor of the *Geographical Review*, in May 1944 and was quickly published in October.[25] Wrigley was delighted. It was "a feast" for readers. Sauer, gratified by her reaction, mentioned that he probably had another couple of articles on early man and plants in the pipeline. "Is there a book in it for the Research Series of the [American Geographical] Society?" she asked.[26] The "Great Leviathan," as Wrigley termed the article, was a tightly argued survey of the entry and dispersal of early humans into both Americas, along with hypotheses about plant distributions and their alteration by humans.

Sauer first reviewed the glacial history of the Americas. He accepted the conventional explanation that lower sea levels had allowed humans from northeast Asia (Berengia) to cross a wide land bridge over what is now the Bering Straits into Alaska and to migrate south via a corridor between the receding ice sheets. What he was not prepared to concede was the late conventional date of that migration at around 10,000 BP, held then by most archaeologists.[27]

Folsom and Yuma man (the earliest known humans in the Americas up to about 1949 when Clovis man was discovered)[28] must have been present, he suggested provocatively, for "at least twenty to twenty-five thousand years." The presence of "Pleistocene man" (i.e., Ice Age man) "can no longer be denied, it is only a question of how far back his title extends in America."[29]

Neither climate change nor disease could account for the total extinction of the large Pleistocene megafauna—mammoths, giant bison, musk ox, giant elk, and giant bear—in the space of a mere few hundred years. Their demise could have been due only to the hunting skills of early humans, who used fire to drive the herds and whose "astonishing perfection of lithic techniques" produced the deadliest of spear heads, equal in quality to those of the Solutrean cultures of France and Spain between 16,500 and 25,000 BP.

Sauer believed that pervasive and destructive fires had facilitated the formation and expansion of the American grasslands. This was not a climatically induced climax vegetation, as was commonly assumed, but rather a biotic transformation that needed over 20,000 years of human use of fire and animal grazing to produce the vast present-day prairies and pampas.[30] He then turned to the routes of dispersal across the continents.

Sauer was pleased with the impact of the article, which brought him into the center of national scholarly discourse. The "steady trickle" of letters from biologists and natural scientists turned into a regular stream. Two of his controversial ideas on early America have been accepted by many—what has become known as the "Pleistocene Overkill" of the megafauna, and that the grasslands came into being as a result of the widespread use of fire. He later amplified this second thesis.[31]

Sauer's long-standing, deep-seated, and almost visceral aversion to academic orthodoxies left him delighted to have helped demolish the "climatic climax" theory of the origin of the grasslands. Although he hoped to "watch the dawn breaking after the long period of dreadful night," to crack the orthodoxy of dating the entry of the first Americans proved far more difficult.[32]

The often acrimonious debate between early and late entry is still not over.[33] Whatever the outcome, Sauer was the first to suggest an early entry on the basis of the time needed to domesticate plants. He challenged "the whole phobia against recognizing paleolithic skills, [allied to] the dogma that any skill recognized in the New World must be later than the date of its

appearance in Europe. I want more time for the background of agricul\
development, quite a lot more than is conceded by archaeologists, and \
glad for every backward extension of man's record in the New World."[34]

Many archaeologists seemed to adhere to a short "Bishop Ussher chronology for the New World," thereby assuming that the natives must have been
"witless oafs until a few centuries ago and then ran a cultural development
at a rate ten times as great as that in the Old World, gaining attainments of
millennia in a short time."[35]

In 1947 and 1948 Sauer again broached the possibility of Pleistocene man
in the New World and the need for a "long backwards glance" at the hunting
cultures that would push the date for the first Paleo-Indians to before the
end of the Wisconsin Ice Age (10,000 BP).[36] Sauer was convinced that the
human record could be dated only by means of more, and yet more, fieldwork. In 1945–50 he visited Mexico nine times in a frantic, though often
unsystematic, search for evidence.[37] He believed that dry lake beds in the
southwestern United States, surrounded by early settlement sites, had been
glacial Pleistocene, not postglacial, water bodies as generally thought. Similar dry lakes and Pleistocene river terraces in northern Mexico might yield
evidence of human occupance going back at least 25,000 years.

In 1946, searching for sites of early man along river terraces in Sonora
with the University of Arizona archaeologist Emil Haury, Sauer was inclined
"to be far more liberal about the age of archaeological vestiges" than Haury,
who "thought at times that he [Sauer] was less critical of the evidence than
he might have been" and probably overestimated the age of the sites.[38]
Likewise in Baja California, Sauer found numerous large shell middens far
inland. He declared them "some of the oldest records of Man in the New
World," despite his former student Peveril Meigs's earlier conclusive proof to
the contrary.[39] These field trips were a prime spur to his speculative imagination. "I can learn more by being in the field than by reading. When I am
fresh from the field I have a new incentive to read, and after I have read for
a time I have an additional reason for getting back in the field. This is the
happy circle which makes being a geographer a very nice way of spending
one's life."[40]

The next trip to Baja California in February 1947 was of great future significance in a way Sauer could never have anticipated. The Berkeley group of

Associates of Tropical Biogeography organized an interdisciplinary team—the botanist Lincoln Constance, the geologist Howel Williams, the paleontologist Reuben Stirton, and three of Sauer's students.[41] It was agreed beforehand that each would work on his own interests, but Sauer dogmatically insisted that all work on his early man project. Williams composed a ditty that showed how overbearing Sauer had been:

> When you go out on a field trip with Sauer
> You collect not a rock, not a flower.
> But when you get to La Paz
> You sit on your ass
> And listen to Sauer by the hour.[42]

One of the students, Edwin Hammond, was awed by Sauer's intuitive grasp of information almost at a glance, but equally was "surprised by the quickness with which he could go out on a limb in interpreting what he saw. This, of course, was very stimulating, while at the same time it occasionally brought to light no small clayiness of the feet. Nor did he take graciously to having his hypotheses undercut by one of us who turned up contrary evidence."[43] Often the desire to prove his by now obsessional preconceived hypothesis on early man distorted his judgment.

Sauer contemplated chartering a ship to go around Baja California to survey the marine terraces he had seen twenty feet up along the coast, many of them with caves thought to have been once inhabited. These terraces might help break down the "dogma" of no Pleistocene man, since he thought the caves were at least 100,000 years old.[44] However, long trips in 1947, 1948, and 1949 yielded nothing that contributed to early man. The cruise never happened.[45]

Yet Sauer kept trying to move back the age of early man in the Americas. He grasped at straws; the news that some European archaeologists had put back the Solutrean period in Europe to around 70,000 years BP "came as a relief," supporting his estimate of the rate of cultural evolution. If the relationship between American hunting cultures and the Solutrean could be proven (largely on the basis of their similar finely crafted spear heads), then early Americans might be pushed back to 50,000 BP.[46] Sauer's obsession had led him onto shaky ground. The idea of the Solutreans sailing to America or trekking over the ice of the North Atlantic from Britain is now mostly discredited. In Europe they never settled north of Paris; they were separated from the American Eastern Seaboard by three thousand miles of ocean; they were not seafaring people; and Solutrean culture ended around 16,500 BP. Recent authorities on the first Americans, however, make a strong case for Solutrean migration to the eastern United States as early as 19,000 to 25,000 BP.[47]

In January 1950 Sauer met Willard Libby, who was visiting Berkeley from Chicago. Libby had just published a paper on radiocarbon dating that completely revolutionized archaeological research, winning him the Nobel Prize in Chemistry in 1960.[48] Libby "shocked" Sauer with the news that the forest bed at Two Creeks, Wisconsin, was only 12,000 years old. "In that case," exploded Sauer, "the culmination of the Mankato [Ice Lobe] could hardly be more than 9,000 years old. That would mean that we had a glacial culmination in mid-Iowa at a time when the ice-cap on the Scandinavian fjell had shrunk to two detached masses and only one thousand to two thousand years before sea levels recorded a retreat of ice to approximately its present extent." This "incredible" finding seemingly confuted Sauer's idea of Pleistocene man in America.[49]

Still reluctant to give up his quest for an "early" man, over the next decade Sauer mounted a spirited defense against the "palaeo police." He had to accept the radiocarbon dates but was not convinced that they carried the authority that archaeologists gave them. "My prejudice, and it is hardly more than that, is that the older dates are too much compressed as to interval and too recent." He still believed human penetration might have occurred much earlier during an interglacial period.[50]

Sauer took heart from the new dates of 12,000 to 13,000 years BP for Clovis man, earlier than before but still not early enough for him. Perhaps humans had lived in the almost iceless Alaskan plains and then skirted the glacial barriers of Canada by moving south along the Pacific shore, or even penetrated eastward and then down the Atlantic coast.[51]

He continued to ruminate on the "horrible dilemma" of the Pleistocene: "We used to think" that "the continental ice sheets disappeared about 25,000 years ago; now we know that the ice cap extended virtually within sight of Des Moines at less than half that time." Even the Canadian corridor was being called into question. He and others had taken "comfort" in the idea of deglaciation between stages of the Wisconsin Ice Sheet, but the only possible gap for entry was 70,000 years ago, which was too early. Postglacial migration into the New World posed an even greater problem: "Is it tenable that all the bearers of the linguistic families, the older ones by inference in South America, rushed in post-glacially, became separated as they did, and lost their identification with Old World languages wholly?"[52]

Many archaeologists now accept an arrival of people in the Americas by at least 15,000 BP. Recently a pre-Clovis site in Texas was confidently dated to 15,500 BP. Additional genetic evidence for an entry between 15,000 to 25,000 BP and the Solutrean hypothesis of 19,000 to 25,000 BP support Sauer to some extent.[53]

Agricultural Origins and Dispersals

After his talk with Libby and mounting validation of carbon dating, Sauer's enthusiasm for tracing early man waned. He could not argue with hard physical science, yet his "apostasy" kept him from fully giving up a pre-Clovis entry. But he had wasted too much precious time on the pursuit of the first Americans, a marginal issue next to plant domestication.

Wrigley's suggestion of a book about domestication finally bore fruit in 1951 when George Kimble, director of the American Geographical Society, invited Sauer to deliver the Bowman Memorial Lectures. What might it be? "Call it what you will; man against nature, nurture versus nature, culture origins and viability, modification of Earth by man. What I'd like most to do is to present [the] major steps in man's becoming the ecological dominant."[54] To do a "geography Toynbee" in five hours might be less impossible than trying to cover the fortunes of humankind in many large volumes.

Three months' writing yielded five lectures, delivered in January and February 1952: "1. Man-Ecologic Dominant; 2. Planters of the Old World and Their Household Animals; 3. The Planters of the New World; 4. Seed and Harvest; 5. Herdsmen and Husbandmen." As usual, he was disappointed that few geographers turned up, but the botanists were friendly and the "participation of anthropologists was excellent, their reaction far more cordial than I dared expect."[55]

Agricultural Origins was published in late 1952. At just over a hund
pages, it was Sauer's longest work since the *Pennyroyal* book in 1927. Synt
sizing his previous thinking about how people had begun to domestic
the world around them, it was typically <u>Sauerian in style</u>—speculative,
global in reach, spanning all human time, and with a sometimes stunning
disregard for evidence that did not fit his general thesis. He regretted the
"meagerness of [the] Mesolithic record," when man learned so much, the
formative unsung prelude to the far better known Neolithic.[56]

Sauer's detailed treatment of individual crops and animals is beyond analysis here, but his basic premises deserve comment. A half century's hind-
sight shows some things he got right, and others he got wrong. Sauer's idea
that the first agriculturalists were sedentary people is widely accepted. But
David Harris, a former Sauer student and leading authority on plant domestication, finds four major assertions that have not stood the test of time:

1. That progressive fishing people in permanent villages close to rivers
and lakes initiated plant and animal domestication.

2. That riverine Southeast Asia was the first "cultural hearth" of domestication, not Southwest Asia (the Levant) as traditionally supposed.

3. That root crop cultivation preceded seed crop cultivation. Root crops
would not have provided sufficient nutrition without recourse to wild animal sources of protein. "In contrast, systems of grain cultivation, especially
the Southwest Asian variant, which integrated domestic herd animals with
crop cultivation, provided a more balanced diet," and therefore spread ex-
tensively during Neolithic times.

4. Finally, Sauer assumed that agriculture began in conditions of plenty
"where people lived at a comfortable margin above the level of want" and
had the "leisure for reflection, experimentation and discussion." But while
agriculture is far more unremittingly laborious and time-consuming than
fishing, hunting, and gathering, it provides "more food per unit area and
can sustain more people in permanent settlements." In contrast, foraging
was very stressful because it was subject to climatic fluctuations and herd
dynamics. Recent archaeology and paleobotanical finds from the Levant
and China controvert Sauer's contention that agriculture "did not originate
from a growing or chronic shortage of food."[57]

These qualifications do not, however, invalidate Sauer's manifold cultural and ecological insights. He brought attention to the great question of how and where agriculture began. A lasting contribution of *Agricultural Origins* was its demonstration of the power of humans to alter the earth. As humanity interfered more and more with the rest of nature, it became essential to understand, through "retrospective study, the responsibilities and hazards of our present and our prospects as lords of creation."[58] Sauer's message was replete with examples of past excesses, befitting a time of dawning environmental concern.

Despite the "stubbornness" of the guest, insights triumph. "the responsibilities and hazards of our present"

> We try to give play to curiosity, restricted
> only by competence.—Carl Sauer to
> Richard Hartshorne, 1946

9

"The Heart of Human Geography"

During the Second World War Sauer's fears that war with Germany would revive anti-German feelings against the "hyphenates" were never realized.[1] But the conflict affected him professionally and personally. John Leighly, whom he relied on heavily for running the department during his frequent absences, and later John Kesseli, were both seconded to Washington, so that Sauer had to stretch his own teaching. Both Sauer's children also went to Washington. Jonathan, soon to marry Hilda Sievers, was drafted as a weather specialist in the Air Force. Daughter Elizabeth had gone there to work with the Latin American division of the Office of Strategic Services and met her future husband, Edward FitzSimmons. The big redwood house on Arch Street now seemed empty.[2]

Sauer's mother's death in 1942 profoundly affected him. A nonbeliever ✳ since his student days in Chicago, he found no consolation in religion; <u>death was brutally final.</u> "It is easy to see why men invented heaven, without which life may seem to be a series of cruel tragedies."[3]

His mother's death was particularly tragic for Sauer. He seemed to need to communicate intimately in writing, and his <u>letters to his mother</u> from 22 yrs 1919 to 1941 were unusually full and frank. When she was no longer there to hear his hopes and fears, his professional correspondence became more overtly personal, including views that could not be expressed in print. For-

tunately, many of these letters have been saved. In them Sauer railed inces-
santly against the poor quality of American professional geography, the sins
of positivism in the social sciences, and American global modernization.

Berkeley Geography Faculty, 1930s to 1940s

"We are rather old fashioned," Sauer wrote a New Zealand geographer who
contemplated visiting Berkeley. His department concentrated on geomorphology, biogeography, and historical geography. With no political geography or urban planning, "we are somewhat lonely in this country."[4] Following the European tradition of a solid grounding in landforms, soils, climate,
and vegetation, Sauer had pioneered his own brand of cultural geography,
again based on European mentors such as Friedrich Ratzel, Eduard Hahn,
and the historical landscape scholar Otto Schlüter.

In the late 1930s the department was still the small, intimate unit Sauer
had created in 1923, with just one more permanent staff member: himself, Leighly, Jan Broek, and Kesseli. In his view expansion was not war-
ranted; geography was but a part of the wider university, and his students
could benefit from, and were encouraged to take, courses in other disciplines with which he had forged close links. The closest were with Alfred
Kroeber—who lived just across the street and would meet Sauer on their
way down the hill to campus, chattering away in German—and Robert
Lowie, both in anthropology. Sauer helped to oversee many anthropology
graduate students. Herbert Mason in botany, Howel Williams in geology,
Hans Jenny in soil science, Wolfram Eberhard in sociology, M. M. Knight
and Paul Taylor in economics, Siegfried Ciriacy-Wantrup and Carl Alsberg
in agricultural economics, Lesley Simpson in Spanish, Herbert Bolton and
others in history, George Stewart in English, and Alden Miller in zoology
were all sympathetic with Sauer's emphasis on cultural and environmental
history, and were virtually "adjuncts of the Geography faculty." A stream of
visiting or long-term lecturers—former student Stanley Jones from Bristol,
the Dutch map historian A. A. Devries, the Russian forest biologist Nicholas
Mirov, and the Austrian anthropologist Edwin Loeb—added variety and
new viewpoints.[5]

Leighly, who had come to Berkeley from Michigan with Sauer as a gradu-

TO PASS ON A GOOD EARTH

ate student in 1923 and was Sauer's first Ph.D., was the staff linchpin. Sauer relied on him completely, not only as a teacher of climatology, cartography, the history of geography, and the regional geography of Scandinavia but also as a precise logician who complemented his own speculative and free-wheeling bent and who deputized when Sauer was absent. The relationship went deep. It was said that Sauer often gave Leighly penultimate drafts of his work for comment, and Leighly would quietly correct careless mistakes. He succeeded Sauer as chair of the department in 1954. ✔

Broek came from the Netherlands in 1931 as a Rockefeller Fellow and soon produced a classic landscape study of the Santa Clara Valley (known today as Silicon Valley).[6] He taught on and off in the department from 1936. But he did not get along with Sauer and left for Minnesota in 1947.[7]

Kesseli, a German Swiss, did his dissertation under Sauer in 1938 on glaciation in the Sierras. He taught introductory physical geography, geomorphology, California, photogrammetry, and map interpretation and led field classes. Emphatic, gruff, impatient, a strict disciplinarian, and brutally frank, he was the scourge of graduate students required to prove reading proficiency in French and German before beginning dissertation research. His thick guttural accent made him difficult to understand in class. The "drill master" of the department, at times he was reprimanded by Sauer.[8]

The influx of students after the end of the Second World War necessitated more teachers. Ph.D. students Erhard Rostlund, in 1945, and James Parsons, in 1948, became lecturers and then tenured faculty. Parsons taught Latin America, economic geography, and later California. Rostlund, a former merchant seaman from Sweden, taught cultural geography and Europe. Sauer was incensed by criticism that the department had become too in-bred, stressing that the staff were "very different in temperament and in their interests."[9] Clarence Glacken, later famed for his monumental *Traces on the Rhodian Shore: Nature and Culture in Western Thought* (1967), came from Johns Hopkins in 1952 to teach the history of geographical thought, cultural geography, and Asia. The department would remain comparatively small, however. In 1955, nearing retirement, Sauer wrote: "It's a kind of nice little department, with all its queer characters, and that is, I think why it's nice. I wonder what they [the administration] make of such a bunch in which everyone pretty well works on whatever he wants to work at. There probably are a few people around the university who envy us our happy state of self-determination."[10]

Sauer made clear his attachment to limited staff numbers and extensive contacts with the wider university in his rejection of an offer in 1944 to head the Johns Hopkins geography department, built up by Isaiah Bowman as one of the largest in the United States. Writing to Bowman, Sauer acknowledged the advantages of proximity to Washington and New York, but for all its marginal isolation, California, specifically Berkeley, had its advantages:

> In this vast *omnium gatherum* there is a tradition of letting each group work out its own salvation. This place has saved itself by that simple device, or lack of one. It is an academic metropolis in its capacity of accommodating all kinds of persons and minds. The departments that want to go after masses of students do so, the others don't. We have had very intimate relations with Anthropology, which in terms of serious scholarship is the strongest corner of the Social Sciences here. We live in cordial cohabitation, and our agricultural faculty has the best part of the natural science strength of the university. As to the meeting of minds we are very fortunately situated.

He lauded the shift from the "dialectic atmosphere" of the building where geographers previously had been housed with the economists and other social scientists to a building with agricultural scientists, "all happily working away on tangible things."

Then there was the Bancroft Library with its incomparable collection of Latin American and California material, the departmental collection of early Spanish documents that he had accumulated over the years, his unfinished work on nearby Mexico, and the botanists and geneticists in Berkeley and Pasadena with whom he had established good working relationships on plant domestication.

> It isn't simply the California climate, which I do enjoy, nor a sessile temperament. I think the work I have to do can be done here better than it could at Baltimore. For me the nearness of Washington would be [a] disadvantage and distraction. I happen to have a fondness for

the provinces and a somewhat emotional attitude that the better world will come through the strengthening of the local centers, not from the great capitals. Don't write this off as a whim of mine; the whole geography of evolution shows arguments in favor of partial isolation. If I should move into the center of the mass, I should feel that the germinal potential was out on the periphery.[11]

Critics: Ackerman, Hartshorne, Spencer

Beyond his major statements on the importance of history in geography Sauer disavowed opining on what geography should or should not be. But he was catapulted back into the methodological fray in mid–1945 by a request from a young geographer, Edward Ackerman of Harvard, to critique his draft essay on research methods and objectives. Sauer found "shocking" Ackerman's contention that geography should train systematic specialists. Worse was his marginalization of cultural geography. All that seemed to matter to East Coast and midwestern urban geographers was the present and its projection into the future. Even communism, which Sauer thought the closest counterpart to the American emphasis on "presentism" and production, was "based on a serious attempt to understand processes of cultural change, for Marx did not start with the contemporary scene."

While for Sauer human geography had "little meaning unless it deals with cultural origins and the mechanisms of their spread, growth, and extinction," in his view most American geographers had no regard for any form of process, developmental, evolutionary, genetic, historical, or whatever. They had succumbed to the illusion of induction, assuming that if enough things were described they would fit into a synthesis, which raised the questions, description of what, description for what? Significant constructive understanding seemed beyond geographers who came out of the hothouse atmosphere of wartime Washington identifying "objects for destruction."

Sauer was "disturbed" that his emphasis on the time element had no meaning to his American colleagues, other than Bowman. Most of them probably said, "Here is Sauer off again on some strange anthropologic trail and it isn't worth reading." That his work nonetheless elicited animated responses from scholars in fields ranging from genetics to modern history, and from geographers outside North America, led him to only one conclusion: "I am not sure that it is myself who has diverged from the proper task of geography; it may be the others who have left the classical objectives of our discipline. Until these others can tell me on what trails of discovery they are embarking their lives, I shall retain my skepticism."[12]

Soon after the Ackerman exchange Sauer received a three-thousand-word letter from Richard Hartshorne, puzzled by a seeming contradiction in Sauer's thinking.[13] The "pernicious anemia of 'but-is-this-geography'" anxiety against which Sauer frequently railed[14] had begun, Hartshorne averred, with Sauer himself, who authoritatively defined the content of geography in his 1925 "Morphology of Landscape" (see chap. 4). Hartshorne conceded that it might seem unjust to saddle Sauer now with a twenty-year-old prescription, yet

those of us who publish methodological studies are somewhat naïve in supposing that other students will not take them as pronouncements. I am sure that you have no idea of the extent to which your earlier papers of the period 1925–1931 were used as the foundation of attack on papers not being geography. You must consider that to the great majority of geographers east of the Sierras you were known primarily in terms of those methodological papers and the interpretation given by former students and other disciplines. Publishing methodological papers is a dangerous business; one may start a chain of thought and action over which one no longer has any control, but in which his writings form a responsible factor.

Parenthetically, he cited Sauer's "geographically sterile pursuit of the genetic method"[15] as evidence of Sauer's disregard of the historical element, to which Sauer penciled in the margin "Did I write such nonsense?" On the role of history, Hartshorne added:

We do not agree on the extent to which the historical method must be used in geography. As you see it, that is so completely necessary that all regional geography becomes historical geography (I hope this interprets you correctly); in my section on "History of Geography," I argue against that thesis. Since reading your address ["Foreword to

Historical Geography"] and [Derwent] Whittlesey's since then, I am not so sure of my arguments.

Hartshorne concluded by asking Sauer what he should say in the second reprint of The Nature of Geography about Sauer's criticism of Hartshorne, in "Foreword to Historical Geography," for relegating historical geography to the margins of the discipline.[16]

Sauer immediately returned "an off-hand reply," since he was leaving for Baja California the next day. He dismissed his forays into methodology as mere "progress reports on my interests as a scholar concerned with investigation. I neither reread such papers myself, nor do I refer students to them after the bloom is off them. They are best considered as successive orientations; they belong to the history of geography, and if they are any good, they represent change and growth." But he was indignant at what he saw as an ignorant misconception of what he had done and was trying to do: "Admitting that one knows one's self least, I said, Good Lord when I read that I had been the originator of geographical vigilance committees. I don't believe that any one who knows me or my work or the studies undertaken by staff and students here could ever get that idea. Such strength as we have is due to the fact that we try to give free play to curiosity, restricted only by competence." Itemizing his own and his students' contributions on Latin America, he concluded, "Is it my fault that geographers east of the Sierras apparently read only 'methodological' papers, and read apparently only the methodological framework in those?" Those papers may have taken less than 5 percent of his time while the other 95 percent of what he did went unnoticed.

What geographers need is more curiosity, not sharper logic. Is a person contributing something new and significant? Geography is what geographers have worked at successfully in the enlargement of knowledge. Our students are not made to wade through your volume, though they know it, nor through any methodological papers. From time to time some one gives a seminar on the history of geography [but] there is incidental attention to method, and [instead more to] the way in which the geographer gets and arranges his evidence and to the actual contributions he has made to knowledge. Life is short and time is fleeting and there is much to be discovered.

We try to whet intellectual appetites. We have not time and less inclination to reconcile the letters of the apostles with each other. I am not writing this in smugness but in heaviness of heart that geographers should use so much energy in beating methodology around the epistemological stump instead of tilling whatever fields they have for production. I'd like to see youngsters get their teeth into real problems and not waste the years finding out their way as I had to do. I wonder what the hell their minds are working on, or why so many of them become academic Fuller brush men, tactful, smooth salesmen of a line in which they are coached.

Sauer ended his response with what he hoped would be his final word on methodology:

Even if I had the time, it would be useless for me to try to match Sauer's tenet 7a against yours or someone else's. In the first place, if I did commit myself at a certain time on a certain approach, that doesn't commit me today. And the only way I know of infecting youngsters' minds is to open up horizons to them by one's own work and by the appreciation of creative work by any one. I trust I shall never write anything methodological again, and I must apologize for what I have done along those lines in the past.[17]

Hartshorne replied promptly and courteously, saying that he admired Sauer, although he disagreed with him, and now understood Sauer's viewpoint about methodological discussion, even if he had got no further in his efforts to "match" Sauer's criticism of *The Nature of Geography* with what he had actually written.[18] The whole exchange with Hartshorne left Sauer bewildered and hurt by the realization that his work and values were so misunderstood.

Earlier in 1946 Sauer could not resist a request from Leonard Wilson of Carleton College to read a draft of his "Geographical Training for the Postwar World." As with young Ackerman, Sauer was remarkably frank.[19] Wilson was a little taken aback by the detail, depth, and feeling of Sauer's reply. In Wilson's published essay Sauer figured largely, which made him feel like "an elder prophet to have you young fellows cite me by chapter and verse, out of essays long past and half forgotten." Remembering his own experience in marshaling his ideas, he thought a bit of soul-searching not a bad thing early in one's career. However, one should not make it a habit, for "methodology can easily become a substitute for inquiry."[20]

Geographers' search for an intellectual home was a promising sign, and Sauer hoped that "the winter of discontent perhaps will be followed by [a] springtime of growth." He had gotten into geography during just such a florescence: "The only good ones we've ever had in this country— [Rollin] Salisbury, W. M. Davis, [Ralph] Tarr, [Ellen] Semple, [Walter] Tower, [John Paul] Goode, and others—were all busily planting seeds." But this was followed by a long-lasting drought. "The failure of nearly an entire generation of American geographers will someday be a significant subject of historical inquiry," he predicted. Sauer was pretty sure it had stemmed from following the current fashionable idea. First it was environmental responses, then regional synopsis, and latterly planning and political studies. The geographer "ceased to be a contributor to knowledge." All geographers seemed to do at present was to produce textbooks.[21] When his former student Joe Spencer suggested that Sauer write a textbook on Latin America, Sauer exploded, "I hope to God that in some bumbling fashion I am still a minor sort of scholar and not a promoter of textbooks."

If Sauer was clear about what he and his department were trying to do, his aims and methods were not obvious to all the students. Although Spencer, who went on to teach at UCLA, had done his doctorate under Sauer in 1936 and revered him, he told him that many geographers were not sure whether what Sauer did was "straight physiography, history, anthropology, archaeology or bullshit." Sauer had simply mystified everyone, said Spencer, who recalled that some of his contemporaries found it "difficult to cut through the sometimes, seemingly, abstruse haze in which you were frequently enveloped." The "Great God Sauer" jibe was used as much by those who misunderstood his work, or resented Sauer's "scholarly aloofness," as it was by others out of pure envy. Most people were unable to understand "the philosophy behind your scholarship." Many balked at the tortuous language of "Morphology of Landscape," and could see no valid rationale for the studies on Arizona and northern Mexico. Sauer had led his reading audience down "a damned tortuous trail" with little or no guidance. There were "so many trees" that the forest was difficult to discern. Spencer thought that Sauer needed to (1) restate his objectives simply and clearly so that we would all know what made the "'Sauer School' tick," and (2) write a rounded study including all the things that meant geography to him: "High scholarship, alone, will not sell a profession, or earn it a place in culture, nor will it bring the field due recognition. There must be some skillful salesmen in the true sense of the word, or that scholarship is but erudite learning in an ivory tower."[22]

Sauer had once told Hartshorne, and reiterated to a later correspondent, "Once I have written something I do not refer to it again, except to refresh my mind as to statements of fact. I thus escape from commitment to previous opinions and conclusions of mine and therefore am not obliged to defend my past self." Spencer said, "Like anyone else, you ARE bound by the precise word you used. If you don't want that one thrown back at you then you have to publically disclaim what you wrote and substitute a better [one]."[23]

What Sauer's reaction was to this blast of criticism from a devoted well-wisher, we can only guess. He might have just pushed Spencer's letter into a drawer to be answered at some future time. Or, he may have dismissed it as the rambling of a young man about to be sent off to wartime combat from which he might not return. Either way, it must have hurt. But did it hit home or was it summarily dismissed as unjust, unwarranted, and ignorant? Like any contemplative scholar, to be sure, he extended and revised his ideas during his sixty-four writing years, but his professed "idiosyncrasy" often verged on the wayward, darting about the geographical scene like some intellectual *Voortrekker*, moving on when he saw another's methodological smoke.[24]

In any case, Sauer's accustomed idyllic intellectual and social milieu was shattered by the Second World War and the subsequent affluence and expansion of higher education. He was unable and unwilling to accommodate to the changes crowding in on him.

Man in Nature

Despite Sauer's aversion to writing textbooks, he produced one for elementary schools: *Man in Nature: America before the Days of the White Man*, believing it important to show children how native people "get their living by knowing how to make use of nature," with which they live in balance.[25] The Bolivian and San Franciscan artist Antonio Sotomayor added numerous maps and illustrations.

Favorably reviewed, *Man in Nature* was well received by teachers but minimally adopted. Reissued a generation later in a pro-Indian climate, it was widely adopted by Native American (Zuni, Crow, Cherokee) and other schools in the United States and Canada. It was recently lauded as "vintage Sauer, capsules of vivid description that portray cultural expressions in a nuanced, engaging manner, . . . reconstructing an unromanticized ethnographic past against which a beleaguered ethnographic present can be better gauged."[26]

Historical Geography: "The Apple of My Eye"

Sauer faulted American geographers for abandoning landforms, climate, and biogeography, and most of all for making historical understanding marginal to the field: "Historical geography is of course the apple of my eye, and I try for converts to the subject on slightest provocation. It is one of the great regrets of my life that most American geographers, and indeed I fear, most social scientists in this country, [see] so little point to historical inquiry." He frequently reiterated his conviction that "those who restrict themselves to today and economics are getting nowhere."[27] "The successions of events are the only feasible means of understanding the processes of geographic differentiation, physical or cultural. What has happened to man around the world is intelligible to me only in terms of historical experiences centered about the skill or lack of foresight with which he has made use of the materials at hand."

How geographers who restricted themselves to the present could hope to understand anything baffled him. None of the social sciences (except, perhaps, psychology) was free from time, origin, change, and extinction, which became explicable only by "joining when with where. The present is an accretion of the past, all human geography is a study of historical processes."[28] "I object strongly to the idea that I am a proper sort of geographer if I set myself up as a geo-politician, but an improper one if I get interested in the way the Jesuits make their mission areas work, in the reasons for the rise and fall of the Pueblo cultures, or in the means that Sinathropus had for living in north China."[29]

In his 1940 presidential address, "Foreword to Historical Geography" (see chap. 4), he had made plain the central importance of the time element in geography and the need to cultivate the shared terrain of history and geography, but for all its direct eloquence, the essay largely fell on deaf ears. It was not taken up by most geographers, whose indifference Sauer reciprocated: "There is so little curiosity about facts and their meanings that I can live advantageously by disregarding almost completely the work they turn out." He skipped most of their work, especially the voluminous papers on economic and political geography.[30]

Defensive Isolation?

Sauer's scholarly stances were admirably humane, but he was increasingly unwilling to engage with critics face-to-face. Reminiscent of his father's aversion to commerce, he abhorred "the slick and smooth salesmen" who were willing to peddle whatever they thought the market liked.[31] His particular bêtes noires were economic and political geographers, whose ahistorical approach and ignorance of physical geography left them "adrift in a boat without compass or rudder," and rural planners who knew no physical geography and even less about how land was actually farmed. Geopolitics was worse—dishonestly partisan nationalistic propaganda presented not on "a factual, intellectual basis" but on a hidden emotional one. Political geographers did not scrutinize underlying political philosophies. Sauer had "respect [for] radicals who declare their position," but not dissemblers who hid it. "The general state of political science in this country indicates that not much science is being practiced."[32]

Yet much good "traditional" geography was being done in the 1940s and 1950s. Sauer might have been less dismissive had he been less averse to meeting other geographers. "Are you aware," asked Spencer, "of the extent to which your colleagues feel that you refuse to meet with them?" "I don't think I have seen you for 25 years," complained J. Russell Smith, a grand old man of American geography. Sauer's longtime friend and staunch ally Duke Jones charged that long ago "you retired into your hole and became Hartshorne's 'Great God Beyond the Sierras.'"[33] While defending Sauer's intellectual contributions, Jones said that he knew "no one who is so dumb in dealing with people, and Carl's obvious scorn of most geographers in the AAG, except his own students, is pretty bad."[34]

Sauer's backward-looking aloofness was almost paranoid. Time and again he basked in the "good meat and plenty of seasoning" of the "golden days" in Chicago. The decline of geography began with the "oldest sons"—Wallace Atwood, Harlan Barrows, and Isaiah Bowman. Bowman, the most able of these, was diverted by administration and public affairs, becoming Franklin Roosevelt's right-hand man in science and political geography. Atwood too went off into administration. That left Barrows in charge at Chicago, which became a factory that turned out "a standardized product in school masters."[35]

When in 1948 a meeting was proposed to discuss where postwar geography was heading, Sauer refused to come if it were held in Chicago, since Barrows would be bound to kill discussion. "The frustrated situation in which geography finds itself is due largely to the bad influences of Chicago since Salisbury."[36] To accommodate Sauer, the meeting was moved to Ann Arbor.

Deeply distressed by prevailing trends in geography, the social sciences, and postwar America, Sauer retreated into the world of research he knew best—plants, early man, destructive exploitation, and Latin America. He still remained active with the Office of Naval Research and the Guggenheim and Rockefeller Foundations, but professionalized geography was anathema to him, increasing his sense of isolation and his reluctance to engage in debate. His diary remark at age eighteen that there was "too much of myself in the way for me" was all too true forty years later.[37]

10

"Born in Another Age"

Sauer's social science disenchantment stemmed largely from his 1930s experiences with New Deal programs that ignored cultural, environmental, and historical circumstances and sought to solve everything by formula. To Sauer, their universalizing abstractions heralded an ominous doctrine of social regimentation. Social science trends in the 1940s only deepened his dismay.[1]

In 1944 Joseph Willits at the Rockefeller Foundation asked Sauer to vet a memorandum on the role of the social sciences by Robert Redfield, a Chicago anthropologist. Redfield had charted the disruption of traditional Mexican lifestyles induced by the spread of trade and modern technology.[2] Sauer faulted Redfield's sociological approach for its dogma, dialectics, and remoteness from reality. Redfield also seemed to assume that the social sciences and the humanities were prima facie antithetical, even incapable of communication. This was abhorrent to Sauer; just as varied researchers concerned with plant domestication easily conversed, so should those from the social sciences and the humanities.

Reliance on quasi-experimental and quasi-statistical methods by those who sought to imitate the natural sciences made for "a rigidity, a complacency, and a surface gloss that bodes ill for the social sciences."[3] While borrowing the numeracy and positivistic stance of the physical sciences, social science had abandoned their awareness of temporal change. Sauer was "grateful for my early training as a student of geology," in which experimental verification was routinely checked against the historical record. Forgetting his critique of William Morris Davis and others in "Foreword to Historical Geography," Sauer insisted that no geologist would "hold lightly any good historical study." Similarly, biologists were interested in the "entire span of organic life." "I feel very strongly that any disdain for any part of the human record is anti-scientific. I suspect any person who [complains] about antiquarianism is covering up a lack of intellect." Presentist social positivism was antithetical to Latin American cultural tradition. "One can't be a Latin and a Catholic and be arrogant about the finite and the infinite."[4]

Likewise in the Social Science Research Council, Sauer saw "the older breed of gentle, modest people [being] swamped out by the aggressive younger generation, sharp in dialectics, hard, and over-confident." Perhaps the time had come for the likes of him to retire to the academic ivory tower "necessary for survival":

I have no interest in far-flung programs of research by which the individual is reduced to piece work with a few, probably spurious masterminds directing and interpreting. We already have the factory system of instruction, and we are too far on the way to the same thing in scholarship to suit me. [There is] too much propaganda that pretends to be science, too much filling of classroom benches by speech makers, and far too little intellectual curiosity.

Sociology and anthropology had become increasingly mechanistic and programmatic. Those who had "their social consciences all straight and their responses to any situation all ready" scared Sauer. Worst were anthropologists who "go, cold, into a strange culture, and psychoanalyze it, or submit it to scrutiny by schedules and questionnaires."[5]

Reacting to a 1945 manifesto entitled "The Social Sciences and Our National Future," Sauer parodied "Onward Christian Soldiers" as "Onward social scientists marching" and murmuring "all right minded people agree."

I'm afraid of experts in my own field, and in others setting about mending this strange world. We shall hear a great deal [about] action programs by which the social sciences are to "catch up" with the physical scientists in arranging the lives of men unknown to them and not understood by them. And I still want none of it. This show of knowledge has nothing in it of wisdom and pity and humility before the Lord. I can't join up with the Gadarene swine.[6]

The universities were no longer agents of enlightenment, but fast becoming vassals of the state. Sauer yearned to "give back the search for truth and beauty to the individual scholar, to grow in grace as best he can."[7]

Unrelenting in his opposition to modernization, Sauer retreated more and more into his own world. Time and again he praised natural scientists who taught one to "observe, label, and describe," and think in terms of temporal processes. "I always have an interesting session with natural scientists on my problems of cultural origins and growths. They sit forward in their chairs and they are likely to [observe] something significant." In contrast, he had "mostly quit trying with my social science friends," who simply did not understand the flux of time, the long view, retrospection.[8] He refused "to be a party to the impoverishment of social studies by the exaggerated accent on contemporaneity."[9]

The Blind Leading the Blind

Like Sauer, his friend Willits was appalled by "the ineptness of the West in bringing its knowledge and skills to bear upon the service of the people that we arrogantly call backward. We work from the top down; we work in a hurry; and we work through their governments and our own government rather than humbly and at grass roots."[10] Enrolling Willits as an honorary member of "the Society of Backward Peoples and the Slowing Down of Progress," Sauer re-voiced his dismay at the erosion of older and sounder ways, and the exploitive destruction of the environment.[11]

Newfound social science interest in "his" Latin American world was motivated, not by any genuine desire to understand Latin American life and livelihood, but by political and military commitments. "They do not realize that cultural values may be very different and that it may be bad to superimpose a [North American] program" destructive of cultural diversity: "After twenty years I am beginning to feel that I can understand some of the problems in Mexico, and perhaps can make an occasional comparison with another Latin American country. A 'planner' sifting statistical and verbal material applying to situations unknown to him, is little better than a blind leader of the blind."[12] As the international dominance of Europe and North America repressed cultural diversity, bureaucratic standardization paralyzed creative innovation.

Modern California was a preview of what Sauer feared the rest of America and ultimately the world were coming to: "We get a fashion of house type, supermarket, basketball competition, betting on races, or mixing drinks, that if successful sweeps the state. Our education programs are becoming more and more interchangeable from school to school. Our goal seems to be that we look alike, have the same manners and the same thoughts." There were still places he knew, like Missouri and southern Illinois, that had not lost their identity and where "introgressive hybridization" (genetic innovation) was gentle enough for "unlike communities" to survive. But no one was studying them. "Normative" social scientists disregarded variety.[13]

America was exploiting and homogenizing the globe. Since the Industrial Revolution, the West had done "a terrific job of gutting the basic resources of the world for pretty ephemeral returns." War and the increased demands for raw materials had scraped the bottom of America's mineral barrel, and now Latin America was being exploited "destructively." Western-led development of the underpopulated tropics was actually "exploitation for the insatiable appetites of the industrial world." America's economics of "conspicuous waste" meant that "we shall follow the procedure until the spring runs dry. What our attitude will be when we find that there is not enough for the material well-being of everyone I don't know. Probably it will mean ✱ intensified nationalism."[14]

A Needed Vision

Refuting America's blinkered optimists, Sauer saw the unmitigated and accelerated looting of the earth to its farthest corners as a "sober fact of history":

Our ever better machines are ever hungrier for raw materials. Happiness comes through increased consumption and increased consumption means ever increasing production and that means growing overdrafts on reserves of resources. The rate and manner in which the world is actually growing poorer day by day is still poorly explored. Man's disturbance of ecological balance constitutes a major and little touched field of enquiry.

Thomas Malthus's prospect of catastrophic population imbalance was "nearly right," but he had failed to foresee the opening of new lands in the lush New World that kept alive faith in "the elastic universe (more and hungrier machines, more production, more consumption, more consumers)."

Civilized man has succeeded temporarily by becoming the most perilous parasite in the history of the earth. He has thrived briefly on destruction and multiplication. I wonder whether he has any real reason to think that his ill-gotten supremacy indicates his ability to take over the role of recreating the world. But should this dream of the brave new world succeed, the whole of Huxley's prospect will be realized.

Aldous Huxley's dystopian future gave Sauer "the cold horrors." It was a carefree, affluent, technologically advanced world in which culture, art, religion, and family life had been eliminated, its people kept permanently happy on government-provided drugs. In place of the conventional calendar, all dates emanated from the "year of our Ford," Henry Ford being idolized as the creator of society, and memorable for declaring "History is bunk," a dictum particularly odious to Sauer.[15]

Sauer was appalled at the growing "shadow of the State over the individual" in all major countries.[16] His premonition of greater state control was exacerbated by President Harry Truman, a fellow Missourian. Sauer read a lot (too much) into the popularity of Truman's 1949 program to promote full employment, and expand Social Security, public housing, and slum clearance. Unable to manage their own lives, the masses surrendered control to authority. The developed world seemed "set for mass conversions and prostrations before the only God [it] recognizes" — the all-embracing state. Sauer trusted only those traditional people whose social values did not derive from "monistic views of social order":

Human survival might depend on there being enough thick-headed peasants who have some dumb awareness that their way of living is good and enduring. I don't think that technicians or professors will save it. My only missionary bent would be to help some places and people from being engulfed in the abyss of accelerated "production," consumption, and population growth that is our pitiful goal.[17]

Intertwined biological and cultural impoverishment and extinction were increasing with every day:

> We are now committed to the extinction of diversity and to the triumph of dominant forms. The birds of the woodland and marsh are going, and the contrast is between starling and house sparrow. The price that will have to be paid for this industrialized civilization is too high and will be collected more and more from those that come after us.

His rueful remaining hope was to give some protection to divergent groups and individuals and "preserve the record of the world that is being wiped out by technology."[18]

For a 1951 talk celebrating University of Minnesota president Guy Stanton Ford (a Sauer hero for rehabilitating Professor William Schaper, hounded out in 1917 on spurious pro-German charges), Sauer offered "to inveigh against specialization, to protest against research administrators, [and] to say a word for letting people do what they really want to do."[19]

Published as "Folkways of Social Science" in 1952, his talk castigated current inquiry that lacked scholarly detachment and sought social ends rather than arising out of curiosity. He bemoaned the lack of competence in foreign languages and cultures in an America obsessed with production and arrogant in its global dominance. "Are we the cleverest people of all time," he asked, "or the blindest because we think neither whence we came nor whither we are bound?"[20] The mantra that "God is good and we are His people and this is God's country" appalled Sauer as congenital American exceptionalism.[21]

"I sing out of tune with my colleagues," he wrote the medical historian Richard Shryock, declining to lecture at Johns Hopkins University. "I take a dim view of contemporary applied science and prevalent social science thinking. I am pessimistic in my outlook on civilization because I think that technology cannot solve the economic problems it caused; nor that any social-political organization that I know will be able to do so."[22] Sauer was also uneasy about subjecting himself to the unhappy atmosphere of a university then wracked by McCarthyite purges. "I wear badly of late under tension and strife, lose the ability to sleep and relax," difficulties brought on by overwork and "snarling" feuds on the Berkeley campus (over a required loyalty oath).[23]

Jesters and Mavericks

The publication of "Folkways of Social Science" took Sauer back to his own past in an unanticipated way. The Texas historian Walter Prescott Webb was "uplifted" by its message. Webb had just published *The Great Frontier* (1951), which, like "Folkways," controversially argued that the fin de siècle end of the New World's easily available land and readily exploited natural resources had led to twentieth-century crisis and boded ill for America's future. But Webb's debt to Sauer went deeper, for Sauer had been the first scholar "to speak favorably of a similar effort of mine long ago" — the startling thesis of *The Great Plains* (1931) that eastern settlers had adapted to the tree-less and water-starved semi-arid Plains by putting up barbed wire fencing, drilling for underground water, and subduing the Indians with the six-shooter revolver. Webb had "always remembered [Sauer's] most generous comment" on his first tentative statement in 1929 against the current historical orthodoxy that credited the horse, the boat, the ax, and the rifle with the conquest of the West.[24]

"We were born in another age," replied Sauer in 1952, glad to be remembered for supporting Webb's assault, "in what a cockeyed period our life-span has happened to fall." Both had "probably been out of step with the intelligentsia for a long time. Not trying to be so, but by some quirk of circumstance, mavericks. As anachronisms or relics, we have a certain entertainment value as 'characters,'" he concluded in the mocking, self-deprecatory tone that became a hallmark of his correspondence in later years. "We wind up as privileged jesters."

Looking back over his own life, Sauer picked out the events that had jolted his views of the conventional wisdom:

My bewilderment began with [Theodore Roosevelt's 1912] Bull Moose [trust-busting Progressive Party] campaign. I was a kid from the country, studying at the University of Chicago. I saw the professors become starry eyed about this millennial movement which I thought they must understand. Then the world blew up in 1914 and the world was to be saved by exorcising German militarism and establishing democracy. I began to doubt the simple worlds of the prophets. The slow and painful Education of Carl Sauer had begun, learning about the backgrounds of the present. I came in at the first of the Children's Crusades that have been repeated until the present. And always led by the intellectuals, with the peasants hanging back dragging their feet, inarticulate but knowing that there was something wrong with the prophets—hysterical lemmings, led by politicos, pundits, and professors. We don't question the circumambient mood of progress as common destiny. We don't really dare release our thinking as to what the industrial revolution has been, the expansion of colonization, the toll of raw materials funneled through world commerce into consumer goods. Nor what is happening to the individual, the non-conformist group, by more and more organization of industrial society.[25]

Two years later Lynn White Jr., a medieval historian and then president of Mills College in Oakland, sought Sauer's support for a manifesto to counter the naive scientism of Vannevar Bush's *Science, The Endless Frontier* (1945), which promised exciting advances from federal funding of large-scale research. White wanted Sauer to write the lead chapter, since no one "surpasses you in wide ranging interest or the vivid sense of the 'growing edge' of your discipline." He was particularly struck by Sauer's conception of geography as "human ecology, as man's relation to his total physical and climatic environment and its fauna, flora, and natural resources, and the effect of these on human thinking, emotions and patterns of organization and action [and] that for thousands of years humans have been the chief element in their own ecology, affecting every aspect of it."[26]

But Sauer simply did not have the time. In America "who wants an historical geographer any more than an Homeric scholar?"

I belong not later than the nineteenth century and the Adams brothers [Brooks and Henry]. My brothers in spirit are in the backwoods of East Tennessee and wherever there are backwoods. I don't like any part of the look ahead or the slogans that are passwords between the forward looking, the socially conscious, the erudite and intellectual. I don't see any connection between formal knowledge and wisdom or freedom of spirit. We're committed to Progress, not variation.[27]

"Out of step," "an anachronism," "born in another age," "the older breed," and "an old cranky stray," Sauer now satirized himself. Like Huxley's *Brave New World* in 1932, Kurt Vonnegut's *Player Piano* in 1952 seemed a realistic forecast of a future in which computer-aided mechanization eliminated human labor, setting wealthy engineers and managers against workers whose skills were no longer needed.[28]

An Interlude of Poets

If Sauer was "an anachronism" in academia, certain avant-garde poets and writers found him to be in tune with the times and highly relevant. The breadth of his inquiring mind, the originality of his insights, and his poetic way with words were much admired by the new literati whose guru he became.[29]

Many of them taught at Black Mountain College in the Appalachians of North Carolina, an experimental community that rebelled against conventional education and practiced an interdisciplinary approach to learning. The faculty included the poets and writers Charles Olson, Robert Creeley, Jonathan Williams, Robert Duncan, and Ed Dorn; architects Buckminster Fuller (of geodesic dome fame) and Walter Gropius; artists Willem de Kooning, Jasper Johns, Robert Motherwell, Joseph Albers, and Robert Rauschenburg; the choreographer and pioneer of modern dance, Merce Cunningham; and the composer John Cage. All went on to make their mark in postwar American cultural life.[30]

Olson, Sauer's principal correspondent among the Black Mountain group, headed the college from 1952 to 1956, when lack of funds forced its closure. A highly influential modernist, Olson's own work owed much to such earlier poets as Ezra Pound and William Carlos Williams. Creeley moved in 1957 to California, befriending Beat poets Allen Ginsberg, Jack Kerouac, and Gary Snyder. During the 1960s the Beat Generation morphed into the hippie counterculture, famed on the Berkeley campus.[31]

Sauer's links with these poets were facilitated by Bob Callahan, whose Turtle Island Foundation in Berkeley published some of Sauer's books. Callahan recalled evenings sitting "with this great old man, often in the darkness of his living room" and taking down his every word. Callahan thought Sauer "the finest historical intelligence of the twentieth century," and "the one person you would read before any other on prehistoric America." The poets were attracted by Sauer's concern with ancient culture, his empathy with traditional land-based folk, and his direct, vigorous, pithy, often pungent prose.[32]

Strangely, it was Sauer's formidably opaque "Morphology of Landscape" that most influenced the poets, for it stressed both the importance of the physical landscape and the aesthetic meanings that lay beyond the visible. Although "an impossible correspondent," Sauer completely entranced Olson.[33] "I am hungry for more, for all Carl Sauer says, in print. Please, please. (I don't know a man whose work I want more to keep abreast of.) I do miss you, wish you were not always there, but were here."[34]

Sauer was baffled, and a bit unnerved, by attention bordering on adulation from so unexpected a quarter. A "most unusual and interesting mind," said Sauer to Callahan of Olson, though "I can hardly understand him at times."[35] But notwithstanding their impressionist diction, these poets at least understood how history linked people and places, and Sauer tried to cope with their queries about such arcane matters as possible Chinese voyages to the New World, the diet of early humans, and the Mayan language.

Desperate to fend off the closing of Black Mountain, Olson tried to enlist Sauer, "the very fatherhead of my being," in "A New American Encyclopedia" of "new" knowledge: "you alone cld. be the Diderot." But Sauer was no Diderot: "If a man is bound to be an encyclopedist, God bless him, but why anybody should want to engage himself in such an endless task is beyond me. It certainly is not my dish. I have never been interested in the summation of all knowledge or even considerable segments of it, but only in the following up of certain quite large queries."[36] Olson asked Sauer to send "a bibliography of every single piece you ever wrote or published," and Sauer's secretary sent him a list. Sauer was reluctant to become further involved.[37]

Beyond Sauer's iconoclastic individualism, his sense of the long span of human history appealed to these writers. His speculations on the first sedentary fishing communities, the origins of agriculture, and human ecological dominance of the earth by fire were accepted as gospel truth. Sauer's advocacy of direct observation and hands-on knowledge echoed their own rebellion against hand-me-down authority. His geographical focus on space, location, and movement charmed poets who grounded their writing in real places and people. And his flair for metaphor and evocative earthy language resonated with them. Sauer and these creative writers may have been poles apart in scholarship, but in empathetic understanding they had a lot in common.

Black Pessimism

Sauer had ever less in common with the social sciences, which he felt were increasingly driven by "some abhorrent dialectic of determinism and a mandatory limitation of curiosity."[38] Of a forthcoming conference aimed at building bridges between cultural historians and behaviorists in anthropology, a disillusioned Sauer wrote:

> I am in a mood of pretty black pessimism. The behavioral lads have won the field in this country and they're out to sweep the world. History is irrelevant or illustrates error (*Was dahinten, das mag schwinden, ich will nichts davon* [What's past is past, I don't want to know about it].[39] Pavlov is Moses, the Promised Land is the World conquered by technocracy. The utilitarian demands of a successfully industrialized world, perhaps reaching eight billion within a century will eradicate the natural and cultural landmarks we cherish. What is the use of studying the history of cultures? The whim of knowing the illuminated letters of a missal, the finding of a Gregorian chant, the tying of a trout fly. That cultural conservancy is critical to the sanity of the world of our kind is as alien to their thinking as nature conservancy used to be.[40]

Disenchantment with the academic world mirrored his disenchantment with the wider world of American policy and international relations. The disregard for other ways of life "depresses and scares the hell out of me." He recalled a platoon of young agronomists sent out to teach the Hopi how to grow corn. Not one of them had a glimmer of a notion that he was dealing with a people traditionally wise in raising corn over centuries of selection in a submarginal climate. The agronomists came to instruct, not to learn. "We have a tragicomic record of meddling in our Point 4 [Truman's technical assistance] program—our present fashion of putting Mother Hubbards on Hawaiians by Connecticut missionaries." "It hurts to see such complacent confidence in American dollars, American know-how and organization as displayed to other breeds. This 'driving power of ignorance' is a major cause of the growing resentment against us. We are the momentary beneficiaries of unearned good fortune and it would become us to learn to walk humbly among the rest of mankind."[41] Sauer considered the rich variety and inventiveness of humankind a splendid storehouse being pillaged and squandered in the guise of progress.

Was he an opinionated, capricious old man who could no longer cope with the changing world—an anachronism, as he put it—or a wise old man, whose wide learning, curiosity, humanity, and compassion fostered his concern about the attrition of the humane? Whichever view one takes, a constant thread ran through his splenetic tirades. As the Berkeley psychology professor John McKae, whose father had known Sauer in Chicago, wrote in sympathy with many of his views, "You appear to be robust, opinionated, iconoclastic, and probably very good company if taken with suitable dollops of well matured brandy."[42]

> How man has *deformed* the pristine . . . is the central theme
> of the Symposium.—William Thomas, "Symposium
> Discussion: Retrospect," 1956

11

"Man's Role in Changing the
Face of the Earth"

At the height of Sauer's black pessimism about the state of learning and academic life, he gained unexpected respite from a major collaborative enterprise.[1] In October 1953 William Thomas, a geographer at the Wenner-Gren Foundation for Anthropological Research in New York, invited him to chair a forthcoming symposium entitled "Man's Impact as a Dynamic Agent in Changing the Face of the Earth," as "the logical person to give impetus to such a vast undertaking." From a list of ninety humanities and social science luminaries, Sauer was asked to select thirty participants. Although "aghast, excited, and somewhat scared" by the boldness and size of the scheme, he accepted at once. The proposal addressed one of his major concerns.[2] "I thought that [it] might be better than most conferences," he wrote Joseph Willits. "It didn't belabor methodology; it saw that it needed minds of varied experience and texture; no attention was paid to officialdom; it required the knowledge of and from other parts of the world."[3] Over the next twenty months Thomas received a torrent of Sauerian advice, queries, reflections, professions, and "confessions."

Retrospect, Process, Prospect

Sauer's inputs were both practical and philosophical. Staging the conference within eight months was impossible; more lead time was essential.

The proposed program needed historical reinforcement from European scholars who knew that "the past is living and that it can be made to speak to us," to counter social scientists' presentist theorizing. He disliked the title's use of "dynamic," an academic catchword among "sons of Daedalus to whom anything that happened before them is antiquarian."[4] Thomas accepted all these suggestions for the symposium, then renamed "Man's Impact in Changing the Face of the Earth," as seen in the past ("Retrospect"), the present ("Process"), and the future ("Prospect").

While lamenting insufficient perspective on the past, Sauer deprecated "crystal ball" gazing into the future. Futuristic scenarios would engender unproductive clashes, since a future that appears "to one in rosy glow gives to another the cold horrors." Social scientists' zeal to remake the globe depressed and frightened him. They claimed "the wisdom to reorganize and operate the world as a planned Utopia. I fail to see how this can be done except by total organization under an entrenched elite, the result as being presented by Aldous Huxley, George Orwell, architect Roderick Seidenberg, and Kurt Vonnegut. Hence my dislike of mastermind social engineers."

Sauer thought social scientists wrong in fact as well as in purpose. "Science must continue to work humbly with the natural order and its limits. Progress is limited and must always be paid for. Man remains within a limited ecological system. My opponents say I've got piety; I'd like to call it prudence in thinking that it's best to let nature take its course, with some corrections of our imprudent actions." Consequently, he told Thomas, he wanted "a minimum of blue-printing the future" in the symposium's Prospect segment and elaboration of the Retrospect segment. The central questions to be addressed were, "How did we get to where we are?" and "How can we construct an intelligible description of where we are?" These keynote queries were passed on to every invited participant.[5]

Symposia at Berkeley on the use of resources had confirmed Sauer's "historically-minded" perspective. These events had lacked interest for social scientists "unaccustomed to think of historical events and processes," and unable to see "that the course of events, if not cyclic, sinusoidal or straight line, was any concern of theirs." On the other hand, biologists and many earth scientists had "the proper enzymes in their rumens and chew such historical cud which to others may be cellulose waste."[6]

Other participants had different concerns. Andrew Clark, a Wisconsin historical geographer, feared the program was "too inclusive."[7] Edgar Anderson, Sauer's erstwhile collaborator on early plant domestication, felt the pace too hurried. The conference was so planned and so complete that there was little opportunity for new ideas to emerge. He urged Thomas and Sauer to "let the thing grow" by leaving gaps for subsequent additions, deletions, and alterations.[8] But Sauer had an increasingly clear idea of what he wanted, and he knew that he could not leave it to chance; it had to be planned.

Sauer was keen to involve Lewis Mumford, a leading intellectual light of the day. Mumford was both complimentary and constructive; he added, deleted, and regrouped potential contributions and authors, and flagged crucial topics thus far neglected. One was industrial atmospheric pollution that might cause permanent climatic change; another was pollution by nuclear fission. More fundamentally, the symposium should assess how humankind's growing demands on finite global resources were to be met. "The causal method alone can deal adequately with past events, [but] a teleological method based on evaluation and purpose must supplement [it] to do justice to creative processes that lie in the future." Among the diverse consequences of man's conquest of nature, some were self-sustaining, others self-destructive. Mumford noted changing attitudes toward land and such ecologically destabilizing trends as widespread air conditioning.[9]

The apprehensions of critics fanned Sauer's "sneaking misgivings" into "serious doubts." "If we've bitten off too much," he wrote Thomas, "the sooner we trim to proper size the better." Sauer envisaged participants who would talk with "authority and grace" about their various specialties. But was he trying to get too many different kinds of people together in too short a time to talk about too many different things? A "warp for the frame" was needed, and more limited objectives.[10]

Thomas was dismayed as he saw his dream crumbling. Yet Anderson's suggestion to let things grow was beginning to work, with the exchange of ideas among Sauer, Mumford, the Ann Arbor zoologist Marston Bates, Paul Sears, Fairfield Osborn, and the zoologist Evelyn Hutchinson, who was invited but did not attend. Sauer mused that disorder was the impetus to order, and "with some stirring it will begin to jell." He urged a venue outside the "air-conditioned catacombs" of New York, for an "atmosphere of informality and exposure to sky and growing things is not entirely irrelevant."[11]

To ensure Mumford's participation, Sauer agreed that the symposium should end with a discussion of the kind of world to which "we are committing ourselves and that is ethically and esthetically satisfying." In this volte-face Sauer mused about inviting two visionary prophets of technological impact, Roderick Seidenberg and Aldous Huxley, along with Charles Galton Darwin, whose The Next Million Years (1952) foresaw a fearsome future in which humans were bred and farmed like livestock. There was a clear need to cast "some new light on where we are going and whether we like it, and whether the course is determined."[12]

Mumford's qualms about a technologically dominated future paralleled Sauer's distress at mounting pressures to maximize production, extraction, and consumption, and at American and Soviet engulfment of other cultures. As he wrote to Thomas, "We in this country have not thought very much about [what] our technics, progress, [and] zeal may spell out for other parts of the world. An imperialism of production may be more dreadful and more final than one of religion or any old fashioned political conquest." Accepting inclusion of a future perspective in the symposium, Sauer recalled his earlier conclusion that "retrospect and prospect are different ends of the same sequence."[13]

The symposium was held June 16–22, 1955, at the Princeton Inn, in Princeton, New Jersey, with Sauer, Mumford, and Bates as cochairmen. Sauer presented "the general thesis" and led the first session on Retrospect—"concern with origins, not antiquarianism." Bates chaired the second session on Process, and Mumford the last on Prospect, "dealing with esthetic and ethical consequences, options and values, and penalties." For invited participants, topics were suggested, not prescribed, because "the people we want most to have may know better what they want to think about than we do," held Sauer. "This is an attempt at a gathering of affinitive minds."[14]

Besides those already mentioned, distinguished scholars among the seventy who came included the economist Kenneth Boulding, the geochemist Harrison Brown, the geographer Clifford Darby, the ecologist Frank Egler, the geomorphologist Luna Leopold, the historian James Malin, the philosopher and paleontologist Pierre Teilhard de Chardin, and the historical sociologist Karl Wittfogel. Twenty-four disciplines were represented from ten countries. Background papers distributed to participants in advance were not read but were discussed at the symposium. Discussions were summarized in the published book, along with fifty-five of the essays.[15] Billed as the "first large-scale evaluation of what has happened and what is happening to the earth under man's impress," *Man's Role in Changing the Face of the Earth*, recently termed a "superb window into mid-twentieth century views on the environment," has remained in print ever since.[16]

To Leave a Good Earth

Sauer's meticulous planning of themes and selection of participants contrasted starkly with the seemingly offhand preparation of his own twenty-page contribution, "The Agency of Man on the Earth." He did little or no new research but drew entirely on his accumulated knowledge, and wrote it rapidly during the months before the symposium. He pulled together the diverse strands of his major intellectual endeavors—cultural diffusion, human migration, Pleistocene humans and their environment, plant domestication, the use of fire, and especially the destructive exploitation of environments and cultures. His journey had led from innocence and enthusiasm for learning to cynicism and disenchantment with academia and alienation from society at large.

During Sauer's lifetime, he felt, careful concern for natural resource use had given way to an economy of waste and accelerated obsolescence. "Living beyond one's means has become a social virtue, thrift antisocial." He despaired of the "spin of change": "As a peasant, I can't understand the exhilaration that people get out of change. I want a car that will have the life and personal attachment of a horse, not a new model every couple of years. I can understand [auto producer Henry J.] Kaiser wishing for more rapid obsolescence, but not why the customers agree with him. Maybe that's why all my life I've enjoyed 'backward areas' where people ask 'is this change necessary?'"

Once a "peasant," he now felt like "a cranky old backwoodsman" who loathed being "sucked into this whirlpool of Progress." America's obsession with ever-expanding production seemed to him "desperately lengthening jumps to keep ahead of the sheriff." And the promise of raising global living standards, he feared, could be met only by greater social regimentation.

Are we living in a "moment of great progress or great aberration?" he asked the economist Frank Knight. A succession of aberrant American moments had educated him in the ways of activist zealots:

> I began having that feeling in the Bull Moose campaign, at the University of Chicago where a lot of previously calm professors began jumping up and down. As a youngster about to cast his first vote I hollered a little, but it seemed to me that Armageddon was [a] considerable overstatement. Then came 1914 and thereafter, I was pretty worried that I was probably just a bonehead, until I found that there were men I respected who were cool spectators, including [University of Michigan] economists Freddie Taylor, [Henry] Adams, and [Leo] Sharfman. Being suspicious of the crusade I began to wonder if all crusades were not suspect as aberrations by mass contagion. And so to wondering whether such contagion did not always come from an initially small group of intellectuals who come to dominate by their assertion and by adhesion of the faint hearted.[17]

These ruminations spurred Sauer to crystallize in "The Agency of Man on Earth" a masterly overview of human modification of the earth from primordial to postglacial times. He emphasized the early role of fire in bringing about change. "Wherever primitive man has had the opportunity to turn fire loose on the land, he seems to have done so." He then summarized changes induced by peasant agriculture and pastoralism, European expansion, commercial agriculture, and industry. "Wherever men live, . . . they have operated to alter the [pristine] aspect of the Earth, both animate and inanimate, be it to their boon or bane." Humans were truly "the lords of creation." But the "ever expanding dynamic economy" of the present had vastly sped the consequent "deformation" of the landscape: "As a native of the nineteenth century I have been an amazed and bewildered witness of the change of tempo that started with the First World War, was given an additional whirl by the Second, and still continues to accelerate."

Moreover, previous fears that society might not use its natural resources thriftily had given way to "an easy confidence" in society's power to do more

ss as it wished. Physical scientists and engineers were "inventing ever
~e daring reorganizations of matter, and, in consequence, whether they
~ire it or not, of social institutions." Social scientists sought to emulate
them and reorder the world. "Capacity to produce and capacity to consume
are the twin spirals of the new age which is to have no end." But it could not
continue indefinitely, for mounting production demanded unsustainable
resource extraction.

Not only natural resources were being depleted, so were human resources. Ever since Columbus, "the spread of European culture has been
continuous and cumulative, borne by immediate self-interest . . . but sustained also by a sense of civilizing mission redefined from time to time."
Now it is called "developing the underdeveloped world." But if the road to
progress was paved with good intentions, much harm came along the way.
Resources were depleted, ecological balances disturbed, and wise and durable indigenous agricultural systems destroyed because modern industry
was "insensitive to other ways and values."

With increasing output now society's prime goal, living beyond one's
needs had become almost "a civic virtue." Citing William Wordsworth's
1807 dictum that "in getting and spending we lay waste our powers," Sauer
judged that "the high moments of history have come not when man was
most concerned with the comforts and displays of the flesh, but when his
spirit was moved to grow in grace." Needed was "an ethic and aesthetic
under which man, practicing the qualities of prudence and moderation,
may indeed pass on to posterity a good Earth." Sauer's "good Earth" was
not only free from exploitative physical deformation, but also graced with
spiritual freedom.[18]

Influence and Significance of Man's Role

Within days of the symposium's end Sauer eagerly departed on sabbatical
leave in Europe. Typical of his treatment of a task, he seldom referred to the
symposium again. Thomas handled all the editing. Nonetheless, given his
meticulous and lengthy planning, one cannot help but wonder whether he
felt it had been worth the effort. Had it produced the "fruitful meditations"
he hoped for? Was it an exemplar of informed inquiry into humans, their
environment, and the legacy of "a good Earth"?

Man's Role was well received in the press and academic journals. Many noted the extraordinary range of specialist input, an interdisciplinary approach at the time quite novel. The tape-recorded reproduction of uninhibited discussion spiced the text with an innovative flavor then rare if not unique and seldom matched since. Nontechnical language made this "a rich and readable feast" by "a first-rate party of scholars," accessible to general readers.[19] There was scarcely a dissenting voice.

Yet few recognized that *Man's Role* was one of the first global, integrative works on human use and misuse of the earth, a pioneering foray on environmental impacts. No reviewer noted Sauer's societal shift from resource thriftiness to "easy confidence" in exploiting nature. Indeed, *Man's Role* appeared at an unreflective intermediate point between these two contrasting takes on environmental issues. Popular works in the 1930s and 1940s by Paul Sears, G. V. Jacks and R. O. Whyte, Russell Lord, Fairfield Osborn, and William Vogt had mostly taken an ameliorative view of environmental problems. Ignorant misuses of land, soil, and water, and uncontrolled fire would be easily remedied by wise and prudent reform measures. Such authors were nevertheless castigated by Earl Parker Hanson as "lugubrious, wailing Neo-Malthusian Jeremiads" for stressing issues of misuse.[20]

Six years after *Man's Role* came Rachel Carson's *Silent Spring*; apocalyptic warnings like hers had not been heard since George Perkins Marsh's *Man and Nature* a century previously (1864). Her "little book of horrors," as one reviewer called it, revolutionized the tenor and thrust of the conservation movement, exposing the interconnected and frequently irremediable ecological consequences of corporate America's willfully irresponsible programs, aided and abetted by lax governmental oversight.[21] Whereas most pre–*Man's Role* volumes on human impacts were limited in regional scope and comfortingly optimistic about the prospects of environmental reform, *Silent Spring* was global, integrative, pessimistic, and doom laden. The environmental debate had moved from science and technology to embrace politics, society, and ethics. One will never know how different *Man's Role* might have been if Carson, whom Sauer had suggested as a participant, had contributed to the symposium.

Aside from Sauer's own pessimistic views, *Man's Role* was closer in outlook to the earlier works than to *Silent Spring*. The ominous consequences of human impacts engaged few contributors. That growing population and technological power meant ever greater damage rarely occurred to discussants. Only Mumford addressed the unexampled, widespread, and fearsomely lethal byproducts of the chemical, biological, and nuclear developments of the 1940s and 1950s.

Although the volume was dedicated to Marsh, and Sauer termed the symposium a "Marsh festival,"[22] Marsh's awareness of humanity's increasing capacity to derange natural processes was conspicuously absent. Sauer's fears of a horrible future were never taken up. Growing public apprehension that the bomb had shown humanity capable of self-annihilation was ignored. Indeed, participants envisaged no role for a concerned public. It was not people in general but "scholars in oncoming generations" that the book was meant to reach.[23] In sum, *Man's Role* was as remarkable for the issues it did not address as for those it did. Perhaps Sauer's choice of participants, guided by his preference for their historical perspective, excluded some who might have speculated more about the future, while his own avowed primitivism distanced him from the contemporary scene much as he cut himself off from the future.

Most contributors took progress largely for granted. Erwin Gutkind saw humankind moving away from ruthless exploitation toward "responsibility and unification," for "the conquest of the air enables mankind for the first time in its history to experience [our impact on nature] in all its innumerable ramifications. . . . Today we can look at the world with a God's-eye view." Clarence Glacken thought heedless impacts were increasingly giving way to rational, conservation-minded manipulation; Warren Thornthwaite believed man "incapable" of significantly changing climatic patterns; Edward Graham lauded soil conservation reform and biotic resource manipulation; John Curtis thought that the ongoing loss of climax deciduous forest had to be accepted; Lester Klimm saw no adverse effects of ports and harbor construction; Michael Graham wrote that "man can hardly sully and cannot appreciably despoil" the oceans; John Bugher envisioned the use of nuclear wastes as benign tracer elements for tracking flows in atmospheric and ocean circulation. The hubristic optimism was overwhelming.[24]

Many participants, including Sauer himself at that time, clung to outdated ecological succession-to-climax concepts. Ecological concern was expressed only when stability seemed threatened or the steady-state situation upset. Fraser Darling called the pastoralist the "climax-breaker." Sauer blamed American technology and ethnocentric imperialism for "destroying wise and durable native systems of living with the land." Only the psychiatrist Iago Galdston noted the demise of belief in any static equilibrium, whether personal or environmental, while Frank Egler commented that traditional ecology was pretty well "on the skids."[25]

Given widespread worry over population growth, *Man's Role* contained surprisingly little on the population "bomb." The demographer Warren Thompson predicted far slower population growth (only 7.2 billion by AD 2100) than has since occurred. James Malin dismissed the "doom" forecast by Malthusians that had "contaminated Western thought since the eighteenth century." Each age had feared the consequences of science and technology, but these fears were again and again dispelled by the adaptive ingenuity of humankind.[26]

More astonishing still, the atomic bomb and its legacies of radiation and nuclear waste went little mentioned, except by Bugher, who grossly minimized the genetic and other risks, and by Mumford, who made an impassioned but generalized plea for "humility and prudence, not cockiness and indecent haste" in the peacetime exploitation of atomic energy. His remedy was love: "Only when love takes the lead will the earth, and life on earth, be safe again." Given widespread public anxiety over looming threats of nuclear warfare, radioactive fallout, waste disposal, and genetic mutations — a congressman from Sauer's home state echoed many in fearing "that the world will be destroyed by the machines and weapons created by our own mind" — this was a pretty limp recipe. *Man's Role*'s total silence "about the fact that the leaders in the Pentagon . . . may destroy the major habitats on the planet," seemed unbelievably strange to Mumford himself a decade later.[27]

Also disappointing was the lack of a substantial summary statement by Sauer. The slot was there for him, but he could not strike the right note. "You won't expect any rhetoric from me; it's neither my line nor appropriate." He would be "relaxed and ruminative," rather than reiterate his overriding concerns about Western commodity fetishism and the death of natural and cultural diversity.[28] He had little faith in the subsequent popular environmental movement, dismissing Earth Day in 1970 as an "ecological binge." Sauer had closed his mind to wider public concerns that were in fact in tune with his own deeply felt convictions.[29]

Man's Role was "useful less for its somewhat labored attempts at synthesis," judged an anthropologist, "than for its presentation of partial understandings . . . for a creative synthesis still to come."[30] Thirty-five years later, environmentally minded successors at a cognate symposium suggested that the lasting influence of *Man's Role* was to have "informed and sometimes inspired several generations of scholars in the natural sciences, social sciences, and humanities."[31] But with a world population doubled since 1955; mounting losses of soils, fresh water, forests, habitats, and species to development; newly perceived threats such as global warming; and growing awareness of human impotence to correct or even curtail such threats, *The Earth as Transformed by Human Action* (1990) was radically more somber and pessimistic than *Man's Role*, even Sauerian in dubiety about progress, though only two of its forty-two essays referred back to Sauer's own concerns.[32]

TO PASS ON A GOOD EARTH

12

A Productive Retirement,

1957–1975

As retirement approached in 1957, Sauer if anything increased his commitments. Between extended stays abroad, he kept up his writing, guest lectur-
ing, and committee work, especially the time-consuming Guggenheim, National Academy of Sciences/National Research Council, and Office of Naval
Research meetings. Planning for the geography department's new home in
the Earth Sciences Building (now McCone Hall) made his last year as head
of the department in 1954 particularly grueling. "The old horse is staggering
down the track, looking no further than the June finish line."[1] The comfortable surplus of time that he had when young now was rushing away from
him. Like his oft-repeated line from Chaucer, "The life so short, the craft
so long to learn," a German student song seemed apt: "Es gibt so manche
Strasse da nimmer ich marschiert. Es gibt so manchen Wein den ich nimmer noch probiert" (There are so many roads that I have never walked. There
are so many wines that I have never tasted).[2]

Uncertain what he really wanted to do, he started by eliminating what
he didn't. "No more committees, no more conferences, no more lectures.
I've been getting requests to teach and I don't want to teach, anywhere. I
don't want a schedule of days and hours that will have to be observed." He
declined many public lectures and would never talk on an assigned subject,

but only on a topic of his choice. He couldn't do fieldwork any longer but enjoyed visiting and advising if it did not require physical exertion. "I don't want to be away from home for more than half a year at the outside. I should be putting in a good deal of time working up notes and studying, for I've got a lot of themes partly roughed out that I can do best here. We have a good home and feel at home here. I don't want to miss out on the grandchildren." As he summed it up, "A spot of travel to learn and a spot of quiet to study and write is about the way I'd like to go on. I am looking forward to starting over in a new life."[3]

The new life's eighteen years were no less busy or productive than those before. There were trips to Europe and, despite his earlier protestations, teaching semesters in a number of U.S. universities, along with continuing Guggenheim and other service. Most impressive was his writing, the fruits of a lifetime's reflective gathering: four books, twenty-one articles, and numerous comments, reviews, and obituaries. This was also the period of his greatest prestige, due largely to *Agricultural Origins and Dispersals* in 1952 and the *Man's Role* volume in 1956. By the late 1950s Sauer had come to seem "sage, philosopher-king, and even oracle."[4]

Travel

The trips to Europe were high points in his new life. They were "a sort of pilgrimage" to find out what was going on where learning was valued for its own sake, untrammeled by the "new fangled" corruptions that bedeviled America. From July to October 1960 he toured German and Austrian geography departments on behalf of the National Science Foundation, but he spent very little time conversing with academic colleagues, whom he found mildly disappointing. In any event, he mainly wanted to soak up the ambience of places in Spain that he had imagined fondly since his youth, and to "visit Germany and Austria, lands of memory to me."[5]

On several occasions he was honored—with the Vega Medal from the Swedish Society for Anthropology and Geography in Stockholm in 1957, the Alexander von Humboldt Medal at the Humboldt Centenary celebration in Berlin in 1959, and an honorary doctorate from the University of Glasgow in 1965. By 1975, when he was awarded the Royal Geographical Society's prestigious Victoria Medal, he was too frail to receive it in person.

TO PASS ON A GOOD EARTH

He found his divorce from the classroom unexpectedly hard to take. All his life he had guided students, and he particularly missed the work with postgraduates. Moreover, many of the ideas he would extemporize in class later found their way into his writing. Hence he held seminars for former students—Homer Aschmann at the University of California, Riverside, in 1958; Joe Spencer at UCLA in 1961[6]—and his son, Jonathan, at Wisconsin in 1965. He gave a final Berkeley seminar in 1964.[7]

An invitation in 1961 to Williamsburg, Virginia's colonial capital, was declined out of his enduring sense of exclusion as a German American:

I have several strains of Europe in me but not a drop of English. I don't know the succession of English kings and queens, prime ministers, nor could I qualify for colonial ancestors, the first of mine having reached Pennsylvania in 1818. As a boy [I] sang "My Country 'Tis of Thee" as lustily as any one, but the Atlantic seaboard can still make me feel like a heavy tongued immigrant.[8]

Other lecture visits were to Indiana, Winnipeg, and Austin, Texas. At a 1972 Louisiana State University symposium on the nature, origin, and human modification of grasslands, Sauer collapsed with a urinary infection and seldom ventured away from Berkeley again.

He spoke at the Pacific Coast Geographers Meeting in San Diego in June 1973, after nineteen of his former students, in a session chaired by Joe Spencer, gave papers in his honor. He ended his remarks with: "At any rate, please God, don't you geographers whoop it up for growth and development."[9] This was his final public appearance.

the last lecture

Continued Writing

"I'm too old a dog to be learning new tricks," wrote Sauer a few years after retiring, "but I am learning more of my old ones." His productivity was indeed predominantly aimed at filling out and reflecting deeply on old themes. He was "largely hung up on the XVI [century] and before with Spanish expansion, and with the spread of cultivated plants and domestic animals." He also continued writing on other familiar themes, notably early humans and their environments, the history of geography, and reminiscences of the midwestern landscapes, economy, and society of his youth nearly seventy years earlier.[10]

Although Sauer had earned a reputation as a pioneer in tracing plant domestication and diffusion, that work had stalled when he realized he lacked the requisite biological expertise. Moreover, his ancillary interest in dating early man in the Americas had come to seem more exciting and productive. But by 1950 that too received a hard blow with Willard Libby's discovery of carbon-14 dating (see chap. 8).

From charting plant variations and dating archaeological sites, Sauer had moved on to a broad, sweeping view of innovation and diffusion in *Agricultural Origins* (1952) and to human transformation of landscape in "The Agency of Man on the Earth" (1956). These works, and most that followed, concerned large themes in a global perspective, deploying Sauer's speculative bent with wide erudition and literary skill.

Asked by the botanist Ray Fosberg to review tropical life with "tropical eyes rather than from [an] alien point of view" for the Ninth Pacific Science Congress in Bangkok in 1957,[11] Sauer penned a sustained attack on the simplistic models that equated vegetation patterns solely with climate. Such "schemes of successive stages and climatic climaxes" did not take into account the flux of climates in the past or the long history of human impact on vegetation. His wide experience came to the fore as he assembled varied evidence.

As Sauer wrote in his conference paper, "Man in the Ecology of Tropical America," post-Columbian settlement of the American tropics was "largely the resettlement of aboriginally occupied areas" where the original population had been swept away by European disease and warfare. That population had "numbered in the millions," and had found niches everywhere in the exuberant forest, particularly along waterside sites, which offered opportunities for a varied diet of fish, turtles, and agricultural crops. Forest dwellers cleared plots for cultivation mainly by girdling (debarking), thus killing trees, which were then burned, creating grassy deforested areas. After the European encounter and Indian demise, forests recovered. Parts of the tropics that then appeared empty were later reoccupied. But "under supposed 'pristine' forest [today] lie the sites of quite advanced cultures."[12] Recent research has tended to confirm this.[13]

Sauer turned again to American cultivated plants in 1959, summarizing what was known about their origin and diffusion across the two continents in "Age and Area of American Cultivated Plants." Southern Central America marked a major cultural divide, he said. To the south and in the Caribbean, vegetative reproduction (new plants grown from cuttings of other plants) prevailed, the lack of fat and protein being made up by aquatic sources and wild animals. To the north, seed production dominated, with protein-rich maize and beans, plus squash. In the same year Sauer elaborated on the crucial nature of the cultural passageway between the two areas in "Middle America as Culture Historical Location." This was followed by the wide-ranging papers "Maize into Europe" in 1962 (discussed in chap. 8) and "Cultural Factors in Plant Domestication" in 1965, which stressed the use of the digging stick to plant seeds and to heap up mounds for cultivation in wetlands.

Sauer had hesitated to plunge back into the maelstrom of dating early humanity in the Americas, but invited by J. B. Jackson to contribute "anything" to his new journal *Landscape*, he could not resist an opportunity to fly a kite again. "Time and Place in Ancient America" was a stirring call for Paleolithic inquiry.[14]

The distant past is being revealed by one discovery after another of human vestiges and by new and more precise means of estimating their age. . . . [Folsom type projectile points suggest] the ancestral elephant hunters had many thousands of years of residence in the Great Plains before the Bison Hunters came along. . . . The barriers across the trails of Ancient Man are down. Discovery now can give attention to evidence and does not need to accommodate itself to doctrine.[15]

The essay was an enormous success, and helped put *Landscape* on the map.

Jackson asked for more from Sauer, whose subsequent letter to the magazine on past and present American culture was a relentless attack on the inanities of American life, its excessive emphasis on mobility, conspicuous consumption, and continuous innovation, as glorified in "our trashiest movies, widely exported, sensational, violent, stupid, and sybaritic."

The automobile industry, most successful in this respect, has called it planned obsolescence. We have made a vast business success of changing styles, even more so than of improved function. Change for the sake of change, discarding what we have, and [preferring] something new because it is new, may be less the progress we like to think it than loss of moderation and stability, a cutting loose from the moorings we need.[16]

From the contentious issue of dating early Americans, Sauer moved to "geographical localizations of cultural beginnings," stimulated by a 1959 Wenner-Gren symposium at Burg Wartenstein, Austria. His own paper sought to reconstruct the social life of early humans, not, as commonly done, by extrapolating from primate physical characteristics and aggressive behavior, but by viewing them as makers of culture essential to their survival. Humans lacked the ability to defend themselves by speed, strength, or bodily weapons such as claws or powerful teeth. Their omnivorous diet, based on a digestive system that accepted a broad range of animal and plant food, enabled them to maximize resource use wherever they were. Moreover, human young were helpless and, unlike infants of most primates, had to be carried. A mother might have had two or more children dependent on her at any one time. Hence primordial humans could not survive like wandering bands of baboons, but became semi-sedentary.

Sauer thus hypothesized that women played a decisive role in early cultural development, which required a habitat that provided shelter, drinking water, and a ready supply of animal and plant food within a reasonable distance. Family formation demanded "the arts and goods of the household, and pacific community life." Fire was all important in hunting, food preparation, and warmth, and it was women who captured wild fire and kept it "alive" for the community.[17]

In 1962 he suggested, contrary to accepted opinion, that seashores and lakesides, with their abundant and diverse plant and animal life, were the original habitat of early man in Africa, rather than the open savanna. "The discovery of the warm tidal ocean gave to emergent humanity an opportunity to learn, increase, and spread coastwise and inland. The seashore offered the best route of dispersal from continent to continent."[18] It was a revolutionary but plausible hypothesis, though difficult to verify, since successive changes in sea level had wiped out most ocean-side sites.

Two years later Sauer brought together his views on the matrifocal nature of early society and the primacy of sedentary seashore locations. That humans were anatomically better adapted and equipped for swimming than other primates clinched the waterside location for him. And with the command of fire came migrations northward: "Having fire, man was enabled to go forth to possess the world; without it, he was a primate narrowly limited to suitable parts of the tropics."[19]

Other papers on early humans and their environment restated and elaborated these topics. One was for a meeting of the International Economic History Association in 1968.[20] Another, presented at the 1972 Baton Rouge conference on the nature, origin, and human modification of grasslands, added new details to his thesis of the importance of fire, particularly from sixteenth-century Spanish and French accounts of early vegetation. Sauer stated unequivocally that the world's prairies, savannas, and other grasslands were not a climatic climax vegetation, but rather human artifacts created and maintained by the repeated use of fire.[21]

Final Books

While controversies over plant domestication and early man continued to demand Sauer's attention, his major postretirement contributions were four books mainly on European expansion in the New World during the sixteenth and seventeenth centuries.[22] Although he complained that no one read and few commented on his historically based work, these final books were widely reviewed.

The Early Spanish Main (1966) portrayed the Caribbean as the Spaniards first found and occupied it, documenting how long-sustained native social and economic systems were broken down and a population of millions reduced to the point of extinction within a few years. Sauer castigated Columbus and the Spaniards for brutality and incompetent administration. "By 1519 the Spanish Main was a sorry shell. The natives . . . were destroyed. . . . Most of its land had been repossessed by wild growth of tropical vegetation."[23]

Frequently cited, the book had several editions and a Spanish translation. But of twenty-five-odd reviews,[24] the most for any of Sauer's books, several took him heavily to task. The noted Spanish historian Salvador de Madariaga was particularly scathing: "The work of a good geographer who is a bad historian. . . . There is no distant view. . . . For lack of this mastering vision, we are left with a loose set of events, a huge lunatic asylum. . . .

Anti-Spanish bias is writ large." The historical demographer Ángel Rosen-blat criticized Sauer's estimate of 1,130,000 Indians on Hispaniola "as an article of faith." The Caribbeanist Bruce Solnick noted the professional historian's "serious reservations about this volume."[25]

In the *Geographical Review*, the historian Thomas McGann praised Sauer's "outpouring of information about crops and customs, tools and technology . . . presented in a lively, compact style," with descriptions of native life for which "he has no peer." But McGann felt that the book lacked "the same rigorous analysis, abundance of synthesized data, and originality, that have characterized Professor Sauer's other major monographs." Moreover, the lengthy treatment of Columbus as a "feckless administrator" had all been done long before.[26] Deeply offended, Sauer withdrew his name from the journal's list of supporting editors: "It cites me as lacking in historical competence, myself having labored so long to win a good place for historical geography."[27] Thus ended more than thirty-five years of warm cooperation between Sauer and the *Geographical Review*, and with this break his isolation from American professional geography became even more pronounced.

On balance, however, most reactions were favorable. "Professor Sauer has written by far the best summary that has yet appeared," wrote the distinguished historian J. H. Parry. "It sheds much new light. . . . A remarkable series of informed, sound, and balanced judgments." The historian Anthony Pagden called it a "classic account of the land, nature, and people Columbus encountered . . . a deeply moral book." The botanist Daniel Austin said it "should be on the 'must read' list for every biology graduate student." The geographer Paul Starrs considered it "brilliant and surgical.[28]

Sauer's next book, *Northern Mists* (1968), about "the faring out to sea during the Middle Ages from Atlantic Europe," seemingly appeared out of nowhere.[29] There is not one reference to it in his correspondence. The title was taken from Fridtjof Nansen's study of sea voyages in the North Atlantic before the time of Columbus.[30] Sauer traced the Norse settlement of Greenland from the late tenth century into the fifteenth. Meanwhile, European fishermen were harvesting abundant marine resources off the shores of Newfoundland, and there were reports of a Vinland in present-day southern New England. Irish monks who left Iceland after the coming of the Vikings, Sauer suggested, could have gone west to Greenland and then Newfoundland, settling around the Gulf of St. Lawrence in the tenth century. "Sauer may well be right in thinking that there were pre-Norse contacts with North America," wrote a reviewer, but "the evidence adduced here is not convincing."[31] Almost forty years later, a geographer found "little of the fact and content has been superseded . . . a pleasure to read, his insights often profound and informed." And it now is clear that there was a Viking settlement in L'Anse aux Meadows in present-day Newfoundland at about the end of the tenth century.[32]

Sauer's *Sixteenth Century North America* (1971) recounts where the early explorers went and what they reported. He discusses Spanish exploration and colonization in detail, less so English and French. Routes of movement and places of settlement were prefigured by Indian experience. Indians had long modified forests and grasslands, notably by means of fire. Europeans on the eastern frontier took over crops, methods, and fields of Indian agriculturalists. "Vintage Sauer," wrote a well-known geographer, "an impressive contribution" by an "original" and "innovative" mind.[33]

By the time *Sixteenth Century North America* came out, Sauer was "far enough along with the *Seventeenth*" to see the conclusion of a series that "I have been doing in my dotage with some sort of notion that there was an unassembled view of the American past that I should get out of my system." As an "incorrigible historical geographer," he saw himself as quite "the opposite of a forward-looking American, looking bright-eyed ahead."[34]

The poet Bob Callahan had founded the avant-garde Turtle Island Foundation and the Netzahualcoyotl Historical Society in Berkeley for the multicultural study of American literature and cultural history. Callahan thought Sauer's empathetic understanding of native peoples held lessons for the alternative society envisaged by activists during the late 1960s. Callahan had republished *Northern Mists* and published *Seventeenth Century North America* in 1980, after Sauer's death.

In a 1981 collection of Sauer's essays Callahan wrote that with Sauer's death America had "lost one of the most articulate scholars this century has yet to produce."

And indeed, the very Earth . . . lost a man who had become the very voice and conscience of benign and intelligent American land-management thinking. Like so many of the leaders of the various Native American

cultures he had come over the years to so very much admire and respect, Carl Sauer, it now seems, may even have been born to teach us
all how to walk softly, and ever so much more knowingly, in balance
with the lasting treasures and resources of our continent.[35]

Seventeenth Century North America fleshes out Sauer's own narrative with
numerous quotations from Spanish and French eyewitnesses—Oñate in
New Mexico, Champlain and Nicollet in Canada and the Great Lakes, the
Jesuits Joliet and Marquette in the Mississippi Valley, La Salle the Lower
Mississippi, coastal plain, and Texas, and many more. "The Indian way of
life was admirable, it was agreed, before it was changed by European influence." The French were less destructive than the Spaniards, but both
brought about the massive "decline of Indian population."[36]

Writing about these final books the historical geographer Donald Meinig
judged that "Sauer's views are not just unorthodox, they are generally unknown or barely acknowledged. . . . Few American historians have been prepared to see the European 'discovery' of the 'New World' as an irruption into
a richly developed continent which was rapaciously conquered and transformed." Sauer's views are part of a "radical revision" of history . . . [an]
"ongoing re-invention of America."[37] This revision has gained substantial
acceptance, especially since the Columbian Quincentennial of 1992.

History and Practice of Geography

Sauer's late writing on geography was largely autobiographical. His second
presidential address to the Association of American Geographers in 1956
recounted his selecting and training of students and staff at Berkeley over
the previous thirty-three years. He stressed informal Socratic teaching and
shunned any prescription of what was and was not geography. He considered interest in geography "immemorial and universal," not the exclusive
domain of professionals. Geographers of many diverse backgrounds and
disciplines shared a liking for maps, an urge to travel, curiosity about what
they saw in the landscape, and a "morphological eye" that embraced "the
fourth dimension of time" as a guiding explanatory principle. He assailed
the abandonment of humane scholarship, the growth of mechanical com-
putation, and the sterility of purely descriptive regional courses. Interpreta-

tion of the origins of landforms, soils, vegetation, and cultural landscapes involved processes that were "largely non-recurrent and involved time spans mainly beyond the short runs available to enumeration." He ended his address with a plea to reach "beyond formal science" to an aesthetic understanding of the "real" world. Vexing questions of the place of humans in nature and their effect on global ecology were the proper domain not of social science but of moral philosophy. "We are moralists," he once said.[38]

A second backward glance was a festschrift essay for his old friend and Mexican traveling companion Gottfried Pfeifer of Heidelberg University. Sauer sketched geography's role in every aspect of American life, from place-names to Jeffersonian public land surveys to contributions to state geological surveys and federal censuses, along with the pioneering influences of individuals such as George Perkins Marsh. Much of the essay dwelt on reminiscences of his experiences at Chicago. It was a personal testimony that fulfilled a personal debt.[39]

At the age of eighty Sauer acknowledged his intellectual debt to Friedrich Ratzel, citing his little known but penetrating articles written for a German newspaper as he traveled across the United States in 1873. Sauer termed these observations "historical geography of grand design."[40]

In his eighty-fourth year Sauer wrote of his escape from the "narrowing professionalism" of Chicago and Michigan to the freedom at Berkeley to do what research he liked amid a "congenial" gathering of scholars from a wide range of disciplines. "Wider horizons were opened to us, perhaps wider than we would have found anywhere else." In Berkeley Sauer became increasingly aware that man "was not the master of an unlimited environment, [and] that technologic intervention in the physical world and its life has become the crisis of his survival and that of his co-inhabitants."[41]

"Scenes of My Youth"

On a 1958 visit to Warrenton, Sauer revisited "the scenes of my youth." Down "old remembered roads" he found upland farming abandoned and old fields replaced by woodland stands of red cedar, persimmon, sassafras, dogwood, sumac, and coveys of quail. Squirrels, raccoons, possums, deer, turkey, and beaver abounded, and wolves had even been sighted there, all these in his youth "remembered only by the oldest settlers."[42]

One area of regrowth was the Little Charrette Valley, the local beauty spot etched in his memory as the scene of picnics, outings, and his courtship of Lorena. He now "inspired" the elderly owner to bequeath the land to the Missouri Conservation Commission, so that "future generations may enjoy the charm of the Little Charrette hills," just as he had. Sauer admired the Missouri Commission as an innovative local organization untrammeled by federal directives, such as those of the Forest Service, whose "official doctrine must be subscribed to." The grassroots approach was far preferable to anything "decreed and executed by the distant Great White Father" in Washington.[43]

His nostalgic Missouri memories prompted two essays recalling the Middle Border at the turn of the century. For a Homestead Centennial Symposium at the University of Nebraska in 1962 he offered a fond look back at "the old days and old folks," showing how American rural life had changed in "mode, mood and meaning," all but wiping out the family farm. He cherished "the native virtues of rural life" and felt America the poorer for their loss.[44]

An even more personal and evocative publication in a German journal detailed changes that made his youthful haunts—Warrenton, the Ozarks, and southern Kentucky—now almost unrecognizable as the result of two world wars, the rise of centralized control by a welfare-oriented government, and the internal combustion engine. His past had vanished. When the first automobiles came to Warrenton there was just "one stretch of eight miles of smooth road to a neighboring town":

> People who had cars soon formed the habit of evening drives back and forth over this stretch for sheer exhilaration of rapid motion, not in order to get to another place. The sedentary home and community centered life began to give way to wider, more frequent, more casual, and more rapid mobility. The American has become habituated to relocating himself beyond the proper call of bettering his position, a new restless nomad.[45]

With movement for the sake of movement, Americans turned their backs on their past.

These eulogies for the lost past marked a shift in Sauer's conservation priorities from concern with resources for the future to satisfaction with nature and man in amicable harmony. Places like Charrette were refuges for the spirit in an ever more frantically hurried age. Carl Sauer was becoming "greener" than he was prepared to admit.

Final Years

Coping with trips aboard and brief spells at American universities, Sauer generally enjoyed good health. He was "hale and hearty, intellectually active and full of vigor," James Parsons said of him in his seventy-fourth year. However, he looked old; John Leighly, who had known him for over sixty years, said that he had developed a wrinkled brow early on. In his last decade David Hooson saw him as a "benign, impressively wrinkled Einsteinian old gentleman," always surrounded by a "ruminative cloud" of pipe smoke.[46]

Nearly every weekday Sauer walked down the hill from Arch Street to his office in the Earth Sciences Building at the north edge of campus, where he did some writing, conversed with colleagues, and counseled graduate students. Frequently he visited the Bancroft Library for specialist historical material, and the general campus library to consult new publications and read the financial news to check his investments. Occasionally he lunched at the Faculty Club, but more often than not he walked back up the hill to eat with Lorena, who was equally fit and well. Hardly a day went by without Lorena digging and planting in the garden, and frequently "she climbs the hills in the morning and visits her incapacitated friends."

At home Sauer worked in his upper-floor study during the afternoon, with an occasional break on the balcony to feed the birds.[47] He read English crime stories, less for their plots than for their vividly depicted landscapes. After the evening meal he enjoyed soaps about the Old West such as *Wagon Train*, *Gunsmoke*, *Bonanza*, and *The Virginian*, which appealed to "widespread nostalgia for the past, lost, but more and more sentimentally remembered." Laura FitzSimmons, his youngest granddaughter, recalls sitting on his lap snuggling close to his chest to hear the chuckles and grunts that accompanied his TV watching.

Many of Sauer's friends had died or retired elsewhere; he found fewer and fewer familiar faces on campus, more and more new, younger ones. With former university president Robert Gordon Sproul vouching for his "personality, character and sociability," he joined the Bohemian Club, a dining and conversation group in San Francisco. But Sauer went only occasionally.[48] Aside from his conservation interests, he gave little attention to Warrenton matters unless the interchange was with old acquaintances. He did not reply to most requests, including one to write an autobiography that would be "interesting and inspiring to many young geographers."[49]

After being briefly hospitalized at a grasslands symposium in Baton Rouge in 1972, Sauer's exercise was limited to a nearby daily walk less steep than that to the campus.[50] Impaired physical health did not undermine his intellectual energy, however, and at the time of his death he was sketching out an outline of a historical geography of the United States, to be entitled "Recessional at the Bicentennial." It would reflect his pessimism concerning the future of humanity in general and, in particular, American hubris over misuses of the land. Dismayed by the relentless plundering and exhaustion of resources that fed an insatiable economy of consumption, he had little hope that technology or political action would check industry's lemming-like rush toward self-destruction.[51]

Sauer was awarded numerous honors over his lifetime. Besides the medals listed earlier, he received honorary degrees from the universities of Glasgow, Heidelberg, Syracuse, and California, Berkeley. He was a Guggenheim Fellow in 1931, and elected to the American Philosophical Society in 1944. He received the Charles P. Daly Medal in 1940 from the American Geographical Society. President of the Association of American Geographers in 1940 and honorary president in 1956, in 1974 he was given a "Special Award" "for a lifetime of exceptional achievement as a scholar."

Lorena Schowengerdt Sauer died peacefully on June 19, 1975, and, as often happens with couples whose lives have so long been intimately shared, Carl simply could not exist without his companion of over sixty-one years. "His heart was broken," said their granddaughter Laura.[52] Just a month later, on July 18, Carl Sauer's long and busy life also came quietly to an end at age eighty-five. A headstone (Carl) and a memorial stone (Lorena) were set up, side by side, in the cemetery in Warrenton, their small midwestern home.

Carl Sauer had fused "an unusual capacity to grasp a wide range of universal knowledge, and . . . to impart intellectual wisdom" with "an uncanny ability to express complex ideas in disarmingly simple language."[53] Insisting that "all geography is essentially historical," he held that modern technological society could and should learn from "simpler cultures, past and present," how to achieve "a humane use of the earth."[54]

Afterword

Abrupt, repetitive [handwritten annotation]

Fulfilled in family and career, and famed as seer and mentor, Carl Sauer felt increasingly alienated from modern ways. In the guise of progress, resources were gutted, landscapes befouled, rural communities impoverished, traditional cultures eviscerated. Sanctimonious do-gooders — St. Bureaucraticus's "more and better jobs" to guide "this wobbly world," and St. Scholasticus's "five-dollar phrases for commonplaces" — ruled government and academe alike. Cultural and agricultural diversity gave way to monocultural uniformity, an arid and rootless sameness of soil and spirit, whether on the American or the Soviet model. Moneyed malefactors backed purblind planners' development programs that squandered finite reserves of soils, water, and forests, ditching humane and aesthetic values for short-term profits.

Out of tune with modernity in general and technocrat improvers in particular, Sauer termed himself an obsolete relic from a bygone era, a "cranky old backwoodsman." Nostalgic for his slow-paced small-town childhood, he relished his "Society of Backward Peoples and the Slowing Down of Progress." Yet for all of Sauer's self-mocking despair, subsequent events make manifest the merits of many of his embattled stances.

Most salient today is Sauer's critique of environmental exploitation. "Civilized man," he pronounced, was "the most perilous parasite in the history of the earth. He has thrived briefly on destruction and multiplication, [but] the world is actually growing poorer day by day." The technological hubris that Sauer then assailed in vain has given way to alarmed awareness of the perils unleashed by human derangement of the Earth. "More damage has been done to the productive capacity of the world" in the past century and a half, judged Sauer, "than in all human history preceding." The half century since has redoubled the damage; we have not yet learned Sauer's "difference between yield and loot." Growing population and mounting power make human agency—burning fossil fuels, accelerating erosion, poisoning air, land, and waters, extirpating species, and crippling ecosystems—the prime threat to our well-being if not survival. From the time of Rachel Carson's *Silent Spring* (1962) to the searing summers of today's global warming, recurrent disasters—lethal oil spills, polluted waterways, eutrophically dead lakes, nuclear meltdowns, plastic-choked oceans and debris-clogged space orbits, antibiotic-resistant pathogens, ozone depletion, melting icecaps—underscore the ecological warnings that Sauer did not originate but of which he was a most eloquent champion.

Sauer's concern for cultural diversity paralleled his pleas to conserve nature. He likened technical assistance "meddling" that sought to "reorder the world" and "reduce it to one system" to missionaries "putting Mother Hubbards on Hawaiians," a vainglorious know-how devoid of "wisdom and pity and humility." He feared that industrial demands would "eradicate the natural and cultural landmarks we cherish" and destroy invaluable heritage. The backward Third World was bidden to eliminate hunger, endemic disease, poverty, and illiteracy, guided by Western planners with "their social consciences all straight and their responses to any situation all ready," scoffed Sauer, "arranging the lives of men unknown to them and not understood by them. That cultural conservancy is critical to the sanity of the world [was] alien to their thinking."

No more. Sauer's stewardship is now de rigueur. Cultural autonomy is sacrosanct, Western tutelage repudiated as neocolonialism. United Nations and UNESCO protocols declare traditional heritage and *genres de vie* inviolable. The arrogant modernizing certitudes that Sauer deplored are replaced, in precept if not in practice, by an ethic of self-determination. However quixotic or impracticable, each people (nation, tribe, or minority) is entitled to set its own goals.

Two events underlie this volte-face. One is the failure of utopian postwar planning. Once-confident social engineers now realize, *pace* Sauer, the futility of one-cure-fits-all to local, complex ailments. Second, cultural along with ecological and genetic diversity has become a precious resource to be sheltered from global conformity and rapacious entrepreneurs. The viability of diverse cultures in distinctive locales is no longer rejected as primitivist folly, but prized as essential to human well-being. Because "there are very few things most sensibly done in one way only," as Sauer argued, "we deal not with Culture, but with cultures." And one day "human survival might depend on there being enough thick-headed peasants who have some dumb awareness that their way of living is good and enduring."

Sauer saw all human experience as historically determined, the present as "an accretion of the past." To understand the present one must learn "how things came to be what they are." Tracing origins and changes "that document formerly dominant, but now old-fashioned conditions," we come at length "to that high moment when the past is clear, and the contrasts to the present are understood." Such study demanded empathetic immersion in unfamiliar paths, wherever they led. Sauer echoed Robert Musil's *The Man without Qualities:* "The way of history is not that of a billiard ball, which, once hit, moves in a straight line, but like drifting clouds, or the path of a man sauntering through the streets, diverted here by a shadow, there by a knot of bystanders or by a striking façade, until at last he arrives at a place he never knew of nor meant to go to."

Along with Sauer's cultural pluralism, his historical bent was anathema to hard-nosed social scientists unable to see, he charged, "that the course of events, if not cyclic, sinusoidal or straight line, was any concern of theirs." Only the present mattered. Applying universal and unchanging laws of human behavior to current social and economic issues, they dismissed Sauer's stress on the past as antiquarian irrelevance. Two generations on, Sauer's historical insight has become conventional wisdom, from astronomy and biology to archaeology and art. Physical science is increasingly historicized, nature seen to share humanity's capricious career. Laws of nature once thought eternal and universal turn out to be time-bound, contingent on unpredictably episodic events. Natural like cultural outcomes are conditioned by Sauer's "frame of time and place."

Zest for knowledge, untrammeled by disciplinary diktat or reformist zeal, animated Sauer and his students. "We try to give free play to curiosity, restricted only by competence. True scholars needed no assignment but merely the leeway to follow their own bent." Such ivory-tower inquiry was condemned as frivolously self-indulgent by "world-improvers" of the New Deal, wartime, and postwar decades. Sauer dreaded their imperious sway. "We already have the factory system of instruction, and we are too far on the way to the same thing in scholarship," the individual "reduced to piece work" under a few "spurious masterminds" bent on "mending this strange world." Team research on topics of immediate utility continued to expand to the detriment of the lone maverick and of global diversity alike. "This curious world is unendingly fascinating," rebuked Sauer. "It is not our business to make it conform to our reason."

Eighty years ago Sauer praised his university for "accommodating all kinds of persons and minds." Colleagues from soil science and history, engineering and economics, anthropology and art history were "working in common to so large an extent" that they no longer needed to demarcate their disciplines. "The pursuit of knowledge cannot afford to frustrate itself," Sauer insisted, "by building fences about narrow plots of learning." Disciplinary narrowness impeded what students most needed: exposure to unfamiliar ways of knowing.

Whereas power to hire and fire, police and promote, sustains disciplinary dominance in academe, innovative research and teaching migrate to Sauer's "germinal potential out on the periphery." Scholars enthralled by broader horizons are needed, both to expand the frontiers of knowledge and to persuade students to take all knowledge as their province. To pass on Sauer's good Earth requires not only ecological expertise and spiritual nous but caring citizens capable of seeing beyond parochial borders.

To that end, Sauer's educational instinct is vitally germane. He had "guessed right several times on heretics who made good" by encouraging contrarian oddballs. "The only way I know of infecting youngsters' minds is to open up horizons to them by one's own work and by the appreciation of creative work by any one." To further "the thrill of turning up an ancient civilization, or discovering a new type of mountain sculpture or of reconstructing the missions of a vanished frontier," Sauer sought to "give back the search for truth and beauty to the individual scholar, to grow in grace as best he can."

David Lowenthal

[NOTES]

Much of this work is based on unpublished correspondence. The Sauer Papers are located in the Bancroft Library of the University of California, Berkeley (Kenzer, 1986). They consist of boxes of correspondence, cartons of manuscripts, conferences, research and class notes, diaries and ledgers, photographs, departmental items, and newspaper clippings. Much of the professional correspondence comes from outside geography.

During his early decades at Berkeley, copies were not made of most of Sauer's letters. Later, many of the originals were sent by the recipients to the Bancroft Library. In the chapter endnotes, academic correspondence in the Sauer Papers is identified by SP. Family letters in the possession of Sauer's daughter, Elizabeth Sauer FitzSimmons, in Berkeley, are identified as "Father," "Mother," "Parents," and wife "Lorena." Michael Williams did not always provide sources for quotations from family correspondence.

Abbreviations

AAG	Association of American Geographers
COS	Carl Ortwin Sauer
CWC	Central Wesleyan College
DL	David Lowenthal
FBI	Federal Bureau of Investigation
IGU	International Geographical Union
MW	Michael Williams
NAS/NRC	National Academy of Sciences/ National Research Council
n.d.	no date
ONR	Office of Naval Research
RFA	Rockefeller Foundation Archive
SP	Sauer Papers (Bancroft Library, Berkeley)
SSRC	Social Science Research Council
USDA	United States Department of Agriculture
WMD	William M. Denevan

Foreword

1. Michael Williams (b. 1935) was Professor of Geography Emeritus and Sir Walter Raleigh Fellow of Oriel College, Oxford University, Fellow of the British Academy, and D. Litt., University of Wales. His books include *The Draining of the Somerset Levels*, 1970; *The Making of the South Australian Landscape*, 1974; *Americans and Their Forests*, 1989; and the magisterial *Deforesting the Earth*, 2003. He died in Oxford on October 26, 2009, shortly after completing a draft of this book, the very day he had been scheduled to give the Carl O. Sauer Memorial Lecture at Berkeley. See Clout, "Professor Michael Williams," 2010, and "Michael Williams," 2011.

2. Notable among numerous tributes are Leighly, "Carl Ortwin Sauer," 1976; Parsons, "Carl Ortwin Sauer," 1976; and Pfeifer, "Carl Ortwin Sauer," 1975. For more than 500 commentaries on Sauer's life and work, see Denevan and Mathewson, *Carl Sauer on Culture*, 2009, 53–86. Essays about Sauer are collected in Kenzer, *Carl O. Sauer*, 1987; Speth, *How It Came to Be*, 1999; and Mathewson and Kenzer, *Culture, Land, and Legacy*, 2003. Sauer's own essays are anthologized in Leighly, *Land and Life*, 1963; Callahan, *Selected Essays*, 1981; and Denevan and Mathewson, *Carl Sauer on Culture*, 2009.

Introduction

1. Thomas, *Man's Role*, 1956.

2. Williams, "Apple of My Eye," 1983; Williams, "Sauer and *Man's Role*," 1987; and Williams, "Carl O. Sauer and the Legacy," 2003.

3. Williams, "Sauer, Carl Ortwin," 2001. Also by Williams on Sauer: "Carl Sauer," 2002; and his foreword to *Carl Sauer on Culture*, 2009.

4. Skeels, "Passage to Premodernity," 1993.

5. Lee, *Body Parts*, 2005.

6. The title of this book, *To Pass On a Good Earth*, is taken from Sauer: "What we need more perhaps is an ethic and aesthetic under which man, practicing the qualities of prudence and moderation, may indeed pass on to posterity a good Earth." Sauer, "Agency of Man," 1956, 68.

Prologue

1. Quotations are from Sauer's short-lived diary, 1907–8.

1. Warrenton of the Middle Border, 1889–1908

1. Garland, *Son of the Middle Border*, 1917, and *Daughter of the Middle Border*, 1921. These were evocative reminiscences of the building of the Midwest between the close of the Civil War and the start of the First World War. Also see Cather's novels, such as *My Antonia*, 1918.

2. Based on Eisenstein, *Walks in Warrenton*, 2002; and an oblique aerial photograph of Warrenton, ca. 1930, with annotations and sketch maps by Elizabeth FitzSimmons.

3. Margaret Schowengerdt, *Historic Sites of Warren County*, 1976, 118–39. She was Lorena Sauer's youngest sister.

4. COS, "Status and Change," 1963. For the draft with the penciled alternative, see SP, Carton 3.

5. Namier, *1848: The Revolution*, 1944.

6. Johnson, "Location of German Immigrants," 1941.

7. Gerlach, "Population Origins in Rural Missouri," 1976.

8. Duden, *Report on a Journey*, [1829] 1980.

9. Kamphoefner, *Westfalians*, 1987, esp. 70–105.

10. Haselmayer, "German Colleges," 1964; Wolff, "History of Central Wesleyan College," 1957.

11. The origin of "Ortwin" is unknown, but may have come from the Westphalian humanist theologian Ortwin Gratius (1475–1542).

12. *Warrenton Banner*, 30 Aug. 1918.

13. COS, "Geography of the Ozark Highland," 1915, v.

14. McClelland, *State, Society, and University*, 1980, 307–8.

15. *Warrenton College Star*, 9 June 1900.

16. Smith, "Geography in Germany," 1902, 430, 426–27.

17. COS to Mother, 16 Aug. 1929; Jonathan Sauer to MW, pers. comm., May 2002.

18. *Warrenton Banner*, 21 Aug. 1901.

19. COS to Parents, 19 Jan., 2 Feb. 1913, 2 Aug. 1914.

20. COS to Lorena, 18 Aug. 1913.

21. Winifred Hess, pers. comm. to MW, Aug. 2003.

22. Diary of COS (hereafter Diary), 6 Mar. 1907.

23. COS to Lorena, 10 Dec. 1919.

24. Diary, 1 Mar. 1908.

25. Diary, 20 June 1907; COS to Mother, 6 Feb. 1933; Diary, 20 Apr. 1907.

26. Diary, 17 June 1907; COS to Parents, 21 May 1913; COS to Lorena, 25 Nov. 1909; Diary, 28 June 1908.

27. Diary, 20 June, 21 May, 28 June, 8 July, 17 Sept., 12 Dec. 1907, 27 Jan., 20 Mar. 1908.

28. Diary, 20 Nov. 1907; *Pulse*, 1908; SP, Bader to COS, 1 July 1966.

29. COS, letter to *Landscape*, 1960.

30. COS to Mother, 13 May 1928.

31. COS to Mother, 29 May 1939. On German immigration, Warrenton, Central Wesleyan College, and Sauer's early years, see Kenzer, "Milieu," 1985; Kenzer, "Like Father, Like Son," 1987.

2. Graduate Studies and New Places, 1908–1915

1. COS to Lorena, 26 May 1910.

2. COS to Parents, 14 Nov. 1909. "Stille Nacht" was the carol "Silent Night"; the

others were musical settings of Heine's "Die Lorelei" (1823) and Goethe's "Heiden-röslein" ("The Heath Rose," 1770), the line quoted being "A young boy saw a wild rose growing."

3. COS to Parents, 19 Nov. 1909, 14 Aug. 1910, 10 Sept. 1909; COS to Lorena, 8 Oct. 1917; COS to Mother, 13 May 1928.

4. COS to Parents, 4 Mar. 1910.

5. COS to Lorena, 12 Nov. 1908.

6. COS to Parents, 27 Jan., 8 Feb. 1908.

7. COS to Lorena, 24 Mar. 1909.

8. COS to Parents, 27 Jan. 1908.

9. COS to Parents, 14 Feb. 1909.

10. COS to Parents, 20 Feb., 16 Mar., 22 Mar. 1909.

11. On Sauer's time at Northwestern, see Kenzer, "Carl O. Sauer," 1985.

12. COS to Parents, 10 Mar. 1909; SP, COS to Jackson, 24 June 1960; COS to Parents, 28 Apr. 1909.

13. COS to Parents, 1 Dec. 1909, 10 Mar., 20 Feb. 1908; COS to Lorena, 22 Oct. 1909; COS to Parents, 10 Sept., 21 Jan. 1909; COS, "On the Background of Geography," 1967, 70.

14. See Pattison, "Rollin Salisbury," 1981.

15. Chamberlin and Salisbury, *Driftless Area,* 1885.

16. COS to Lorena, 11 Oct. 1909; COS, "Background of Geography," 1967, 69, 70; COS to Parents, 10 Sept., 15 Oct. 1909.

17. COS to Parents, 15 Oct. 1909; COS, "Background of Geography," 1967, 69; COS to Parents, 10 Sept. 1909.

18. COS to Lorena, 11 Oct., 22 Oct. 1910.

19. COS to Lorena, 10 Jan., 7 Jan., 13 May 1910.

20. Doing research for Barrows, Sauer first came across Van Hise's *Conservation of Natural Resources,* 1910; the works of the French geographer Elisée Reclus; and studies of American resources such as Gannett's *Report of the National Conservation Commission,* 1908.

21. COS to Parents, 10 Sept., 19 Nov., 1 Dec. 1909, 7 Oct. 1910; SP, COS to Willits, 16 Jan. 1944.

22. G. J. Martin, "John Paul Goode," 1984.

23. COS, "Ellen Churchill Semple," 1934; Colby, "Ellen Churchill Semple," 1933; Bushong, "Ellen Churchill Semple," 1984.

24. Fitzpatrick, *History's Memory,* 2002, 76–77; Wanklyn, *Friedrich Ratzel,* 1961, 30–33.

25. Semple, "Anglo-Saxons of the Kentucky Mountains," 1901; Semple, *American History and Its Geographic Conditions,* 1903; and Semple, *Geography of the Mediterranean Region,* 1931.

26. COS to Parents, 7 Jan. 1910; COS, "Background of Geography," 1967, 71; COS to McDermott, 5 Nov. 1970 (MW thanks Ronald Grim, then at the Library of Congress, for a copy of this letter).

27. Roscher, *Principles of Political Economy*, [1854] 2009; Bushong, "Ellen Churchill Semple," 1984, 89; COS to Mother, 6 Apr. 1931.

28. COS to Parents, 28 Jan., 4 Mar. 1910; COS, "Background of Geography," 1967, 71; COS, "Formative Years of Ratzel," 1971; COS to Parents, 22 Oct. 1910.

29. COS to Parents, 28 Jan. 1910; COS to Lorena, 10 Sept. 1909.

30. COS to Lorena, 22 Oct., 10 Dec. 1909; COS to Parents, 8 Dec. 1909.

31. COS to Parents, 15 Jan. 1910; COS to Lorena, 9 Feb. 1910.

32. COS to Lorena, 30 Mar., 21 Apr., 28 Apr., 5 May, 20 May 1910.

33. COS to Parents, 10 July 1910; COS to Lorena, 8 July 1910.

34. COS to Parents, 11 Dec., 27 Oct., 4 Dec. 1910.

35. COS, *Geography of the Upper Illinois Valley*, 1916.

36. COS to Parents, 13 Feb., 6 Mar., 8 May 1911, 21 July 1912, 17 Aug. 1913; COS, Cady, and Cowles, *Starved Rock State Park*, 1918.

37. COS to Parents, 24 July 1910. Most of this passage was in English, which he always lapsed into when he felt very strongly about something. COS to Lorena, 24 July 1910.

38. COS to Parents, 3 Dec. 1910.

39. COS to Parents, 22 Oct., 27 Oct, 4 Dec. 1910.

40. COS to Lorena, 27 Nov. 1910; COS to Parents, 1 May 1911.

41. COS to Parents, 16 Mar., 22 Mar. 1909.

42. COS to Lorena, 3 Jan., 22 Oct. 1910, 4 Nov. 1909, 6 June, 27 Jan., 28 Feb. 1910.

43. COS to Parents, 12 Mar. 1910. He later said that the money from the book (*Educational Opportunities in Chicago*, 1911) was essential to supporting himself at the university. SP, COS to Fejos, 17 Sept. 1955.

44. COS to Parents, 2 Mar., 8 May 1911.

45. COS to Parents, 6 June, 12 Nov., 3 Dec. 1911, 7 Jan., 13 Feb. 1912.

46. SP, COS to Hewes, 24 Dec. 1955; COS to Parents, 12 Aug., 28 July 1912, 16 Feb. 1913, 25 Aug. 1912.

47. COS to Parents, 8 Sept. 1912, 19 Jan. 1913; COS to Lorena, 16 Feb., 6 Sept., 11 Sept., 21 Sept. 1913.

48. COS to Parents, 20 Aug. 1913; COS to Lorena, 16 Oct., 19 Oct. 1913.

49. COS to Lorena, 19 Nov., 24 Nov., 26 Nov. 1913

50. COS to Lorena, 23 Nov., 28 Nov., 3 Dec., 1 Dec. 1913.

51. COS to Lorena, 25 Aug., 27 Oct., 2 Nov. 1913.

52. COS to Parents, 5 Dec., 9 Dec. 1913; Elizabeth FitzSimmons to MW, pers. comm., n.d.

53. COS to Atwood, 3 June 1914; reproduced in Berman, "Distinctly Professional," 1988, 36. Atwood was an early influence, but later Sauer became critical, rating him a "nit-wit." COS to Mother, 25 Oct. 1930.

54. COS to Parents, 4 Jan., 11 Jan. 1914. Most scholars now doubt that Roger Williams lived in the house Sauer mentioned, which was probably built later in the seventeenth century.

55. COS to Parents, 25 Jan., 12 Apr., 17 May, 27 May 1914; Huntington, "Memoir of Sumner Webster Cushing," 1921.

56. COS to Parents, 11 Jan., 18 Jan., 1 Feb., 15 May 1914.

57. COS to Parents, 11 Jan., 1 Feb., 24 Apr., 7 June 1914.

58. COS to Parents, 18 Jan., 27 May 1914. On the elm and its decline, see Campanella, *Republic of Shade*, 2003.

59. Bowman and Huntington were outstanding geographers in entirely different ways. Martin, *Ellsworth Huntington*, 1973; Martin, *Life and Thought of Isaiah Bowman*, 1980; COS, "Geography and the Gerrymander," 1918.

60. SP, COS to J. R. Smith, 15 Nov. 1948.

61. The literature on the "hillmen," or "hillbillies," as they were commonly known, is vast. Harold Bell Wright romanticized the rough hill life in his novel *Shepherd of the Hills*, 1907. See also Rayburn, *Ozark Country*, 1941; Miller, "Ozark Culture Region," 1968.

62. COS to Lorena, early Sept., 25 Sept., 15 Sept. 1914. For the French and German traditions, see Cozzens, "Conservation in German Settlements," 1943; Carrière, *Tales from the French Folklore*, 1937.

63. COS to Lorena, early Sept., 15 Sept., 1 Oct. 1914.

64. COS to Lorena, 15 Sept., 30 Oct., 2 Nov., 3 Nov., 30 Oct. 1914. See COS, *Geography of the Ozark Highland*, 1920, ix and vii; COS, "Homestead and Community," 1962, 1963. For a recent assessment, see Ketchell, *Holy Hills of the Ozarks*, 2007, 132–34, 256n8.

65. COS to Lorena, 15 Oct. 1914.

66. COS to Lorena, 1 Nov., mid Nov., 5 Nov., 15 Nov. 1915. Semple had been active on his behalf. SP, Semple to COS, 16 July 1916.

67. COS, "Geography of the Ozark Highland," 1915; published 1920 with same title.

68. COS to Lorena, 6 Dec., 8 Dec., 25 Nov., 14 Dec. 1915.

3. Michigan, 1916–1923

1. COS to Lorena, 7 Oct. 1917.

2. COS to Lorena, 6 Oct. 1917.

3. COS to Parents, 13 Feb. 1916.

4. SP, COS to James, 9 Nov. 1951; James, "University of Michigan Field Station," 1983; Karan, "Regional Studies in Kentucky," 1983; James and Mather, "Role of Periodic Field Conferences," 1977.

5. During the first year a student arrived in his flashy $5,000 Mercer, "the wonder of the countryside." COS to Lorena, 4 July 1921.

6. Karan, "Regional Studies in Kentucky," 1983.

7. COS to Lorena, 4 July 1921; James, "University of Michigan Field Station," 1983, 73–74.

8. Wittke, *German-Americans*, 1936. For similar campaigns against prominent German Americans, see Rodgers, *Mencken*, 2005, 175–89.

9. Conzen, "German-Americans," 1985; Tolzmann, *German-American Experience*, 2000, 232–95; Luebke, *Bonds of Loyalty*, 1974.

10. COS to Mother, 3 May 1922.

11. COS to Lorena, 11 Nov. 1914.

12. COS to Parents, 15 Jan. 1915.

13. COS to Parents, 7 Feb. 1915.

14. COS to Parents, 6 Aug. 1914.

15. COS to Mother, 12 Apr. 1917.

16. Tolzmann, *German-American Experience*, 2000, 273.

17. COS to Mother, 12 Apr. 1917; COS to Lorena, 7 Oct. 1917. "Hyphenated American" was a disparaging term much used by Theodore Roosevelt in 1909. After 1915 it was applied almost exclusively to German Americans.

18. "Prof. Hobbs spoke of you in very glowing terms and has a high estimate of your ability. I told him that yours was one of the finest minds that [I] had ever come across in my classes." SP, Semple to COS, 16 July 1918.

19. COS to Mother, 2 Apr. 1922.

20. COS to Mother, 3 May 1922.

21. COS, "Man's Influence," 1916; Fischer, "Mensch als geologischer Faktor," 1915.

22. COS, quoted in Visher, "Rollin D. Salisbury," 1953, 6.

23. COS, *Geography of the Upper Illinois Valley*, 1916, 15, 28.

24. COS to Parents, 20 Aug. 1910.

25. COS, Cady, and Cowles, *Starved Rock*, 1918, 59–66; COS to Parents, 8 May 1911.

26. COS, *Geography of the Ozark Highland*, 1920, viii.

27. COS, *Geography of the Ozark Highland*, 1920, vii–ix.

28. COS, *Geography of the Pennyroyal*, 1927, ix–x.

29. Martis, "Original Gerrymander," 2008.

30. COS, "Geography and the Gerrymander," 1918, 404, 412–14.

31. Morrill, "Ideal and Reality in Reapportionment," 1973; Morrill, "Electoral Geography and Gerrymandering," 1999; Iyer and Gaskins, *Redistricting and Congressional Control*, 2012.

32. Steer, *Lumber Production*, 1948.

33. Sargent, *Report on the Forests*, 1884, 550; Williams, *Americans and Their Forests*, 1989, 193–237.

34. COS, "Proposal of an Agricultural Survey," 1917, 79–86. The Michigan Academy was the state's major forum for scientific ideas, often referred to by policy makers and administrators. See Schmaltz, "Academia Gets Involved," 1979, 41–46.

35. COS, "Soil Classification for Michigan," 1918, 83; COS, "Mapping the Utilization," 1919.

36. COS, "Problem of Land Classification," 1921, 3. Sauer drew on his knowledge of German geographical literature. Just as he had referred to Norbert Krebs's 1912 study of the Austrian Alps in his last Michigan paper ("Proposal of an Agricultural Survey," 1917, 84), so he referred to the German *Bonitierung*, or eightfold classificatory system, in his "Land Classification" paper (4). Throughout his career, linguistic familiarity and natural inclination led him to regard German academic work as superior.

37. COS, "Problem of Land Classification," 1921, 6, 15. Clearing stumps with dynamite and huge winches cost from $20 to $60 an acre. H. Thompson and Strait, *Cost and Methods*, 1914.

38. Schmaltz, "P. S. Lovejoy," 1975, 73–74. Paul Bunyan was a super hero of Herculean physique, the popular embodiment of the North American lumberjack, a symbol of virility, physical might, ingenuity, and American enterprise. He was usually accompanied by his huge blue ox, Babe. See Bethke, "Paul Bunyan," 1983.

39. Lovejoy, "Farms v. Forests," 1919.

40. COS to Mother, 3 Mar. 1921.

41. SP, Carton 3, COS, unpublished report, "The Cut-over Lands of Michigan: A Geographic Study in Land Utilization," 1922.

42. Schmaltz, "Michigan's Land Economic Survey," 1978.

43. COS to Lorena, 4 July, 17 July 1920; Leighly, "Scholar and Colleague," 1978, 118–20.

44. COS to Mother, 2 Apr. 1922; COS to Lorena, Apr. 1922.

45. COS to Mother, 25 May 1922; SP, R. F. Holway to COS, 29 May 1921; COS to Holway, 30 May 1921; COS to J. Parsons, 22 Aug. 1959.

46. James and Mather, "Role of Periodic Field Conferences," 1977; COS to Mother, 3 May 1922.

47. SP, COS to C. Jones, 9 Nov. 1951. After Sauer left, Michigan's survey and the cutovers in the Great Lakes states became one of the most widely publicized agricultural topics in the United States. See Black and Gray, *Land Settlement and Colonization*, 1925; Sparhawk and Brush, *Economic Aspects*, 1929; Hartman and Black, *Economic Aspects*, 1931; Hartman, *State Land-Settlement Problems*, 1933.

4. Berkeley: An Insider, 1923–1941

1. SP, COS to S. Dodge, 19 Oct. 1938; COS to Mother, 27 Nov. 1927 or 1928.

2. COS, "Survey Method in Geography," 1924; COS, *Geography of the Pennyroyal*, 1927.

3. COS to Mother, 15 Feb. 1926, 3 Aug. 1921, 25 May 1922.

4. COS to Mother, 20 Sept., 24 Oct. 1924.

5. COS to Mother, 20 Sept. 1927, 10 Sept. 1928, 5 Feb. 1929, 5 Aug. 1930. His properties in 1945 were in Canalou, MO; Moweaqua, IL; Medford, OK (from his mother); Jackson, MO (from Albert?), with a gross return of $6,923. Whitewater showed no return. SP, COS to Windrem, 24 Feb. 1945.

6. COS to Mother, Thanksgiving, Nov. 1926, 18 Oct., 21 Nov. 1927, 17 Apr. 1929. He would not visit Warrenton during vacations, the only times available for fieldwork.

7. COS to Mother, 26 Jan. 1930, 21 Aug. 1927, 16 June 1929.

8. COS to Mother, Aug. 1923, 1 Feb. 1924.

9. Wolff, *History of Central Wesleyan College*, 1957; Kenzer, "Central Wesleyan College Archives," 1985. MW is indebted to Judith May-Sapko, former Archivist and Special Collections Librarian, Pickler Memorial Library, Truman State University.

10. "Moderate in opinion, punctilious in workmanship, and sane in judgment, he prepared a sound basis for the development of physical geography on the western coast." COS, "Memorial of Ruliff S. Holway," 1929.

11. "I should be very glad indeed to approach the task of building at California a teaching staff, devoted also to productive scholarship." COS to D. Barrows, 8 Mar. 1923. See Macpherson, "Preparing for the National Stage," 1987, esp. 71–75.

12. Dunbar, "Geography in the University of California," 1981, 7; Speth, "Berkeley Geography," 1981, 224.

13. COS to Mother, 21 Aug. 1927; Macpherson, "Preparing for the National Stage," 1987, 76, 80.

14. COS to Mother, Dec. n.d., 6 Sept., 20 Sept., 2 Oct. 1927.

15. COS to Mother, 21 Nov., 27 June 1927, 29 June 1928, 10 Nov., 24 Nov. 1930. When J. P. Goode congratulated Sauer, somewhat enviously, on his "great good luck" in moving to Berkeley, Sauer agreed. SP, COS to Goode, 26 Jan. 1932.

16. COS to Mother, 7 Oct., 26 Oct. 1924. See Mathewson, "Sauer South by Southwest," 1987, esp. 97–99.

17. COS to Mother, 1 Aug. 1927, 10 Sept., 22 Sept. 1928. In fact, Hoover was one of a minority against the folly of imposing crippling reparations on Germany.

18. COS to Mother, 19 Oct. 1928, 2 Oct. 1932.

19. COS to Mother, 30 Dec. 1925.

20. SP, COS to Hartshorne, 22 June 1946.

21. "The Morphology of Landscape was an early attempt to say what the common experience was in the European tradition." COS, "Fourth Dimension of Geography," 1974, 191. Of the monograph's 59 references, 38 were German, 7 French, 4 English, 2 Swedish, and 1 each from Italy and Holland. Only 6 were American, and 2 of these were to anthropologists.

22. SP, COS to Hartshorne, 22 June 1946; COS to Mother, 17 Aug. 1924.

23. Quotation is from COS, "Morphology of Landscape," 1925, 48. For Goethe's

ideas of morphology, see Williams, "Apple of My Eye," 1983, esp. 5–6; Speth, "Berkeley Geography," 1981, esp. 229–34.

24. "Morphology of Landscape" grew out of the Pennyroyal experience. SP, COS to J. R. Smith, 2 Aug. 1937.

25. COS to Mother, 9 Mar. 1929.

26. SP, COS to Hartshorne, 22 June 1946; also G. Martin, "From the Cycle of Erosion," 2003. See Penn and Lukermann, "Chorology and Landscape," 2003.

27. SP, L. Wilson to COS, 15 Apr. 1948.

28. Parsons, "Later Sauer Years," 1979, 13.

29. Dryer, review of "Morphology," 1926; SP, Hartshorne to Sauer, 18 June 1946; Williams, "Apple of My Eye," 1983, 6.

30. COS to Mother, 21 Mar. 1926.

31. Van Cleef, review of Gradmann's *Süddeutschland*, 1931; Peattie and Van Cleef, review of Früh's *Geographie der Schweiz*, 1932; COS, "Correspondence [on physical geography]," 1932, 528.

32. SP, Wrigley to COS, 15 Mar. 1932; COS to Wrigley, 22 Apr. 1932.

33. Stoddart, "Carl Sauer," 1997, 343.

34. COS to Mother, 2 Oct. 1927.

35. COS, "Fourth Dimension of Geography," 1974, 190.

36. "Salisbury was the only man in the country who enjoyed a fracas with old W.M.D. [W. Davis] and twitted the latter about having discovered the final scheme of things." COS to Kroeber, 10 July 1934, Kroeber Papers, Bancroft Library, University of California, Berkeley.

37. See Leighly, "Drifting into Geography," 1979, 7–8.

38. COS to Mother, 9 Mar. 1929.

39. Stoddart, "Carl Sauer: Geomorphologist," 1997, 353, 354, 360.

40. Bryan and Wickson, "W. Penck Method of Analysis," 1931; COS, "Land Forms in the Peninsular Range," 1929. Also see Bryan, "Retreat of Slopes," 1940.

41. SP, COS to R. J. Russell, 24 Feb. 1932; COS to Mother, n.d.

42. SP, COS to T. G. Taylor, 3 July 1932.

43. SP, COS to Calkins, 6 Dec. 1949.

44. Spencer, "Carl Sauer," 1975, 83–84. On courses taught, see Speth, "Berkeley Geography," 1981.

45. Ann Nicholls Marshall to MW, pers. comm., n.d.

46. Bruman, "Carl Sauer in Midcareer," 1987, 129, 135; Spencer, "Carl Sauer," 1975, 84; SP, COS to Suhl, 14 July 1937; COS to Sears, 20 May 1940.

47. Mikesell, "Sauer and 'Sauerology,'" 1987; personal reminiscences from David Lowenthal and David Hooson, 2001–6, as told to MW.

48. COS, *Seventeenth Century North America*, 1980, 9.

49. Constance, "With Carl Sauer in Baja California," 1987, 88; SP, COS to Bowman, 11 Oct. 1938; Mikesell, "Sauer and 'Sauerology,'" 1987, 148.

50. COS to Price, quoted in Gale, "Award," 1989.

51. SP, COS to Suhl, 19 Apr. 1932; Storm [Suhl] to COS, 4 Aug. 1943. See Zelinsky, "Women in Geography," 1973. Between 1923 and Sauer's retirement in 1957, 16 women received master's degrees in geography at Berkeley. The first female Ph.D. was Patricia McBride Bartz in 1949. See Parsons and Vonnegut, 60 Years of Berkeley Geography, 1983, 39, 154.

52. SP, Trowbridge to COS, 10 Dec. 1935; COS to Trowbridge, 18 Dec. 1935.

53. COS to Mother, 29 Jan. 1928. Whereas Americans regarded education as a "secondary matter," in "the 'old' country almost every avenue has gates that can be passed only by those who have formal educational qualifications." COS to Mother, 7 July 1929.

54. "Germany Not Seeking Conquest, says German." Moritz Julius Bonn, quoted in the New York Times, 6 Aug. 1916.

55. COS to Mother, 10 May 1933; Weidermann, Das Buch der verbrannten Bücher, 2009.

56. COS to Mother, 14 Jan. 1934.

57. SP, COS to W. Jones, 3 Dec. 1936; COS to Mother, 14 Apr. 1938; SP, COS to Bowman, 6 Apr. 1937.

58. SP, COS to May, 30 Nov. 1934; COS to Roberts, 15 Oct. 1934.

59. SP, COS to Thomas, 12 Apr. 1937; COS to G. Carter, 3 Mar. 1937[?]; Bowman to COS, 22 Aug. 1936.

60. SP, COS to Trewartha, 27 Jan. 1937; COS to Credner, 5 Dec. 1938; COS to Waibel, 24 Dec. 1937. COS to Mother, 10 Apr. 1937.

61. SP, Von Hagen to COS, 8 Sept., 27 Dec. 1940.

62. SP, COS to Pfeifer, 14 Oct. 1936; COS to S. Jones, 13 Apr., 19 Dec. 1938.

63. SP, COS to Hoover, 13 Feb. 1932; Bowman to COS, 1 Sept. 1932; COS to Bowman, 8 Sept. 1932; COS to Dodge, 4 Apr. 1932.

64. SP, COS to Blom, 20 Aug. 1934; COS to G. Carter, 31 Mar. 1936; COS to S. Dodge, 5 Nov., 26 Nov. 1936, 19 Oct. 1938; COS, "Geography: Cultural," 1931.

65. SP, Bowman to COS, 14 Feb. 1939; COS to Bowman, 2 Mar. 1939.

66. Hartshorne's book was first published by the Association of American Geographers, and so appeared to have the imprimatur of the association.

67. COS, "Foreword to Historical Geography," 1941, 4, 9, 17–23, 24; Faulkner, Requiem for a Nun, 1951, 92.

68. COS to James, 27 Mar. 1940.

69. COS, "Foreword to Historical Geography," 1941, 8–16. Clüver, Germania antiqua, 1616, and Italia antiqua, 1624; Humboldt, Political Essay, 1811–14; Meitzen, Siedelung und Agrarwesen, 1895; Peake and Fleure, Corridors of Time, 1927–56; E. G. R. Taylor, Tudor Geography, 1930, and Late Tudor, 1934.

70. COS, "Foreword to Historical Geography," 1941, 8, 24.

71. Lowenthal, *George Perkins Marsh*, 2000.

5. Larger Horizons of Place and Time: Mexico and the Southwest, 1923–1935

1. West, *Carl Sauer's Field Work*, 1979. The record of his trips is sometimes uncertain because he frequently omitted the year date; where there is doubt, they are ordered according to internal evidence.

2. COS to Lorena, 16 Feb. 1910; SP, COS to Willits, 20 Sept. 1940.

3. Spencer, quoted in West, *Carl Sauer's Field Work*, 1979, 64.

4. COS to Mother, 26 Jan. 1930; Kelly quoted in West, *Carl Sauer's Field Work*, 1979, 64.

5. COS to Mother, 10 June, 4 July 1933; SP, COS to James, 14 Aug. 1935.

6. Exceptions are COS, "Personality of Mexico," 1941, and COS, *Colima of New Spain*, 1948.

7. SP, COS to J. R. Smith, 15 Nov. 1948.

8. "As long as we had the long winter vacation we turned south because that was where the good weather was and through that back door we got into Latin American and Indian geography. Having struck good pay-dirt there we never got into California or Northwestern problems." SP, COS to S. Jones, 9 Nov. 1951.

9. COS to Mother, 30 Dec. 1925.

10. SP, COS to Meigs, 18 June 1926[?]; COS to Mother, 21 Mar. 1926.

11. COS and Meigs, "Lower California Studies," 1927.

12. Leighly, in West, *Carl Sauer's Field Work*, 1979, 36.

13. Rowe, "Alfred Louis Kroeber," 1962.

14. T. Kroeber, *Alfred Kroeber*, 1970.

15. Beals, "Kroeber, Alfred L.," 1968.

16. SP, COS to Speth, 30 June 1971, 3 Mar. 1972. See Murphy, *Robert H. Lowie*, 1972; and Lowie's memoir, *Robert H. Lowie*, 1959. Kramer, "Eduard Hahn," 1967.

17. COS and Brand, "Pueblo Sites," 1930, 416.

18. COS to Mother, 9 Mar., 7 Apr. 1929; Meyer, *The Cristero Rebellion*, 1976.

19. COS to Mother, 16 June 1929.

20. COS to Mother, 6 Nov. 1929.

21. COS to Mother, 26 Jan. 1930; reminiscences of Gottfried Pfeifer, in West, *Carl Sauer's Field Work*, 1979, 50–51.

22. COS, "Thirty-two Ancient Sites," 1930.

23. COS to Mother, 21 Mar., 13 Mar. 1930.

24. COS and Brand, "Prehistoric Settlements of Sonora," 1931, 67, 71–74; Turney, *Prehistoric Irrigation*, 1929, 72–73. Recent research refutes Sauer and Brand's conclusions about the nonagricultural use of the *trincheras*. By 1970 thousands more were found: many were agricultural terraces, others remnant urban structures with reservoirs,

ball courts, and houses. Doolittle, *Cultivated Landscapes*, 2000, 302–6; Fish, Fish, and Vallalpando, *Trincheras*, 2007.

25. COS to Mother, 1 June 1930.

26. COS to Mother, 12 Mar., 10 June 1931.

27. COS to Mother, 10 June, 5 July 1931.

28. COS to Mother, 5 July, 27 July 1931.

29. COS to Mother, 5 July 1930. Sauer was particularly entranced by the seventeenth-century Jesuit Father Caisag, son of a Croatian nobleman, who established two settlements for several thousand Indians in Baja California, and "by simple strength of character and devotion built churches, planted fields and gardens, constructed houses and hospitals" where none had existed before.

30. Las Casas, *Historia de Las Indias*, [1527–64] 1961, 2:549.

31. SP, COS to Leighly, 27 Aug. 1931; COS to Mother, 27 July 1931.

32. COS to Mother, 17 Aug. 1931.

33. SP, COS to Leighly, 5 Nov. 1931; COS to Mother, 26 Sept., 19 Nov. 1931.

34. COS to Mother, 16 Aug. 1929.

35. COS and Brand, "Prehistoric Settlements of Sonora," 1931; COS and Brand, *Aztatlán*, 1932; COS, *Road to Cíbola*, 1932.

36. COS and Brand, *Aztatlán*, 1932, 43, 61–62.

37. SP, COS to Jackling, 17 Oct. 1939.

38. COS, "Discovery of New Mexico," 1937, 270; COS to Mother, 28 Feb. 1932. In later years Sauer published three more articles on Spanish exploration in the American Southwest, all essentially spin-offs from *The Road to Cíbola*: "Spanish Expeditions," 1935; "Discovery of New Mexico," 1937; "Credibility," 1941.

39. SP, COS to L. Wright, 6 Dec. 1932; COS to J. R. Smith, 2 Feb. 1939.

40. COS to Mother, 1 June, 10 June 1933. More than 30 years later, his last doctoral student, Harry Sawatzky, worked on these colonies. Sawatzky, *They Sought a Country*, 1971.

41. COS to Mother, 10 June 1933.

42. Sapper, "Die Zahl und die Volksdichte," 1924, 100; Rivet, Stresser-Péan, and Loukotka, "Langue américaines," 1924, 661; Spinden, "Population of Ancient America," 1928, 660.

43. A. L. Kroeber, "Native American Population," 1934, 24; Steward, "Native Population," 1949, 656.

44. COS, *Distribution of Aboriginal Tribes*, 1934; A. L. Kroeber, *Uto-Aztecan Languages*, 1934.

45. A. L. Kroeber, *Cultural and Natural Areas*, [1939] 1963, 177.

46. E.g., Cook and Borah, *Essays in Population History*, 1971–79; Dobyns, "Estimating Aboriginal American Population," 1966. The history of calculations of population size

is reviewed in Denevan, *Native Population of the Americas*, [1976] 1992, 1–4. For Sauer's contribution, see Denevan, "Carl Sauer and Native American," 1996. See Henige, *Numbers from Nowhere*, 1998, for a conservative critique.

47. Keen, "Recent Writing," 1985, 163.

6. The Frontiers of Knowledge

1. SP, COS to J. R. Smith, 2 Feb. 1939.

2. Chaucer, "Parliament of Fowls," [ca. 1380] 1957, 310.

3. COS to Mother, 30 Nov. 1930, 24 Apr. 1931.

4. See Kramer, "Eduard Hahn," 1967.

5. COS to Mother, 28 Apr. 1935; West, *Carl Sauer's Fieldwork*, 1979, 80–81; Kelly, *Excavations at Chametla*, 1938.

6. COS to Mother, 26 June 1935; COS to Elizabeth Sauer, 31 May 1935.

7. COS, "American Agricultural Origins," 1936, 291–92, 294, 296.

8. SP, COS to McBryde, 9 Oct. 1935.

9. SP, COS to Alsberg, 23 Oct. 1935.

10. SP, COS to Alsberg, 26 Dec. 1935.

11. SP, COS to Alsberg, 6 Nov., 26 Nov. 1935.

12. Sauer also unsuccessfully proposed Vavilov for the prestigious Hitchcock Visiting Professorship at Berkeley. SP, COS to Kofoid, 15 Oct. 1935; COS to C. B. Hutchinson, 28 Apr. 1936; COS to Kidder, 31 Aug. 1936. On Vavilov, see Nablan, *Where Our Food Comes From*, 2009.

13. SP, COS to Nash, 23 Mar. 1939.

14. Hays, *Conservation*, 1959, 1–5; COS to Parents, 5 Apr. 1914.

15. SP, COS to Vance, 1948.

16. McGee, *Proceedings of a Conference*, 1909.

17. COS, *Geography of the Upper Illinois Valley*, 1916, 140, 143.

18. Brunhes, "Specific Characteristics," 1913; Lowenthal, *George Perkins Marsh*, 2000, 204, 509n31; Koelsch, "The Legendary 'Rediscovery' of George Perkins Marsh," 2012, 510–11; Lowenthal, "Marsh and Sauer," 2013, 410–11.

19. COS, "Man's Influence," 1916; Woeikof, "De l'influence de l'homme," 1901; Lucas, "Man as a Geographical Agency," 1914; Fischer, "Der Mensch als geologischer Faktor," 1915. See Whitaker, "World View of Destruction," 1940, 149–53.

20. COS, "Notes on the Geographic Significance," 1922, 189.

21. COS, *Geography of the Pennyroyal*, 1927, 181.

22. COS, "Recent Developments in Cultural Geography," 1927, 188–89; Brunhes, *Human Geography*, [1910] 1920; Friedrich, "Wesen und geographische Verbreitung," 1904. See Costanza, *Ecological Economics*, 1991, 121–22.

23. SP, COS, "Grassland Climax," 1950, 18; COS to Wade, 5 Jan. 1946.

24. SP, COS to Wickson, 13 Apr. 1936; COS, "Prospect for Redistribution," 1937, 8.

25. SP, Ciriacy-Wantrup to COS, 2 Mar. 1939.

26. SP, COS to Zimmermann, 2 Nov. 1937; COS, "Destructive Exploitation," 1938, 494, 499.

27. COS, "Theme of Plant and Animal Destruction," 1938, 765–66, 773, 775.

28. COS, "March of Agriculture," [1940] 1981, 56.

29. SP, COS to A. Meyer, 8 Nov. 1934.

30. SP, COS to Spethman, 21 Aug. 1934; Jordan, *Machine-Age Ideology*, 1994, 1–10, 232–52, 255–79.

31. SP, COS to Willits, 9 Dec. 1935; Willits to COS, 11 Dec. 1935. See Goodrich, *Migration and Economic Opportunity*, 1936, vi, 268. Tugwell's Farm Resettlement Administration was a ham-fisted disaster, but his Farm Security Administration photography project enabled Dorothea Lange and other photographers to record vividly the poverty and social upheaval of mid–1930s rural America, a concern of Sauer's. Lange and her husband, Paul Taylor, a radical economist at Berkeley, were frequent dinner guests of the Sauers.

32. SP, COS to D. Young, 23 Sept. 1936.

33. COS, "Regional Reality," SP, Carton 3, Box 3. This address remained unpublished until Kenzer's 1984 edition. Kenzer's commentary says the address was never given, but Sauer's letters indicate otherwise. See COS to Mother, 20 Dec. 1936, 6 Jan. 1937.

34. COS, "Regional Reality," [1936] 1984, 38, 40.

35. SP, Box 3, MS, "Theme of Plant and Animal Destruction," 1938. The prefatory outburst is not in the published version.

36. COS, "Regional Reality," [1936] 1984, 46.

37. SP, COS to Appleton, 12 May 1937.

38. SP, COS to Carter, 3 Jan. 1938. The sociologist Bruno Lasker had inquired about maps of the Pacific. "If social scientists are getting to the point where maps are important to them," replied Sauer, "I shall personally take a more cheerful view of the social sciences." SP, COS to Lasker, 4 Jan. 1938.

39. SP, COS to Stacy May, 8 May 1938.

40. SP, COS to May, 8 Feb. 1938; COS to E. Wilson, 15 Feb. 1938.

41. SP, COS to Aydelotte, 6 June 1938; COS to J. R. Smith, 19 Apr. 1938.

7. "The Great God West of the Sierras"

1. SP, W. Jones to COS, 18 Nov. 1937.

2. At the AAG meeting in 1937, "Glenn Trewartha informed Hartshorne that Carl Sauer had stated 'if you could not see it, then it was not geography.' Hartshorne replied, 'It is time to question this great god west of the Sierras.'" G. Martin, "Richard Hartshorne," 1994, 484; interview of Hartshorne by Martin; Martin to WMD, pers. comm., 2012. For other accounts, see SP, Kniffen to COS, 11 Feb. 1938; McBryde to COS, 13 Jan. 1938; Thornthwaite to COS, 7 Jan. 1938; W. Varney to COS, 17 Jan. 1938.

Shortly thereafter, Sauer opposed Hartshorne's bid for a Guggenheim Fellowship on the philosophy of geography: "He did good work in his Silesian studies and if he were now applying for a tangible piece of research he might have a case; as it is his present proposal could only lead to a superficial work." SP, Carton 7, Minutes of Guggenheim meeting, 20–21 Jan. 1938.

3. SP, COS to Meigs, 27 Jan. 1938; J. Parsons, "Carl Sauer's Vision," 1996.

4. SP, Vandenberg to COS, 13 May 1948; COS to Vandenberg, 18 May 1948; COS to Kenny, 19 Jan., 7 Mar. 1950.

5. SP, COS to Alsberg, 29 Jan. 1934; Bowman to COS, 26 Jan. 1934; COS, "Preliminary Report," 1934. The title of this section of the chapter is from Faulkner, *Requiem for a Nun*, 1951, 235.

6. SP, Bowman to COS, 15 June 1934; Sauer, "Preliminary Report," 1934. The Soil Erosion Service became the Soil Conservation Service in 1935.

7. SP, Lowdermilk to COS, 28 June 1934; Bennett to COS, 18 July 1934; COS to Dosch, 4 Nov. 1937. Lowdermilk's daughter, Winifred Hess, later became Sauer's secretary.

8. SP, Thornthwaite to Bowman, 13 Aug. 1936.

9. SP, COS to Colton, 8 Oct. 1934; COS to Bowman, 20 Nov. 1934.

10. SP, Thornthwaite to COS, 10 Dec. 1935; COS to Thornthwaite, 7 Feb. 1936.

11. SP, Bryan to Bowman, 28 July 1936; see, e.g., Bryan, *Papago Country, Arizona*, 1925.

12. SP, Thornthwaite to Bowman, 13 Aug. 1936; Bowman to Thornthwaite, 15 Aug. 1936; Bryan to Bowman, 26 Aug. 1936.

13. SP, COS to F. Morris, 9 Jan. 1936; COS to Raup, 15 Dec. 1934; COS, "American Agricultural Origins," 1936.

14. SP, Thornthwaite to COS, 22 Nov., 9 Dec. 1935; COS to F. Morris, 9 Jan. 1936; COS to Thornthwaite, 13 Jan. 1936.

15. SP, Gladstone to COS, 28 Feb. 1936; Thornthwaite to COS, 20 Mar. 1936; Ireland to COS, 7 Apr. 1936; COS to Ireland, 13 Apr. 1936; COS to Thornthwaite, 9 Apr. 1936.

16. SP, COS to Thornthwaite, 30 June 1936.

17. SP, appended to Thornthwaite to COS, 3 July 1936; COS to Mother, 4 July 1936.

18. SP, Phyllis Morris to MW, pers. comm., 17 Mar. 1981. Two articles were written by F. Grave Morris: "Soil Erosion," 1937, and "Environment and Regional Development," 1937.

19. Lyell, *Second Visit*, 1849, 25–29; SP, COS to Thornthwaite, 20 July 1936.

20. For other results of the Piedmont project, see Sharpe's *Landslides*, 1938; Ireland, Sharpe, and Eargle, *Principles*, 1939; SP, Thornthwaite to COS, 7 Jan. 1938. In the same year, Sam Dicken, another Sauer ex-student, studied erosion in the karst lands of Kentucky; see SP, COS to Dicken, 4 July 1936. See Stoddart, "Carl Sauer," 1997, 366–70.

21. Trimble, *Man-Induced Soil Erosion*, 1974; Trimble, "Perspectives on the History," 1985; Helms, "Soil and Southern History," 2000.

22. SP, COS to Moe, 31 Oct. 1935.

23. COS to Mother, Jan. 1936; SP, COS to Moe, 30 Jan. 1936.

24. SP, COS to Canning, 10 Mar. 1938. "The old man" was a phrase Sauer used frequently. "The old man is getting dull—wait until you find out what senility is." SP, COS to Mosk, 26 Nov. 1935. He was merely 46 at the time.

25. SP, COS to Moe, 26 Mar. 1936, 8 Dec. 1937.

26. SP, COS to Moe, 2 Apr. 1936. Said to be "the last man who knew everything," Veblen, born to Norwegian immigrant parents, wrote seminal books on class, the American way of life, and the disadvantages of affluence. A witty critic of capitalism long dismissed by mainstream economists as a wacky eccentric, he coined the phrase "conspicuous consumption." Jorgensen and Jorgensen, *Thorstein Veblen*, 1999, 241, 255; Fine, "Social Construction," 1994.

27. SP, COS to Moe, 31 Mar. 1938.

28. SP, Willits to COS, 11 Dec. 1933. On Willits, see Fisher, *Fundamental Development*, 1993, 52–58.

29. See Constance, "Berkeley and the Latin American Connection," 1978; SP, COS to Blom, 20 Aug. 1934.

30. Parsons, "Carl Sauer's Vision," 1996, 379; SP, COS to May, 30 July 1937, 8 Feb. 1938.

31. SP, COS to Wilder, 31 July 1940. Curator of the Jeanine Taylor Folk Art Museum in Colorado Springs, Wilder had raised Sauer's awareness of the fragility of folk art in a modernizing world.

32. SP, COS to Dobzhansky, 13 Oct. 1945.

33. SP, COS to Willits, 23 Sept. 1940.

34. SP, COS to Kelly, 12 Nov. 1940; COS to Moe, 22 Oct., 24 Oct., 26 Oct. 1940.

35. Guggenheim later established a separate fellowships program for Latin Americans.

36. SP, Willits to COS, 8 Feb., 7 Mar., 21 Apr. 1941; Willits to Sproul, 8 Aug. 1941; Sproul to Willits, 14 Aug. 1941. In addition to Sauer's grant, Rockefeller funded Paul Taylor's studies of Mexican labor migration.

37. RFA, Willits to W. Stewart, 9 Mar. 1942; Memorandum, Willits to Staff, 2 Apr. 1942; Willits to COS, 25 June 1942. MW does not discuss the letters, but all 24 are reproduced in full in West, *Andean Reflections*, 1982.

38. SP, COS to Willits, 25 Aug. 1942, "Letter 26: A Summary Statement," in West, *Andean Reflections*, 127–32.

39. SP, Quam to COS, 7 Nov. 1951. See West, *Carl Sauer's Fieldwork*, 1979, 150–55.

8. The Farthest Corridors of Human Time

"The farthest corridors of time," a phrase in Sauer's "Foreword to Historical Geography," 1941, 13, was taken from Peake and Fleure's 10-volume *Corridors of Time*, 1927–56, which Sauer admired greatly. Fleure stayed several weeks with the Sauers in 1945. SP, Fleure to COS, 28 July 1945.

1. SP, COS to Treanor, 13 Sept. 1932.

2. SP, COS to E. Anderson, 29 July 1943; COS to Wrigley, 29 Jan. 1943. See Jennings, *Foundations*, 1988, 50–57, 192.

3. See West, *Andean Reflections*, 1982.

4. SP, COS to E. Anderson, 27 Oct. 1941; Anderson to COS, 5 Nov. 1941.

5. SP, COS to E. Anderson, 10 Oct. 1941; Anderson to COS, 13 Oct. 1941.

6. SP, COS to E. Anderson, 10 Nov. 1941, 20 Aug., 31 Aug. 1942.

7. SP, COS to Mason, 10 Aug. 1943.

8. SP, COS to E. Anderson, 8 Oct. 1942. Mangelsdorf and Anderson had been roommates at Harvard.

9. Mangelsdorf and Reeves, *Origin of Indian Corn*, 1939.

10. This complex progression is documented in Kleinman, "Edgar Anderson," 1999.

11. SP, COS to E. Anderson, 8 Oct. 1942; Anderson to COS, 10 Oct., 16 Nov. 1942; Anderson, "What We Do Not Know," 1968; COS, "Cultivated Plants," 1950, 491–92.

12. Kleinman, "His Own Synthesis," 1999.

13. SP, COS to E. Anderson, 14 Nov. 1942.

14. SP, E. Anderson to COS, 7 July 1943; COS to Ekholm, 26 Apr. 1943.

15. SP, COS to E. Anderson, 22 July, 10 Aug. 1943; COS to Bruman, 17 May 1944; COS, "Maize into Europe," 1962. On possible evidence for pre-Columbian maize in India, see Johannessen, "Early Maize in India?," 2003.

16. E. Anderson, *Plants, Man, and Life*, 1945, v, 91; Kleinman, "His Own Synthesis," 1999, 314. Anderson dedicated his *Plants, Man, and Life* to Orland E. White, Oakes Ames, and Carl Sauer, "who turned my attention in this direction."

17. COS, "Geographic Sketch," 1944.

18. SP, COS to LeCron, 22 May 1943.

19. SP, COS to Floyd, 19 Nov. 1943.

20. SP, COS to G. H. Smith, 19 Apr. 1938; COS to Maddox, 15 Sept. 1948; COS to [Percy] Bidwell, 9 Dec. 1952; COS to Roberts, 7 Dec. 1945; COS to Bronk, 28 Apr. 1952.

21. SP, Steward to COS, 1 June 1943; COS to Steward, 11 June 1943; COS, "Cultivated Plants," 1950; see Gade, "Carl Sauer," 1999, 189–95. COS, "Geography of South America," 1950.

22. West, *Carl Sauer's Fieldwork*, 1979, 114–22.

23. SP, COS to Kelly, Apr. 1945.

24. SP, COS to Wade, 5 Jan. 1946.

25. COS, "Geographic Sketch," 1944; SP, COS to Wrigley, 16 May 1944.

26. SP, Wrigley to COS, 23 May, 24 July 1944; COS to Wrigley, 17 July 1944; Wrigley to COS, 6 Sept. 1944.

27. The origin and route was first suggested in 1590 by the Spanish cleric José de Acosta, *Natural and Moral History*, [1590] 2002, 63, 71. See Fiedel, "Peopling of the New

World," 2000, 39. For ice extent and vegetation see Adams, Foote, and Otte, "Could Pre-Glacial Maximum Humans Have Existed?," 2001.

28. Delicately fluted spear points alongside mammoth bones were identified at Blackwater Draw, near Clovis, New Mexico, in 1949 at a level below Folsom points, dated between 12,900 and 13,200 BP. Until recently, it was customary to talk of Clovis as the earliest Americans; Sellards, *Early Man in America*, 1952.

29. COS, "Geographic Sketch," 1944, 550, 539, 531, 536; COS, "Time and Place," 1956.

30. Oscar Schmieder, who worked briefly in Sauer's department, had come to this conclusion nearly 20 years earlier; see Schmieder, "The Pampa," 1927. Sauer must have benefited from this work.

31. SP, COS to Wrigley, 19 Oct. 1944; Romer to COS, 23 Oct. 1944; P. S. Martin, *Twilight of the Mammoths*, 2005; SP, COS to Eiseley, 13 Nov. 1944; Rawitscher to COS, 30 Jan. 1946. See COS, "Grassland Climax," 1950.

32. SP, COS to Roberts, 7 Dec. 1945. But also see COS, "Grassland Climax," 1950.

33. See, e.g., Parfit, "Dawn of Humans," 2000; Flannery, "Who Came First?," 2003; Adams, Foote, and Otte, "Could Pre-Glacial Maximum Humans Have Existed?," 2001; Stanford and Bradley, *Across Atlantic Ice*, 2012.

34. SP, COS to Roberts, 7 Dec. 1945.

35. SP, COS to McBryde, 14 Feb. 1946. Archbishop Ussher had calculated the date of Creation in the book of Genesis as being 4004 BC.

36. COS, "Early Relations," 1947; COS, "Environment and Culture," 1948.

37. During this period Sauer also produced *Colima of New Spain*, 1948. This provides an additional chapter on the destruction of the Indies and is his final substantial foray into Spanish Mexican history.

38. Haury to West, 2 July, 16 July 1979; quoted in West, *Carl Sauer's Fieldwork*, 1979, 124–26.

39. SP, COS to Roberts, 31 Jan. 1946; COS to McBryde, 14 Feb. 1946; Meigs, "Vegetation on Shellmounds," 1938.

40. SP, COS to Wrigley, 22 Oct. 1946.

41. West, *Carl Sauer's Fieldwork*, 1979, 129.

42. Howel Williams, quoted in West, *Carl Sauer's Fieldwork*, 1979, 131; also in Constance, "Berkeley," 1978, 28. See Constance, "With Carl Sauer," [1986] 2011.

43. Hammond to West, 10 Jan. 1979; quoted in West, *Carl Sauer's Fieldwork*, 1979, 132.

44. SP, COS to C. L. Hubbs, 3 Apr., 24 Apr. 1947; COS to Sefton, 7 Dec. 1948.

45. West, *Carl Sauer's Fieldwork*, 1979, 145.

46. SP, COS to Gladwin, 29 Oct. 1946.

47. Straus, "Solutrean Settlement," 2000; Gugliotta, "First Americans," 2013; Stanford and Bradley, *Across Atlantic Ice*, 2012, 188, 247.

48. R. Taylor, "Beginnings of Radiocarbon Dating," 1985; Libby, Anderson, and Arnold, "Age Determination," 1949.

49. SP, COS to McCown, 26 Jan. 1950.

50. SP, COS to Orr, 7 Dec. 1954; Orr to COS, 13 Dec. 1954; COS to Fay, 2 Aug. 1954.

51. COS, "End of the Ice Age," 1957. Sauer's idea of early settlement in Alaska is refuted by Bever, who found that "none of the sites in Alaska are significantly older than early sites elsewhere in the New World." Bever, "Too Little, Too Late?," 2006, 615.

52. Apparently SP, Sauer to W. Taylor, late 1961.

53. Pringle, "1st Americans," 2011, 38; Pringle, "Texas Site Confirms," 2011.

54. SP, Kimble to COS, 6 June 1951; COS to Kimble, 17 July, 19 Oct. 1951. Kimble had been a visiting professor in Sauer's department in the fall of 1947.

55. SP, Light to COS, 26 Feb. 1952; COS to Broek, 10 Nov. 1952.

56. COS, *Agricultural Origins*, 1952, 23.

57. Harris, "Farther Reaches of Human Time," 2002. Also, Gade, "Carl Sauer," 1999, 207–8.

58. COS, *Agricultural Origins*, 1952, 104.

9. *"The Heart of Human Geography"*

1. SP, COS to Kelly, 6 July, 5 May 1944.

2. The Sauers lived in the house until their deaths in 1975.

3. SP, COS to Kelly, 19 Nov. 1947 or 1949; Elizabeth FitzSimmons, pers. comm. to MW, n.d.

4. SP, COS to Cumberland, 5 Oct. 1946.

5. Parsons, "Later Sauer Years," 1979, 13.

6. Broek, *Santa Clara Valley*, 1932.

7. SP, COS to Bowman, 21 May 1944.

8. Winifred Hess, pers. comm. to MW, 2002; SP, COS to Bowman, 30 Mar. 1937; Parsons, "Later Sauer Years," 1979.

9. SP, COS to Kerr, 10 Dec. 1953; COS to Davis, 10 Feb. 1953; COS to Sproul, 12 Jan. 1951; Davis to COS, 7 May 1951.

10. COS to Hess, 1 Nov. 1955.

11. SP, COS to Bowman, 21 May 1944. Bowman entirely understood Sauer's reasons and had anticipated that he would never leave California. SP, Bowman to COS, 27 May 1944.

12. SP, Ackerman to COS, 14 Aug. 1945; Ackerman, "Geographic Training," 1945; SP, COS to Ackerman, 5 Feb. 1946.

13. SP, Hartshorne to COS, June 1946.

14. COS, "Foreword to Historical Geography," 1941, 4.

15. In "Morphology of Landscape," 1925, 33, Sauer had actually written "sterile pursuit of the pure genetic method," criticizing geomorphologists' simplistic age-stages, which neglected history. However, the phrase did cause endless confusion among those who, like Hartshorne, read it carelessly.

16. SP, Hartshorne to COS, 18 June 1946. Whittlesey, "Horizon of Geography," 1945. See also Hartshorne, "Notes toward a Bibliobiography," 1979, 65, 67.

17. SP, COS to Hartshorne, 22 June 1946.

18. SP, Hartshorne to COS, 29 June 1946. Hartshorne did make some major alterations to his section entitled "The Relation of History and Geography" in the 1949 edition of *The Nature of Geography*, 175–88. Also see Hartshorne, "On the Mores of Methodological Discussion in American Geography," 1948, a strange, abstruse addition, unintelligible unless seen in the light of the foregoing correspondence, parts of which are included but not acknowledged as such. Hartshorne's *Perspective on the Nature of Geography*, 1959, 81–107, subsequently reversed his views on the time element in geography, influenced by Andrew Clark, a Wisconsin historical geographer and Sauer Ph.D.

19. SP, COS to L. Wilson, 6 Apr. 1946.

20. SP, L. Wilson to COS, 15 Apr. 1948; COS to L. Wilson, 6 June 1948; and L. S. Wilson, "Geographical Training," 1948, in which Sauer's work was highlighted (see 575–79, 581–82).

21. SP, COS to L. Wilson, 6 June 1948.

22. SP, Spencer to COS, 20 Sept. 1943; COS to Spencer, 24 Sept. 1943.

23. SP, Kinvig to COS, 24 Feb. 1953; COS to Kinvig, 19 Mar. 1953; Spencer to COS, 20 Sept. 1943.

24. For other critics of Sauer, see Stoddart, "Carl Sauer," 1997; Symanski, "Coconuts," 2002; and Mathewson, "Carl Sauer and His Critics," 2009.

25. COS, *Man in Nature*, 1939, 5.

26. Lovell, "First Book in Geography," 2003, 332.

27. SP, COS to F. Morris, 9 Jan. 1939.

28. SP, COS to L. Wilson, 6 June 1948.

29. SP, COS to Willits, 11 May 1944.

30. SP, COS to Willits, 18 June 1943. See also SP, COS to James, 3 June 1944; COS to Shryock, 17 Oct. 1944.

31. SP, COS to J. R. Smith, 12 Sept. 1942; COS to Coulter, 18 Mar. 1946; COS to Guthrie, 22 July 1946; COS to Lowell, 18 Feb. 1948; COS to Spencer, 4 Nov. 1950.

32. SP, COS to T. Nichols, 25 May 1948; COS to Kollmorgen, 15 Nov. 1948.

33. SP, Spencer to COS, 20 Sept. 1943; J. R. Smith to COS, 22 Jan. 1949; W. Jones to COS, 28 Sept. 1946.

34. SP, W. Jones to Whittlesey, 9 Feb. 1941 (Harvard University Mss. HUG 4877.410).

35. Of the next generation of geographers, Sauer named only Vernor Finch at Wisconsin, O. E. Baker at Maryland, "and myself." In the younger group there were Richard Russell, Leighly, Warren Thornthwaite, Fred Kniffen, Jan Broek, and Horace Byers (five of the six were from Berkeley); Ralph Brown at Minnesota; John Orchard, Hartshorne, Lester Klimm, and Glenn Trewartha, all at Wisconsin; and Clarence

Jones at Clark. Of the youngest group, there were his own students, of course, and "there must be others, but the pickings are pretty poor." SP, COS to Willits, 15 Jan. 1944.

36. SP, COS to J. K. Wright, 4 Apr. 1948.

37. Diary, 1 Mar. 1908.

10. *"Born in Another Age"*

1. SP, COS to Willits, 18 June 1943.

2. Redfield, *Tepoztlán*, 1930; Redfield and Villa Rojas, *Chan Kom*, 1934.

3. SP, COS to Willits, 16 June 1944.

4. SP, COS to Willits, 11 May 1944.

5. SP, COS to E. B. Wilson, 17 Oct., 4 Nov. 1944.

6. SP, COS to Willits, Sept. 1945. MW does not give a source for the manifesto.

7. COS, "Folkways of Social Science," 1952, 109.

8. SP, COS to Willits, 18 Dec. 1947.

9. SP, COS to Willits, 26 Feb. 1948.

10. SP, Willits to COS, 17 Nov. 1948.

11. SP, COS to Willits, 20 Nov. 1948.

12. SP, COS to Willits, n.d.; COS to Moe, 17 Nov. 1942. See chap. 7.

13. SP, COS to Willits, 24 Feb. 1948.

14. SP, COS to Warren, 28 Sept. 1943; COS to [Percy] Bidwell, 9 Dec 1952.

15. SP, COS to R. Russell, 20 Oct. 1948; Huxley, *Brave New World*, 1932.

16. SP, COS to Harper, 8 Oct. 1945.

17. SP, COS to Bronk, 28 Apr. 1952.

18. SP, COS to Willits, 20 Jan. 1950.

19. Matsen, "Professor William S. Schaper," 1988; SP, COS to W. Andersen, 4 Jan. 1951.

20. COS, "Folkways of Social Science," 1952, 109.

21. COS to R. Russell, 20 Oct. 1948.

22. SP, COS to Shryock, 21 Jan., 25 Feb., 15 Apr. 1952.

23. SP, COS to Shryock, 16 May 1952.

24. W. P. Webb, "Great Plains," 1930; also see Webb, *Great Plains*, 1931. SP, Webb to COS, 22 Apr. 1952.

25. SP, COS to Webb, 8 May 1952.

26. SP, L. White to COS, 28 Oct. 1954; White, *Frontiers of Knowledge*, 1956.

27. SP, COS to L. White, 16 Nov. 1954.

28. SP, COS to Moe, 20 Oct. 1953.

29. Parsons, "'Mr. Sauer' and the Writers," 1996.

30. See Duberman, *Black Mountain*, 1972.

31. Davidson, *San Francisco Renaissance*, 1980.

32. Callahan, "Correspondences," 1979, 137; Callahan, "Bob Callahan on Turtle Island," 1978.

33. SP, Olson to COS, 20 Oct. 1949. Several Olson-COS letters are published in Callahan, "Correspondences," 1979.

34. SP, Olson to COS, 25 Oct. 1950.

35. Callahan, "Correspondences," 1979, 137.

36. SP, COS to Olson, 17 Nov. 1949; Olson to COS, 14 June 1960, 20 May 1954; COS to Olson, 26 July 1954.

37. SP, Olson to COS, 14 June 1960; McClish (COS's secretary) to Olson, 24 Aug. 1960.

38. SP, COS to Fejos, 14 Mar. 1955.

39. The German phrase is from a hymn by Hiller, "Ich will streben nach dem Leben," 1767.

40. SP, COS to Fejos, 8 Dec. 1958.

41. SP, COS to F. Osborn, 24 Oct. 1958.

42. On curiosity, see Gade, "Anima Curiositas," 2011; SP, J. McKae to COS, ca. 1954.

11. "Man's Role in Changing the Face of the Earth"

Some of this chapter is revised from Williams's "Sauer and Man's Role," 1987, and "Carl Sauer and the Legacy," 2003. The Man's Role correspondence is in SP, Box 5.

1. SP, COS to A. Lee, 3 Dec. 1953.

2. SP, Thomas to COS, 1 Oct., 5 Oct. 1953; COS to Thomas, 14 Oct. 1953.

3. SP, COS to Willits, 25 June 1954.

4. SP, COS to Thomas, 14 Oct. 1953; Thomas to COS, 21 Oct. 1953; COS to Thomas, 27 Oct., 5 Nov. 1953.

5. SP, COS to Thomas, 6 Nov. 1953, 12 Jan. 1954.

6. SP, COS to Thomas, 17 and 23 Nov. 1953.

7. SP, A. Clark to Thomas, 15 Feb. 1954.

8. SP, E. Anderson to Thomas, 5 Mar. 1954.

9. SP, COS to Mumford, 13 Jan. 1954; Mumford to Thomas, Feb. 1954; COS to Thomas, 16 Mar. 1954.

10. SP, COS to Thomas, 5 Feb. 1954.

11. SP, COS to Thomas, 5 and 25 Feb. 1954.

12. SP, COS to Thomas, 25 Feb. 1954; COS to Mumford, 2 Mar. 1954. Seidenberg and Darwin came; Huxley did not.

13. COS to Thomas, 16 Mar. 1954; COS, "Foreword to Historical Geography," 1941, 9.

14. SP, COS to Mumford, 8 Apr. 1954; COS to Thomas, 26 and 27 May 1954.

15. Thomas, "Introductory," 1956, xxiii.

16. R. M. Wilson, "Retrospective Review of Man's Role," 2005, 564.

17. SP, COS to F. Knight, 1 Oct., 18 Nov., 2 Dec. 1954.

18. COS, *Agricultural Origins*, 1952, 104; COS, "Agency of Man," 1956, 55, 49, 66, 68. Wordsworth, "World Is Too Much," [1807] 1973.

19. *American Scientist*, review of *Man's Role*, 1957; Green, review of *Man's Role*, 1957.

20. COS, "Agency of Man," 1956, 66; Sears, *Deserts on the March*, 1935; Jacks and Whyte, *Rape of the Earth*, 1939; Lord, *To Hold This Soil*, 1938; Osborn, *Our Plundered Planet*, 1948; Vogt, *Road to Survival*, 1948; Hanson, *New Worlds Emerging*, 1949, x–xi. The Osborn and Vogt books were recommended reading for Sauer's students.

21. Carson, *Silent Spring*, 1962; Marsh, *Man and Nature*, 1864; Williams, "Conservation and Environmental Concern," 2011, 589. Also see F. Graham, *Since Silent Spring*, 1970.

22. Sauer, "Agency of Man," 1956, 49.

23. Thomas, "Introductory," 1956, xxii.

24. Gutkind, "Our World from the Air," 1956, 27; Glacken, "Changing Ideas," 1956, 85–88; Thornthwaite, "Modification of Rural Microclimates," 1956, 582; E. H. Graham, "Re-creative Power of Plant Communities," 1956, 690; Curtis, "Modification," 1956, 734–35; Klimm, "Man's Ports and Channels," 1956, 539; M. Graham, "Harvests of the Seas," 1956, 501–2; Bugher, "Effects of Fission Material," 1956, 847.

25. COS, "Agency of Man," 1956, 55, 56, 58; Darling, "Man's Ecological Dominance," 1956, 779; Iago Galdston and Frank Egler in Thomas, "Symposium Discussion: Process," 1956, 941. See Lowenthal, "Awareness of Human Impacts," 1990, 124–26.

26. The expression "the population bomb" was first used in 1954; Ehrlich, *Population Bomb*, 1968, front note. W. S. Thompson, "Spiral of Population," 1956, 979–80; Malin, in Thomas, "Symposium Discussion: Prospect," 1956, 1127.

27. Mumford, "Summary Remarks: Prospect," 1956, 1148–52; Dewey Jackson Short, in *New York Times*, 30 July 1955, 9, quoted in Lowenthal, "Awareness of Human Impacts," 1990, 124–26; Mumford, "Closing Statement," 1966, 723.

28. SP, COS to Thomas, 15 Sept. 1955.

29. Leighly, "Ecology as Metaphor," 1987. "The ecology binge needs historical perspective." SP, COS to Pennington, 28 Sept. 1971.

30. Wolf, review of *Man's Role*, 1957, 1089.

31. Kates, Turner, and Clark, "Great Transformation," 1990, 4.

32. Turner, et al. *Earth as Transformed*, 1990.

12. An Active Retirement, 1957–1975

1. COS to Thomas, 10 Oct. 1956.

2. Emanuel Geibel, "Der Mai ist gekommen," 1841.

3. SP, COS to Thomas, 12 Dec. 1956; COS to Spencer, 18 Jan. 1957.

4. Hooson, "Carl O. Sauer," 1981, 166. Sauer claimed to be "in a state of shock at having been tabbed the doyen [of geographers]. I've even been asked to write my memoirs!" SP, COS to Thomas, 28 Nov. 1956.

5. SP, COS to Fejos, 14 Mar. 1955.

6. SP, COS to Aschmann, 3 Feb. 1958; COS to Spencer, 1 Nov. 1960; COS, *Plant and Animal Exchanges*, 1963.

7. COS, "Now This Matter of Cultural Geography," [1964] 1987.

8. SP, COS to Dunbar, 15 May 1961.

9. COS, "Casual Remarks," 1976, 76.

10. SP, COS to Spencer, 1 Nov. 1960.

11. SP, Fosberg to COS, 19 Dec., 31 Dec. 1956.

12. COS, "Man in the Ecology," 1958, 106, 110.

13. Denevan, "Rewriting," 2012.

14. SP, Jackson to COS, 4 June 1956; COS to Jackson, 17 Aug. 1956. Sauer had seen Sellards's "Oldest Traces of Early Man," 1956. SP, Sellards to COS, 31 Jan. 1957.

15. COS, "Time and Place," 1956, 8, 13.

16. COS, "Letter," *Landscape*, 1960.

17. COS, "Sedentary and Mobile Bents," 1961, 266.

18. COS, "Seashore—Primitive Home of Man?," 1962, 47.

19. COS, "Concerning Primeval Habitat," 1964, 524.

20. COS, "Human Ecology," 1968.

21. COS, "Man's Dominance," 1975. However, pollen data indicate that some grasslands date to prehuman times.

22. MW pays much more attention to Sauer's late articles than to his final four books. This probably reflects his illness and urgency to complete the manuscript. DL and WMD have added additional information on these books and their reception.

23. COS, *Early Spanish Main*, 1966, 194, 195.

24. Denevan and Mathewson, *Carl Sauer*, 2009, 55–56.

25. Madariaga, "Passionate History," 1967; Rosenblat, "Population of Hispaniola," 1976, 61; Solnick, review of *Early Spanish Main*, 1969.

26. McGann, review of *Early Spanish Main*, 1968.

27. COS to W. B. Fairchild, editor of *Geographical Review*, 15 Apr. 1968.

28. Parry, "Discoverers or Desperados?," 1966, 25; Pagden, foreword to *Early Spanish Main*, 1992, cover, x; Austin, review of *Early Spanish Main*, 1992; Starrs, "Looking for Columbus," 1992, 370, 373.

29. COS, *Northern Mists*, 1968, 1.

30. Nansen, *In Northern Mists*, 1911.

31. Evans, review of *Northern Mists*, 1969, 298.

32. Madland, "Real 'Sleeper,'" 2006; Ingstad and Ingstad, *Viking Discovery*, 2000.

33. De Vorsey, review of *Sixteenth Century*, 1973, 412.

34. SP, COS to Dunbar, mid-Sept. 1971; COS to Hart, 19 Nov. 1973.

35. Callahan, *Selected Essays*, 1981, see introduction, xv.

36. COS, *Seventeenth Century*, 1980, 245–49, 253.

37. Meinig, review of *Seventeenth Century*, 1981, 433, 434.

38. COS, "Education of a Geographer," 1956, 298–99; Leighly, introduction to *Land and Life*, 1963, 4.

39. COS, "Background of Geography," 1967.

40. Ratzel, *Städte- und Culturbilder*, 1876; Ratzel, *Vereinigten Staaten*, 1878–80; COS, "Formative Years of Ratzel," 1971, 253.

41. COS, "Fourth Dimension of Geography," 1974, 191, 192; SP, COS to Hart, 19 Nov. 1973. See also Williams, "Relations of Environmental History," 1994 ("however, in that review I did not realize the true significance of Sauer's contribution to the debate").

42. SP, COS to F. Osborn, 25 Oct., 10 Nov. 1958.

43. SP, Reifsnider to COS, 12 Nov. 1958; COS to Reifsnider, 21 Nov. 1958; COS to F. Osborn, 10 Nov., 3 Dec. 1958. Deeded by Bertha Reifsnider, this is now the 1,400-acre Frank, Emma Elizabeth, and Edna Reifsnider State Forest.

44. COS, "Homestead and Community," 1962, 7. A different, fuller version, with the same title, appeared in 1963. See Hewes, "Carl Sauer," 1983, 144.

45. COS, "Status and Change," 1963, 365.

46. Hooson, "Carl O. Sauer," 1981, 165.

47. SP, J. Parsons to Fretter, 25 Jan. 1963; COS to Kelly, 1970; reminiscences of Winifred Hess, pers. comm. to MW, n.d..

48. COS to Gilbert, 28 July 1970. On Sauer's television watching, Elizabeth Fitz-Simmons and Laura FitzSimmons, pers. comm. to MW; and SP, COS to Wilder, n.d. For the Bohemian Club, see SP, Sproul to Entwistle, 22 Sept. 1964.

49. SP, Ballas to COS, 14 Dec. 1972.

50. SP, COS to Vermeer, 2 May 1972.

51. Leighly, "Carl Ortwin Sauer," 1976, 344.

52. Laura FitzSimmons to MW, pers. comm., n.d.

53. Gade, "Thoughts on Bibliographic Citations," 2009, 31.

54. *New York Times*, "Carl O. Sauer Dies," 1975; Leighly, introduction to *Land and Life*, 1963, 7.

[BIBLIOGRAPHY]

Ackerman, Edward A. 1945. "Geographic Training, Wartime Research, and Immediate Professional Objectives." *Annals of the Association of American Geographers* 35:121–43.

Acosta, José de. [1590] 2002. *Natural and Moral History of the Indies*. Durham: Duke Univ. Press.

Adams, Jonathan M., G. R. Foote, and M. Otte. 2001. "Could Pre-Glacial Maximum Humans Have Existed in North America Undetected? An Interregional Approach to the Question." *Current Anthropology* 42:563–66.

American Scientist. 1957. Review of *Man's Role in Changing the Face of the Earth*, edited by William L. Thomas Jr. 45:50A.

Anderson, Edgar. 1945. *Plants, Man, and Life*. Berkeley: Univ. of California Press.

———. 1968. "What We Do Not Know about Zea Mays." *Transactions of the Kansas Academy of Science* 71:373–78.

Austin, Daniel F. 1992. Review of *The Early Spanish Main*, by Carl O. Sauer. *Bulletin of the Torrey Botanical Club* 119:343.

Beals, Ralph. 1968. "Kroeber, Alfred L." In *International Encyclopedia of the Social Sciences*, edited by David L. Sills, 8:454–63. New York: Macmillan.

Berman, Mildred. 1988. "Distinctly Professional: The Development of Geography at Salem State College." In *Geography in New England*, edited by John E. Harmon and Timothy J. Rickard, 30–39. New Britain, CT: New England/St. Lawrence Valley Geographical Society.

Bethke, Robert D. 1983. "Paul Bunyan." In *The Encyclopedia of American Forest and Conservation History*, edited by Richard C. Davis, 1:51–53. New York: Macmillan.

Bever, Michael R. 2006. "Too Little, Too Late? The Radiocarbon Chronology of Alaska and the Peopling of the New World." *American Antiquity* 71:596–620.

Black, John D., and L. C. Gray. 1925. *Land Settlement and Colonization in the Great Lakes States*. USDA Bulletin No. 1295. Washington, DC: Government Printing Office.

Broek, Jan O. M. 1932. *The Santa Clara Valley, California: A Study in Landscape Change*. Utrecht, Netherlands: Osthoek.

Bruman, Henry J. 1987. "Carl Sauer in Midcareer: A Personal View by One of His Students." In *Carl O. Sauer: A Tribute*, edited by Martin S. Kenzer, 125–36. Corvallis: Oregon State Univ. Press.

Brunhes, Jean. 1913. "The Specific Characteristics and Complex Character of the Subject Matter of Human Geography." *Scottish Geographical Magazine* 29:304–22, 558–74.

———. [1910] 1920. *Human Geography*. New York: Rand McNally.

Bryan, Kirk. 1925. *The Papago Country, Arizona*. United States Geological Survey, Water Supply Paper 499. Washington, DC: Government Printing Office.

———. 1940. "The Retreat of Slopes." *Annals of the Association of American Geographers* 30:254–67.

Bryan, Kirk, and Gladys G. Wickson. 1931. "The W. Penck Method of Analysis in Southern California." *Zeitschrift für Geomorphologie* 6:287–91.

Bugher, John C. 1956. "Effects of Fission Material on the Air, Soil, and Living Species." In *Man's Role in Changing the Face of the Earth*, edited by William L. Thomas Jr., 831–48. Chicago: Univ. of Chicago Press.

Bush, Vannevar. 1945. *Science: The Endless Frontier*. Washington, DC: Government Printing Office.

Bushong, Allen D. 1984. "Ellen Churchill Semple, 1863–1932." *Geographers Biobibliographical Series* 8:87–94. London: Mansell.

Callahan, Bob. 1978. "Bob Callahan on Turtle Island: An Interview with Michael Helm." *City Miner* 3 (3): 24–26, 33–39.

———. 1979. "The Correspondences: Charles Olson and Carl Sauer." *New World Journal* 1 (4): 136–68.

Campanella, Thomas J. 2003. *Republic of Shade: New England and the American Elm*. New Haven: Yale Univ. Press.

Carrière, Joseph M. 1937. *Tales from the French Folk-lore of Missouri*. Northwestern Univ. Studies in the Humanities, no. 1. Evanston.

Carson, Rachel. 1962. *Silent Spring*. Boston: Houghton Mifflin.

Cather, Willa S. 1918. *My Antonia*. Boston: Houghton Mifflin.

Chamberlin, Thomas C. 1909. "Soil Wastage." In *Proceedings of a Conference of Governors in the White House, Washington, D.C., May 13–15, 1908*, edited by W J McGee, 75–83. Washington, DC: Government Printing Office.

Chamberlin, Thomas C., and Rollin D. Salisbury. 1885. *The Driftless Area of the Upper Mississippi*. Sixth Annual Report of the United States Geological Survey. Washington, DC: Government Printing Office.

———. 1904–6. *Geology*. 3 vols. New York: Henry Holt.

Chase, Stuart. 1936. *Rich Land, Poor Land*. New York: Whittlesey House.

Chaucer, Geoffrey. [ca. 1380] 1957. "The Parliament of Fowls." In *The Works of Geoffrey Chaucer*, edited by F. N. Robinson, 310–18. 2nd ed. Boston: Houghton Mifflin.

Clout, Hugh. 2010. "Professor Michael Williams 1935–2009." *Geographical Journal* 176:111–14.

———. 2011. "Michael Williams, 1935–2009." *Memoirs of Fellows, X: Proceedings of the British Academy* 172:354–75.

Clüver, Philipp. 1616. *Germania antiqua*. Leiden.

———. 1624. *Italia antiqua*. Leiden.

Colby, Charles C. 1933. "Ellen Churchill Semple." *Annals of the Association of American Geographers* 23:229–40.

Constance, Lincoln. 1978. "Berkeley and the Latin American Connection." The Twentieth Bernard Moses Memorial Lecture. Berkeley: Regents of the Univ. of California.

———. [1986] 2011. "With Carl Sauer in Baja California." In *Lincoln Constance, Versatile Berkeley Botanist*, interview by Ann Lage, 88–91. Calisphere, Univ. of California Digital Library, Berkeley.

Conzen, Kathleen Neils. 1985. "German-Americans and the Invention of Ethnicity." In *America and the Germans: An Assessment of a Three-Hundred-Year History*, edited by Frank Trommler and Joseph McVeigh, 1:131–47. Philadelphia: Univ. of Pennsylvania Press.

Cook, Sherburne F., and Woodrow Borah. 1971–79. *Essays in Population History*. 3 vols. Berkeley: Univ. of California Press.

Costanza, Robert. 1991. *Ecological Economics: The Science and Management of Sustainability*. New York: Columbia Univ. Press.

Cozzens, Arthur B. 1943. "Conservation in German Settlements of the Missouri Ozarks." *Geographical Review* 33:286–98.

Curtis, John T. 1956. "The Modification of Mid-Latitude Grasslands and Forests by Man." In *Man's Role in Changing the Face of the Earth*, edited by William L. Thomas Jr., 721–36. Chicago: Univ. of Chicago Press.

Darling, F. Fraser. 1956. "Man's Ecological Dominance through Domesticated Animals on Wild Lands." In *Man's Role in Changing the Face of the Earth*, edited by William L. Thomas Jr., 778–87. Chicago: Univ. of Chicago Press.

Darwin, Charles Galton. 1952. *The Next Million Years*. London: Hart-Davis.

Davidson, Michael. 1980. *The San Francisco Renaissance: Poetics and Community at Mid-Century*. Cambridge: Cambridge Univ. Press.

Davis, William Morris. [1909] 1954. *Geographical Essays*. Edited by Douglas W. Johnson. New York: Dover.

Denevan, William M., ed. [1976] 1992. *The Native Population of the Americas in 1492*. 2nd ed. Madison: Univ. of Wisconsin Press.

———. 1996. "Carl Sauer and Native American Population Size." *Geographical Review* 86:385–97.

———. 2012. "Rewriting the Late Pre-European History of Amazonia." *Journal of Latin American Geography* 11:9–24.

Denevan, William M., and Kent Mathewson, eds. 2009. *Carl Sauer on Culture and Landscape: Readings and Commentaries*. Baton Rouge: Louisiana State Univ. Press.

De Vorsey, Louis, Jr. 1973. Review of *Sixteenth Century North America*, by Carl O. Sauer. *Geographical Review* 63:412–13.

Dobyns, Henry F. 1966. "Estimating Aboriginal American Population: An Appraisal of Techniques with a New Hemispheric Estimate." *Current Anthropology* 7:395–449.

Doolittle, William E. 2000. *Cultivated Landscapes of Native North America*. Oxford: Oxford Univ. Press.

Dryer, Charles R. 1926. Review of "The Morphology of Landscape," by Carl O. Sauer. *Geographical Review* 16:348–50.

Duberman, Martin B. 1972. *Black Mountain: An Exploration in Community*. Evanston: Northwestern Univ. Press.

Duden, Gottfried. [1829] 1980. *Report on a Journey to the Western States of North America*, translated by Wayne M. Senner. Columbia: Univ. of Missouri Press.

Dunbar, Gary S. 1981. "Geography in the University of California (Berkeley and Los Angeles), 1868–1941." Marina del Rey, CA: DeVorss.

Ehrlich, Paul R. 1968. *The Population Bomb*. New York: Ballantine.

Eisenstein, Julian. 2002. *Walks in Warrenton*. With the assistance of Roxie Schroeder. Warrenton, MO: Warren County Historical Society.

Evans, E. Estyn. 1969. Review of *Northern Mists*, by Carl O. Sauer. *Geographical Review* 59:297–98.

Faulkner, William. 1951. *Requiem for a Nun*. New York: Random House.

Fiedel, Stuart J. 2000. "The Peopling of the New World: Present Evidence, New Theories, and Future Directions." *Journal of Archaeological Research* 8:39–103.

Fine, Gary Alan. 1994. "The Social Construction of Style: Thorstein Veblen's 'The Theory of the Leisure Class' as Constructed Text." *Sociological Quarterly* 35:457–72.

Fischer, Ernst. 1915. "Der Mensch als geologischer Faktor." *Zeitschrift der Deutschen Geologischen Gesellschaft* 67:106–48.

Fish, Suzanne K., Paul R. Fish, and M. Elisa Vallalpando, eds. 2007. *Trincheras: Sites in Time, Space, and Society*. Tucson: Univ. of Arizona Press.

Fisher, Donald. 1993. *Fundamental Development of the Social Science Research Council*. Ann Arbor: Univ. of Michigan Press.

Fitzpatrick, Ellen. 2002. *History's Memory: Writing America's Past, 1880–1980*. Cambridge, MA: Harvard Univ. Press.

Flannery, Tim. 2003. "Who Came First?" *New York Review of Books* 12 June, 51–53.

Fox, Cyril. 1932. *The Personality of Britain: Its Influence on Inhabitants and Invaders*. London: Royal Anthropological Institute.

Friedrich, Ernst. 1904. "Wesen und geographische Verbreitung der 'Raubwirtschaft.'" *Petermanns Mitteilungen* 50:68–79, 92–95.

Früh, Johann Jacob. 1930. *Geographie der Schweiz*. Saint Gallen, Switz.: Fehr.

Gade, Daniel W. 1999. "Carl Sauer and the Andean Nexus in New World Crop Diversity." In *Nature and Culture in the Andes*, 184–213. Madison: Univ. of Wisconsin Press.

———. 2009. "Thoughts on Bibliographic Citations to and by Carl Sauer." In *Carl Sauer on Culture and Landscape: Readings and Commentaries*, edited by William M. Denevan and Kent Mathewson, 29–52. Baton Rouge: Louisiana State Univ. Press.

———. 2011. "*Anima Curiositas*: Carl Sauer." In *Curiosity, Inquiry and the Geographical Imagination*, 97–114. New York: Peter Lang.

Gale, Fay. 1989. "Award. Griffith Taylor Medalist. Ann Marshall." *Australian Geographical Studies* 27:247–50.

Gannett, Henry. 1908. *Report of the National Conservation Commission*. Washington, DC: Government Printing Office.

Garland, Hamlin. 1917. *A Son of the Middle Border*. New York: Macmillan.

———. 1921. *A Daughter of the Middle Border*. New York: Macmillan.

Gerlach, Russell L. 1976. "Population Origins in Rural Missouri." *Missouri Historical Review* 71:1–21.

Glacken, Clarence J. 1956. "Changing Ideas of the Habitable World." In *Man's Role in Changing the Face of the Earth*, edited by William L. Thomas Jr., 70–92. Chicago: Univ. of Chicago Press.

———. 1967. *Traces on the Rhodian Shore: Nature and Culture in Western Thought from Ancient Times to the End of the Eighteenth Century*. Berkeley: Univ. of California Press.

Goode, John Paul. 1923–. *Goode's School [World] Atlas*. Skokie, IL: Rand McNally.

Goodrich, Carter, et al. 1936. *Migration and Economic Opportunity: The Report of the Study of Population Redistribution*. Philadelphia: Univ. of Pennsylvania Press.

Gradmann, Robert. 1931. *Süddeutschland*. Stuttgart: Engelhorn.

Graham, Edward H. 1956. "The Re-creative Power of Plant Communities." In *Man's Role in Changing the Face of the Earth*, edited by William L. Thomas Jr., 677–91. Chicago: Univ. of Chicago Press.

Graham, Frank, Jr. 1970. *Since Silent Spring*. Boston: Houghton Mifflin.

Graham, Michael. 1956. "Harvests of the Seas." In *Man's Role in Changing the Face of the Earth*, edited by William L. Thomas Jr., 487–503. Chicago: Univ. of Chicago Press.

Green, F. H. W. 1957. Review of *Man's Role in Changing the Face of the Earth*, edited by William L. Thomas Jr. *Geographical Review* 123:111–12.

Gugliotta, Guy. 2013. "The First Americans." *Smithsonian Magazine*, February, 36–47.

Gutkind, E. A. 1956. "Our World from the Air: Conflict and Adaptation." In *Man's Role in Changing the Face of the Earth*, edited by William L. Thomas Jr., 1–44. Chicago: Univ. of Chicago Press.

Hanson, Earl Parker. 1949. *New Worlds Emerging*. New York: Duell, Sloan and Pearce.

Harris, David R. 2002. "The Farther Reaches of Human Time: Retrospect on Carl Sauer as Prehistorian." *Geographical Review* 92:526–44.

Hartman, William A. 1933. *State Land-Settlement Problems and Policies in the United States*. USDA Technical Bulletin No. 357. Washington, DC: Government Printing Office.

Hartman, William A., and John B. Black. 1931. *Economic Aspects of Land Settlement in the Cut-Over Region of the Great Lakes States*. USDA Circular, 160. Washington, DC: Government Printing Office.

Hartshorne, Richard. 1939. *The Nature of Geography: A Critical Survey of Current Thought in the Light of the Past*. 3rd rev. ed., 1949. Lancaster, PA: Association of American Geographers.

——. 1948. "On the Mores of Methodological Discussion in American Geography." *Annals of the Association of American Geographers* 38:113–25.

——. 1959. *Perspective on the Nature of Geography*. Chicago: Rand McNally.

——. 1979. "Notes toward a Bibliobiography of the Nature of Geography." *Annals of the Association of American Geographers* 69:63–76.

Haselmayer, Louis A. 1964. "German Colleges in the West." *Methodist History*, ser. 2 (3): 33–43.

Hays, Samuel P. 1959. *Conservation and the Gospel of Efficiency: The Progressive Conservation Movement, 1890–1920*. Cambridge, MA: Harvard Univ. Press.

Helms, Douglas. 2000. "Soil and Southern History." *Agricultural History* 74:723–58.

Henige, David. 1998. *Numbers from Nowhere: The American Indian Contact Population Debate*. Norman: Univ. of Oklahoma Press.

Hewes, Leslie. 1983. "Carl Sauer: A Personal View." *Journal of Geography* 82:140–47.

Hooson, David. 1981. "Carl O. Sauer." In *The Origins of Academic Geography in the United States*, edited by Brian Blouet, 165–74. Hamden, CT: Archon.

Humboldt, Alexander von. 1811–14. *Political Essay on the Kingdom of New Spain*, translated by John Black. 4 vols. London.

Huntington, Ellsworth. 1921. "Memoir of Sumner Webster Cushing." *Annals of the Association of American Geographers* 11:109–11.

Huxley, Aldous. 1932. *Brave New World*. London: Harper Collins.

Ingstad, Helge, and Anne Stine Ingstad. 2000. *The Viking Discovery of America: The Excavation of a Norse Settlement in L'Anse aux Meadows, Newfoundland*. St. Johns, NF: Breakwater Books.

Ireland, Hubert A., Charles F. S. Sharpe, and Dolan H. Eargle. 1939. *Principles of Gully Erosion in the Piedmont of South Carolina*. USDA Technical Bulletin No. 633. Washington, DC: Government Printing Office.

Iyer, Sundeep, and Keesha Gaskins. 2012. *Redistricting and Congressional Control: A First Look*. New York: Brennan Center for Justice, NYU School of Law.

Jacks, G. V., and R. O. Whyte. 1939. *The Rape of the Earth: A World Survey of Soil Erosion*. London: Faber and Faber.

James, Preston E. 1983. "The University of Michigan Field Station at Mill Springs,

Kentucky, and Field Studies in American Geography." In *The Evolution of Geographic Thought in America*, edited by Wilford A. Bladen and Pradyumna P. Karan, 59–85. Dubuque, IA: Kendall/Hunt.

James, Preston E., and Cotton Mather. 1977. "The Role of Periodic Field Conferences in the Development of Geographical Ideas in the United States." *Geographical Review* 67:446–61.

Jennings, Bruce H. 1988. *Foundations of International Agricultural Research: Science and Politics in Mexican Agriculture*. Boulder, CO: Westview Press.

Johannessen, Carl L. 2003. "Early Maize in India? A Case for Multiple-Working Hypotheses." In *Culture, Land, and Legacy: Perspectives on Carl O. Sauer and Berkeley School Geography*, edited by Kent Mathewson and Martin S. Kenzer, 19–53. Baton Rouge: Louisiana State Univ. Geoscience Publications.

Johnson, Hildegard Binder. 1951. "The Location of German Immigrants in the Middle West." *Annals of the Association of American Geographers* 41:1–41.

Jordan, John M. 1994. *Machine-Age Ideology: Social Engineering and American Liberalism, 1911–1939*. Chapel Hill: Univ. of North Carolina Press.

Jorgensen, Elizabeth Watkins, and Henry Irvin Jorgensen. 1999. *Thorstein Veblen: Victorian Firebrand*. London: M. E. Sharpe.

Kamphoefner, Walter D. 1987. *The Westfalians: From Germany to Missouri*. Princeton: Princeton Univ. Press.

Karan, Pradyumna P. 1983. "Regional Studies in Kentucky and American Geography." In *The Evolution of Geographic Thought in America: A Kentucky Root*, edited by Wilford A. Bladen and Pradyumna P. Karan, 87–111. Dubuque, IA: Kendall/Hunt.

Kates, Robert W., B. L. Turner II, and William C. Clark. 1990. "The Great Transformation." In *The Earth as Transformed by Human Action*, edited by B. L. Turner II et al., 1–17. Cambridge: Cambridge Univ. Press.

Keen, Benjamin. 1985. "Recent Writing on the Spanish Conquest." *Latin American Research Review* 20:161–71.

Kelly, Isabel T. 1938. *Excavations at Chametla, Sinaloa*. Ibero-Americana, 14. Berkeley: Univ. of California Press.

Kenzer, Martin S. 1985. "Carl O. Sauer: Nascent Human Geographer at Northwestern." *California Geographer* 25:1–11.

———. 1985. "The Central Wesleyan College Archives at Northeast Missouri State University: A Very Special Collection." *Special Collections* (Northeast Missouri State Univ.) 2 (4): 13–20.

———. 1985. "Milieu and the 'Intellectual Landscape': Carl O. Sauer's Undergraduate Heritage." *Annals of the Association of American Geographers* 75:258–70.

———. 1986. "Carl Sauer and the Carl Ortwin Sauer Papers." *History of Geography Newsletter* 5:1–9.

———. 1987. "Like Father, Like Son: William Albert and Carl Ortwin Sauer." In

Carl O. Sauer: A Tribute, edited by Martin S. Kenzer, 40–65. Corvallis: Oregon State Univ. Press.

———, ed. 1987. *Carl O. Sauer: A Tribute.* Corvallis: Oregon State Univ. Press.

Ketchell, Aaron K. 2007. *Holy Hills of the Ozarks: Religion and Tourism in Branson, Missouri.* Baltimore: Johns Hopkins Univ. Press.

Kleinman, Kim. 1999. "Edgar Anderson: Interdisciplinary Authority on What Was Not Known about Corn." *Endeavour* 23:114–17.

———. 1999. "His Own Synthesis: Corn, Edgar Anderson, and Evolutionary Theory in the 1940s." *Journal of Historical Biology* 32:293–320.

Klimm, Lester E. 1956. "Man's Ports and Channels." In *Man's Role in Changing the Face of the Earth*, edited by William L. Thomas Jr., 522–41. Chicago: Univ. of Chicago Press.

Koelsch, W. A. 2012. "The Legendary 'Rediscovery' of George Perkins Marsh." *Geographical Review* 102:510–24.

Kramer, Fritz L. 1967. "Eduard Hahn and the End of the 'Three Stages of Man.'" *Geographical Review* 57:73–89.

Kroeber, Alfred L. 1934. "Native American Population." *American Anthropologist* 36:1–25.

———. 1934. *Uto-Aztecan Languages of Mexico.* Ibero-Americana, 8. Berkeley: Univ. of California Press.

———. [1939] 1963. *Cultural and Natural Areas of Native North America.* Berkeley: Univ. of California Press.

Kroeber, Theodora. 1970. *Alfred Kroeber: A Personal Configuration.* Berkeley: Univ. of California Press.

Las Casas, Bartolomé de. [1527–64] 1961. *Historia de Las Indias*, vol. 2, Biblioteca de Autores Españoles, vol. 96. Madrid: Ediciones Atlas.

Lee, Hermione. 2005. *Body Parts: Essays in Life Writing.* London: Chatto and Windus.

Leighly, John, ed. 1963. *Land and Life: A Selection from the Writings of Carl Ortwin Sauer.* Berkeley: Univ. of California Press.

———. 1976. "Carl Ortwin Sauer, 1889–1975." *Annals of the Association of American Geography* 66:337–48.

———. 1978. "Scholar and Colleague: Homage to Carl Sauer." *Yearbook of the Association of Pacific Coast Geographers* 40:117–33.

———. 1979. "Drifting into Geography in the Twenties." *Annals of the Association of American Geographers* 69:4–9.

———. [1976] 1987. "Ecology as Metaphor: Carl Sauer and Human Ecology." *Professional Geographer* 39:405–12.

Libby, Willard F., E. C. Anderson, and J. R. Arnold. 1949. "Age Determination by Radiocarbon Content: World-Wide Assay of Natural Radiocarbon." *Science* 109 (2827): 227–28.

Lord, Russell. 1938. *To Hold This Soil*. USDA Miscellaneous Publication No. 331. Washington, DC: Government Printing Office.

Lovejoy, Parrish Storrs. 1919. "Farms v. Forests." Lecture to the Botanical Section of the Michigan Academy of Science. Sauer Papers, Carton 3. Berkeley: Bancroft Library.

Lovell, W. George. 2003. "'A First Book in Geography': Carl Sauer and the Creation of *Man in Nature*." In *Culture, Land, and Legacy: Perspectives on Carl O. Sauer and Berkeley School Geography*, edited by Kent Mathewson and Martin S. Kenzer, 323–38. Baton Rouge: Louisiana State Univ. Geoscience Publications.

Lowenthal, David. 1990. "Awareness of Human Impacts: Changing Attitudes and Emphases." In *The Earth as Transformed by Human Action: Global and Regional Changes in the Biosphere over the Past 300 Years*, edited by B. L. Turner II et al., 121–35. Cambridge: Cambridge Univ. Press.

———. 2000. *George Perkins Marsh: Prophet of Conservation*. Seattle: Univ. of Washington Press.

———. 2013. "Marsh and Sauer: Reexamining the Rediscovery." *Geographical Review* 103:409–14.

Lowie, Robert H. 1959. *Robert H. Lowie, Ethnologist: A Personal Record*. Berkeley: Univ. of California Press.

Lucas, C. P. 1914. "Man as a Geographical Agency." *Geographical Journal* 44:479–92.

Luebke, Frederick C. 1974. *Bonds of Loyalty: German Americans and World War I*. Dekalb: Northern Illinois Univ. Press.

Lyell, Charles. 1849. *A Second Visit to the United States of North America*. Vol. 2. London: John Murray.

Macpherson, Anne. 1987. "Preparing for the National Stage: Carl Sauer's First Ten Years at Berkeley." In *Carl O. Sauer: A Tribute*, edited by Martin S. Kenzer, 69–89. Corvallis: Oregon State Univ. Press.

Madariaga, Salvador de. 1967. "Passionate History." Review of *The Early Spanish Main*, by Carl Ortwin Sauer. *New York Review of Books*, 1 Dec.

Madland, Lee G. 2006. "A Real 'Sleeper' on Early Norse and Irish Atlantic Ventures." *Amazon Review*, 17 July.

Mangelsdorf, Paul G., and Robert G. Reeves. 1939. *The Origin of Indian Corn and Its Relatives*. Texas Agricultural Station Bulletin, no. 574. College Station: Agricultural and Mechanical College of Texas.

Marsh, George Perkins. 1864. *Man and Nature: Or Physical Geography as Modified by Human Action*. New York: Scribner.

Martin, Geoffrey J. 1973. *Ellsworth Huntington: His Life and Thought*. Hamden, CT: Shoe String Press.

———. 1980. *The Life and Thought of Isaiah Bowman*. Hamden, CT: Shoe String Press.

———. 1984. "John Paul Goode, 1862–1932." *Geographers Biobibliographical Studies* 8:51–5. London: Mansell.

———. 1994. "Richard Hartshorne, 1899–1992." *Annals of the Association of American Geographers* 84:480–92.

———. 2003. "From the Cycle of Erosion to 'The Morphology of Landscape': Or Some Thought Concerning Geography As It Was in the Early Years of Carl Sauer." In *Culture, Land, and Legacy: Perspectives on Carl O. Sauer and Berkeley School Geography*, edited by Kent Mathewson and Martin S. Kenzer, 19–53. Baton Rouge: Louisiana State Univ. Geoscience Publications.

Martin, Paul S. 2005. *Twilight of the Mammoths: Ice Age Extinctions and Rewilding of America*. Berkeley: Univ. of California Press.

Martis, Kenneth C. 2008. "The Original Gerrymander." *Political Geography* 27:833–39.

Mathewson, Kent. 1987. "Sauer South by Southwest: Antimodernism and the Austral Impulse." In *Carl O. Sauer: A Tribute*, edited by Martin S. Kenzer, 90–111. Corvallis: Oregon State Univ. Press.

———. 2009. "Carl Sauer and His Critics." In *Carl Sauer on Culture and Landscape: Readings and Commentaries*, edited by William M. Denevan and Kent Mathewson, 9–28. Baton Rouge: Louisiana State Univ. Press.

Mathewson, Kent, and Martin S. Kenzer, eds. 2003. *Culture, Land, and Legacy: Perspectives on Carl O. Sauer and Berkeley School Geography*. Baton Rouge: Louisiana State Univ. Geoscience Publications.

Matsen, William E. 1988. "Professor William S. Schaper: War Hysteria and the Price of Academic Freedom." *Minnesota History* 51 (4): 130–37.

McClelland, Charles E. 1980. *State, Society, and University in Germany, 1700–1914*. Cambridge: Cambridge Univ. Press.

McGann, Thomas F. 1968. Review of *The Early Spanish Main*, by Carl O. Sauer. *Geographical Review* 58:316–17.

McGee, W J, ed. 1909. *Proceedings of a Conference of Governors in the White House, Washington, D.C., May 13–15, 1908*. Washington, DC: Government Printing Office.

Meigs, Peveril. 1938. "Vegetation on Shellmounds, Lower California." *Science* 88:346.

Meinig, Donald W. 1981. Review of *Seventeenth Century North America*, by Carl O. Sauer. *Journal of Historical Geography* 7:432–34.

Meitzen, August. 1895. *Siedelung und Agrarwesen der Westgermanen und Ostgermanen, der Kelten, Römer, Finnen und Slawen*. 3 vols. and atlas. Berlin: Hertz.

Meyer, Jean. 1976. *The Cristero Rebellion: The Mexican People between Church and State, 1926–1929*. Cambridge: Cambridge Univ. Press.

Mikesell, Marvin W. 1987. "Sauer and 'Sauerology': A Student's Perspective." In *Carl O. Sauer: A Tribute*, edited by Martin S. Kenzer, 144–50. Corvallis: Oregon State Univ. Press.

Miller, E. Joan Wilson. 1968. "The Ozark Culture Region as Revealed by Traditional Materials." *Annals of the Association of American Geographers* 58:51–77.

Morrill, Richard L. 1973. "Ideal and Reality in Reapportionment." *Annals of the Association of American Geographers* 63:463–77.

———. 1999. "Electoral Geography and Gerrymandering: Space and Politics." In *Reordering the World: Geopolitical Perspectives on the Twenty-First Century*, edited by George J. Demko and William B. Wood, 117–38. Boulder, CO: Westview Press.

Morris, F. Grave. 1937. "Environment and Regional Development in the Colonial Period." *Social Forces* 16:12–23.

———. 1937. "Soil Erosion in South-Eastern United States." *Geographical Journal* 90:363–70.

Mumford, Lewis. 1956. "Summary Remarks: Prospect." In *Man's Role in Changing the Face of the Earth*, edited by William L. Thomas Jr., 1141–52. Chicago: Univ. of Chicago Press.

———. 1966. "Closing Statement." In *Future Environments of North America: Transformation of a Continent*, edited by F. Fraser Darling and John P. Milton, 718–29. Garden City, NY: Natural History Press.

Murphy, Robert F. 1972. *Robert H. Lowie*. New York: Columbia Univ. Press.

Nabhan, Gary Paul. 2009. *Where Our Food Comes From: Retracing Nikolay Vavilov's Quest to End Famine*. Washington, DC: Island Press.

Namier, Lewis B. 1944. *1848: The Revolution of the Intellectuals*. London: Oxford Univ. Press.

Nansen, Fridtjof. 1911. *In Northern Mists: Arctic Exploration in Early Times*, translated by Arthur G. Chater. New York: F. A. Stokes.

New York Times. 1975. "Dr. Carl O. Sauer Dies: Dean of Geographers, 85." 21 July.

Osborn, Fairfield. 1948. *Our Plundered Planet*. New York: Grosset and Dunlap.

Pagden, Anthony. 1992. Foreword to *The Early Spanish Main*, by Carl Ortwin Sauer, 4th printing, vii–x. Berkeley: Univ. of California Press.

Parfit, Michael. 2000. "The Dawn of Humans: Hunt for the First Americans." *National Geographic*, December, 40–67.

Parry, J. H. 1966. "Discoverers or Desperados?" Review of *The Early Spanish Main*, by Carl O. Sauer. *Saturday Review*, 2 July, 24–25.

Parsons, James J. 1976. "Carl Ortwin Sauer, 1889–1975." *Geographical Review* 66:83–89.

———. 1979. "The Later Sauer Years." *Annals of the Association of American Geographers* 69:9–17.

———. 1996. "Carl Sauer's Vision of an Institute for Latin American Studies." *Geographical Review* 86:377–84.

———. 1996. "'Mr. Sauer' and the Writers." *Geographical Review* 86:22–41.

Parsons, James J., and Natalia Vonnegut, eds. 1983. *60 Years of Berkeley Geography, 1923–1983.* Berkeley: Department of Geography, Univ. of California.

Pattison, William D. 1981. "Rollin Salisbury and the Establishment of Geography at the University of Chicago." In *The Origins of Academic Geography in the United States,* edited by Brian W. Blouet, 151–63. Hamden, CT: Shoe String Press.

Peake, Harold J. E., and H. J. Fleure. 1927–56. *The Corridors of Time.* 10 vols. Oxford: Clarendon Press.

Peattie, Roderick, and Eugene Van Cleef. 1932. Review of *Geographie der Schweiz,* by Jacob Früh. *Geographical Review* 22:175–76.

Penck, Walther. 1924. *Die morphologische Analyse: Ein Kapitel der physikalischen Geologie.* Geographische Abhandlungen 2 (2). Stuttgart: J. Engelhorns Nachf.

Penn, Mischa, and Fred Lukermann. 2003. "Chorology and Landscape: An Internalist Reading of 'The Morphology of Landscape.'" In *Culture, Land, and Legacy: Perspectives on Carl O. Sauer and Berkeley School Geography,* edited by Kent Mathewson and Martin S. Kenzer, 233–59. Baton Rouge: Louisiana State Univ. Geoscience Publications.

Pfeifer, Gottfried. 1975. "Carl Ortwin Sauer, 24.12.1889–18.7.1975." *Geographische Zeitschrift* 63:161–69.

Pringle, Heather. 2011. "The 1st Americans." *Scientific American,* November, 36–45.

———. 2011. "Texas Site Confirms Pre-Clovis Settlement of the Americas." *Science* 331:1512.

Ratzel, Friedrich. 1876. *Städte- und Culturbilder aus Nordamerika.* Leipzig: Brockhaus.

———. 1878–80. *Die Vereinigten Staaten von Nord-Amerika.* Munich: Oldenbourg.

———. 1882, 1891. *Anthropogeographie.* 2 vols. Stuttgart: J. Engelhorn.

Rayburn, Otto Ernest. 1941. *Ozark Country.* New York: Duell, Sloan and Pearce.

Reclus, Élisée. 1868. *La Terre: Description des phénomènes de la vie du globe.* 2 vols. Paris: Hachette.

Redfield, Robert. 1930. *Tepoztlán: A Mexican Village.* Chicago: Univ. of Chicago Press.

Redfield, Robert, and Alfonso Villa Rojas. 1934. *Chan Kom: A Maya Village.* Carnegie Institution of Washington Publication, no. 448. Washington, DC: Carnegie Institution.

Rivet, Paul, G. Stresser-Péan, and C. Loukotka. 1924. "Langues américaines." In *Les langues du monde,* edited by A. Meillet and M. Cohen, 16:597–712. Paris: Société de Linguistique de Paris.

Rodgers, Marion Elizabeth. 2005. *Mencken, the American Iconoclast: The Life and Times of the Bad Boy of Baltimore.* New York: Oxford Univ. Press.

Roscher, Wilhelm [Georg Friedrich]. [1854] 2009. *Principles of Political Economy.* Redford, VA: Wilder.

Rosenblat, Ángel. 1976. "The Population of Hispaniola at the Time of Columbus." In

The Native Population of the Americas in 1492, edited by William M. Denevan, 43–66. Madison: Univ. of Wisconsin Press.

Rowe, John Howland. 1962. "Alfred Louis Kroeber, 1876–1960." *American Antiquity* 27:395–412.

Salisbury, Rollin D. 1907. *Physiography*. New York: Henry Holt.

Sapper, Karl. 1924. "Die Zahl und die Volksdichte der indianischen Bevölkerung in Amerika vor der Conquista und in der Gegenwart." *Proceedings of the 21st International Congress of Americanists* 1:95–104. Leiden: E. J. Brill.

Sargent, Charles S. 1884. *Report on the Forests of North America (Exclusive of Mexico). Tenth Census of the United States (1880)*, vol. 9. Washington, DC: Government Printing Office.

Sauer, Carl O. 1907–8. Unpublished Diary. In the possession of Elizabeth Sauer FitzSimmons.

———. 1911. *Educational Opportunities in Chicago*. Chicago: Council for Library and Museum Extension.

———. 1915. "The Geography of the Ozark Highland of Missouri." Ph.D. dissertation, Univ. of Chicago.

———. 1916. *Geography of the Upper Illinois Valley and History of Development*. Illinois State Geological Survey, Bulletin No. 27.

———. 1916. "Man's Influence upon the Earth." *Geographical Review* 1:462.

———. 1917. "Proposal of an Agricultural Survey on a Geographic Basis." *Michigan Academy of Science, 19th Annual Report*, 79–86.

———. 1918. "Geography and the Gerrymander." *American Political Science Review* 12:403–26.

———. 1918. "A Soil Classification for Michigan." *Michigan Academy of Science, 20th Annual Report*, 83–91.

———. 1919. "Mapping the Utilization of the Land." *Geographical Review* 8:47–54.

———. 1920. *The Geography of the Ozark Highland of Missouri*. Geographic Society of Chicago, Bulletin No. 7.

———. 1921. "The Problem of Land Classification." *Annals of the Association of American Geographers* 11:3–16.

———. 1922. "Notes on the Geographic Significance of Soils: A Neglected Side of Geography." *Journal of Geography* 21:187–90.

———. 1924. "The Survey Method in Geography and Its Objectives." *Annals of the Association of American Geographers* 14:17–33.

———. 1925. "The Morphology of Landscape." *Univ. of California Publications in Geography* 2 (2): 19–53. Berkeley.

———. 1927. *Geography of the Pennyroyal*. Kentucky Geological Survey, ser. 6, vol. 25.

———. 1927. "Recent Developments in Cultural Geography." In *Recent Developments in the Social Sciences*, edited by Edward C. Hayes, 154–212. Philadelphia: Lippincott.

———. 1929. "Land Forms in the Peninsular Range of California as Developed about Warner's Hot Springs and Mesa Grande." *Univ. of California Publications in Geography* 3 (4): 199–290. Berkeley.

———. 1929. "Memorial of Ruliff S. Holway." *Annals of the Association of American Geographers* 19:64–65.

———. 1930. "Basin and Range Forms in the Chiricahua Area." *Univ. of California Publications in Geography* 3 (6): 339–414. Berkeley.

———. 1930. "Thirty-two Ancient Sites on Mexican West Coast." *El Palacio* 29:335–36.

———. 1931. "Geography: Cultural." *Encyclopaedia of the Social Sciences,* 6:621–24. New York: Macmillan.

———. 1932. Correspondence [on physical geography in regional works], *Geographical Review* 22:527–28.

———. 1932. "Land Forms in the Peninsula Range." *Zeitschrift für Geomorphologie* 7:246–48.

———. 1932. *The Road to Cíbola.* Ibero-Americana, 3. Berkeley: Univ. of California Press.

———. 1934. *The Distribution of Aboriginal Tribes and Languages in Northwestern Mexico.* Ibero-Americana, 5. Berkeley: Univ. of California Press.

———. 1934. "Ellen Churchill Semple (1863–1932)." *Encyclopaedia of the Social Sciences,* 13:661–62. New York: Macmillan.

———. 1934. "Preliminary Report to the Land-Use Committee on Land Resource and Land Use in Relation to Public Policy." In *Report of the Science Advisory Board, July 31, 1933 to September 1, 1934,* 165–260. Washington, DC.

———. 1935. *Aboriginal Population of Northwestern Mexico.* Ibero-Americana, 10. Berkeley: Univ. of California Press.

———. 1935. "Spanish Expeditions into the Arizona Apacheria." *Arizona Historical Review* 6:3–13.

———. 1936. "American Agricultural Origins: A Consideration of Nature and Culture." In *Essays in Anthropology Presented to A. L. Kroeber in Celebration of His Sixtieth Birthday, June 11, 1936,* 278–97. Berkeley: Univ. of California Press.

———. 1936. *Handbook for Geomorphologists: The Inauguration of Geomorphological Research in the Southwest.* Washington, DC: Division of Climatic and Physiographic Research, Soil Conservation Service, Department of Agriculture.

———. 1937. "The Discovery of New Mexico Reconsidered." *New Mexico Historical Review* 12:270–87.

———. 1937. "The Prospect for Redistribution of Population." In *Limits of Land Settlement: A Report on Present-Day Possibilities,* edited by Isaiah Bowman, 7–24. New York: Council on Foreign Relations.

———. 1938. "Destructive Exploitation in Modern Colonial Expansion." In *Comptes*

Rendus du Congrès International de Géographie, Amsterdam, 1938, 2:494–99. Leiden: E. J. Brill.

———. 1938. "Theme of Plant and Animal Destruction in Economic History." Journal of Farm Economics 20:765–75.

———. 1939. Man in Nature: America before the Days of the White Man: A First Book in Geography. New York: Scribner's.

———. 1941. "The Credibility of the Fray Marcos Account." New Mexico Historical Review 16:233–43.

———. 1941. "Foreword to Historical Geography." Annals of the Association of American Geographers 31:1–24.

———. 1941. "The Personality of Mexico." Geographical Review 31:353–64.

———. 1944. "A Geographic Sketch of Early Man in America." Geographical Review 34:529–73.

———. 1945. "The Relation of Man to Nature in the Southwest." Huntington Library Quarterly 8 (2): 116–25; discussion 125–49.

———. 1947. "Early Relations of Man to Plants." Geographical Review 37:1–25.

———. 1948. Colima of New Spain in the 16th Century. Ibero-Americana, 29. Berkeley: Univ. of California Press.

———. 1948. "Environment and Culture during the Last Deglaciation." Proceedings of the American Philosophical Society, 92:65–77.

———. 1950. "Cultivated Plants of South and Central America." In Handbook of South American Indians, edited by Julian H. Steward, 6:487–543. Bureau of American Ethnology, Bulletin 143. Washington, DC: Smithsonian Institution.

———. 1950. "Geography of South America." In Handbook of South American Indians, edited by Julian H. Steward, 6:319–44. Bureau of American Ethnology, Bulletin 143. Washington, DC: Smithsonian Institution.

———. 1950. "Grassland Climax, Fire, and Man." Journal of Range Management 3:16–21.

———. 1952. Agricultural Origins and Dispersals. Bowman Memorial Lectures, series 2. New York: American Geographical Society.

———. 1952. "Folkways of Social Science." In The Social Sciences at Mid-Century: Papers Delivered at the Dedication of Ford Hall, April 19–21, 1951, 100–109. Minneapolis: Univ. of Minnesota Press.

———. 1956. "The Agency of Man on the Earth." In Man's Role in Changing the Face of the Earth, edited by William L. Thomas Jr., 49–69. Chicago: Univ. of Chicago Press.

———. 1956. "The Education of a Geographer." Annals of the Association of American Geographers 46:287–99.

———. 1956. "Time and Place in Ancient America." Landscape 6 (2): 8–13.

———. 1957. "The End of the Ice Age and Its Witnesses." *Geographical Review* 47:29–43.

———. 1958. "Man in the Ecology of Tropical America." *Proceedings of the Ninth Pacific Science Congress,* 20:104–10.

———. 1959. "Age and Area of American Cultivated Plants." *Actas del XXXIII Congreso Internacional de Americanistas, San José, Costa Rica, 1958,* 1:215–29.

———. 1959. "Middle America as Culture Historical Location." *Actas del XXXIII Congreso Internacional de Americanistas, San José, Costa Rica, 1958,* 1:115–22.

———. 1960. Letter [on past and present American culture]. *Landscape* 10 (1): 6.

———. 1961. "Sedentary and Mobile Bents in Early Societies." In *Social Life of Early Man,* edited by Sherwood L. Washburn, 258–66. Viking Fund Publications in Anthropology, no. 31. Chicago: Aldine.

———. 1962. "Homestead and Community on the Middle Border" (abridged). *Landscape* 12 (1): 3–7.

———. 1962. "Maize into Europe." *Akten des 34. Internationalen Amerikanistenkongresses: Wien, 18–25 Juli 1960,* 777–88. Horn: F. Berger.

———. 1962. "Seashore—Primitive Home of Man?" *Proceedings of the American Philosophical Society* 106:41–47. Philadelphia.

———. 1963. "Homestead and Community on the Middle Border." In *Land Use Policy in the United States,* edited by Howard W. Ottoson, 65–85. Lincoln: Univ. of Nebraska Press.

———. 1963. *Plant and Animal Exchanges between the Old and the New Worlds: Notes from a [1961] Seminar Presented by Carl Ortwin Sauer,* edited by Robert M. Newcomb. Los Angeles: Los Angeles State College. (Mostly notes on Sauer's comments, only partially verbatim; includes remarks by Newcomb and others.)

———. 1963. "Status and Change in the Rural Midwest—a Retrospect." *Mitteilungen der oesterreichischen geographischen Gesellschaft* 105:357–65.

———. 1964. "Concerning Primeval Habitat and Habit." In *Festschrift für Ad. E. Jensen,* 513–24. Munich: Klaus Renner Verlag.

———. 1965. "Cultural Factors in Plant Domestication in the New World." *Euphytica* 14:301–6.

———. 1966. *The Early Spanish Main.* Berkeley: Univ. of California Press.

———. 1967. "On the Background of Geography in the United States." *Festschrift für Gottfried Pfeifer, Heidelberger Geographische Arbeiten* 15:59–71.

———. 1968. *Northern Mists.* Berkeley: Univ. of California Press.

———. 1968. "Human Ecology and Population." In *Population Economics,* edited by Paul Deprez, 207–14. Winnipeg: Univ. of Manitoba Press.

———. 1971. "The Formative Years of Ratzel in the United States." *Annals of the Association of American Geographers* 61:245–54.

———. 1971. *Sixteenth Century North America: The Land and the People as Seen by the Europeans.* Berkeley: Univ. of California Press.

———. 1974. "The Fourth Dimension of Geography." *Annals of the Association of American Geographers* 64:189–92.

———. 1975. "Man's Dominance by Use of Fire." In *Grasslands Ecology: A Symposium*, edited by Richard H. Kesel, 1–13. Baton Rouge: Louisiana State Univ. Geoscience Publications.

———. 1976. "Casual Remarks." Offered at the Special Session in Honor of Carl O. Sauer: Fifty Years at Berkeley, Association of Pacific Coast Geographers, 1973, edited by David Hornbeck. *Historical Geography Newsletter* 6 (1): 70–76.

———. 1980. *Seventeenth Century North America*. Berkeley: Turtle Island Foundation.

———. [1940] 1981. "The March of Agriculture across the Western World." In *Selected Essays: 1963–1975: Carl O. Sauer*, edited by Bob Callahan, 45–56. Berkeley: Turtle Island Foundation.

———. 1981. *Selected Essays, 1963–1975*, edited by Bob Callahan. Berkeley: Turtle Island Foundation.

———. [1936] 1984. "Regional Reality in Economy," edited with a commentary by Martin S. Kenzer. *Yearbook of the Association of Pacific Coast Geographers* 46:35–49.

———. [1964] 1987. "'Now This Matter of Cultural Geography': Notes from Carl Sauer's Last Seminar at Berkeley," edited by James J. Parsons. In *Carl O. Sauer: A Tribute*, edited by Martin S. Kenzer, 153–63. Corvallis: Oregon State Univ. Press.

Sauer, Carl O., and Donald Brand. 1930. "Pueblo Sites in Southeastern Arizona." *Univ. of California Publications in Geography* 3 (7): 415–59. Berkeley.

———. 1931. "Prehistoric Settlements of Sonora, with Special Reference to Cerros de Trincheras." *Univ. of California Publications in Geography* 5 (3): 67–148. Berkeley.

———. 1932. *Aztatlán: Prehistoric Mexican Frontier on the Pacific Coast*. Ibero-Americana, 1. Berkeley: Univ. of California Press.

Sauer, Carl O., Gilbert H. Cady, and Henry C. Cowles. 1918. *Starved Rock State Park and Its Environs*. The Geographic Society of Chicago, Bulletin No. 6.

Sauer, Carl O., and Peveril Meigs. 1927. "Lower California Studies. I, Site and Culture at San Fernando de Velicatá." *Univ. of California Publications in Geography* 2 (9): 271–302. Berkeley.

Sawatzky, Harry L. 1971. *They Sought a Country: Mennonite Colonization in Mexico*. Berkeley: Univ. of California Press.

Schmaltz, Norman J. 1975. "P. S. Lovejoy: Michigan's Cantankerous Conservationist." *Journal of Forest History* 18:73–81.

———. 1978. "Michigan's Land Economic Survey." *Agricultural History* 52:232–39.

———. 1979. "Academia Gets Involved in Michigan Forest Conservation." *Michigan Academician* 12:25–46.

Schmieder, Oscar. 1927. "The Pampa: A Natural or Culturally Induced Grassland?" *Univ. of California Publications in Geography* 2 (8): 255–70. Berkeley.

Schowengerdt, Margaret C., ed. 1976. *Historic Sites of Warren County*. Warrenton, MO: Warren County Historical Society.

Sears, Paul B. 1935. *Deserts on the March*. Norman: Univ. of Oklahoma Press.

Sellards, Elias H. 1952. *Early Man in America: A Study in Prehistory*. Austin: Univ. of Texas Press.

———. 1956. "Oldest Traces of Early Man in the Americas." *Science* 124 (3218): 396–97.

Semple, Ellen Churchill. 1901. "The Anglo-Saxons of the Kentucky Mountains." *Geographical Journal* 17:588–623.

———. 1903. *American History and Its Geographic Conditions*. Boston: Houghton Mifflin.

———. 1931. *The Geography of the Mediterranean Region: Its Relation to Ancient History*. New York: Henry Holt.

Shaler, Nathaniel Southgate. 1905. *Man and the Earth*. New York: Duffield.

Sharpe, Charles F. S. 1938. *Landslides and Related Phenomena: A Study of Mass-Movements of Soil and Rock*. New York: Columbia Univ. Press.

Skeels, Anna C. 1993. "A Passage to Premodernity: Carl Sauer Repositioned in the Field." Master's thesis, Univ. of British Columbia.

Smith, J. Russell. 1902. "Geography in Germany. I. The Primary and Secondary Schools." *Journal of Geography* 1:420–57.

Solnick, Bruce B. 1969. Review of *The Early Spanish Main*, by Carl O. Sauer. *Terrae Incognitae* 1:79.

Sparhawk, William Norwood, and Warren David Brush. 1929. *The Economic Aspects of Forest Destruction in Northern Michigan*. USDA Technical Bulletin No. 92. Washington, DC: Government Printing Office.

Spencer, Joseph E. 1975. "Carl Sauer: Memories about a Teacher." *California Geographer* 15:83–86.

Speth, William W. 1981. "Berkeley Geography, 1923–33." In *The Origins of Academic Geography in the United States*, edited by Brian W. Blouet, 221–44. Hamden, CT: Archon Books.

———. 1999. *How It Came to Be: Carl O. Sauer, Franz Boas and the Meanings of Anthropogeography*. Ellensburg, WA: Ephemera Press.

Spinden, Herbert J. 1928. "The Population of Ancient America." *Geographical Review* 18:641–60.

Stanford, Dennis J., and Bruce A. Bradley. 2012. *Across Atlantic Ice: The Origin of America's Clovis Culture*. Berkeley: Univ. of California Press.

Starrs, Paul F. 1992. "Looking for Columbus." *Geographical Review* 82:367–74.

Steer, Henry Bake. 1948. *Lumber Production in the United States, 1799–1946*. USDA Miscellaneous Publication No. 669. Washington, DC: Government Printing Office.

Steward, Julian H. 1949. "The Native Population of South America." In *Handbook of*

South American Indians, edited by Julian H. Steward, 5:655–68. Bureau of American Ethnology Bulletin No. 143. Washington, DC: Government Printing Office.

Stoddart, David R. 1997. "Carl Sauer: Geomorphologist." In *Process and Form in Geomorphology*, edited by David R. Stoddart, 340–79. London: Routledge.

Straus, Lawrence Guy. 2000. "Solutrean Settlement of North America? A Review of Reality." *American Antiquity* 65:219–26.

Symanski, Richard. 2002. "Coconuts on a Lava Flow in the Chiricahua Mountains." In Richard Symanski, *Geography Inside Out*, 103–14. Syracuse: Syracuse Univ. Press.

Taylor, Eva G. R. 1930. *Tudor Geography, 1485–1583*. London: Methuen.

———. 1934. *Late Tudor and Early Stuart Geography, 1583–1650*. London: Methuen.

Taylor, R. E. 1985. "The Beginnings of Radiocarbon Dating in American Antiquity: A Historical Perspective." *American Antiquity* 50:309–25.

Thomas, William L., Jr., ed. 1956. *Man's Role in Changing the Face of the Earth*. Chicago: Univ. of Chicago Press.

———. 1956. "Introductory." In *Man's Role in Changing the Face of the Earth*, edited by William L. Thomas Jr., xxi–xxxviii. Chicago: Univ. of Chicago Press.

———. 1956. "Symposium Discussion: Process." In *Man's Role in Changing the Face of the Earth*, edited by William L. Thomas Jr., 915–58. Chicago: Univ. of Chicago Press.

———. 1956. "Symposium Discussion: Prospect." In *Man's Role in Changing the Face of the Earth*, edited by William L. Thomas Jr., 1069–128. Chicago: Univ. of Chicago Press.

———. 1956. "Symposium Discussion: Retrospect." In *Man's Role in Changing the Face of the Earth*, edited by William L. Thomas Jr., 399–409. Chicago: Univ. of Chicago Press.

Thompson, Harry, and Earl D. Strait. 1914. *Cost and Methods of Clearing Land in the Lake States*. USDA Bulletin No. 91. Washington, DC: Government Printing Office.

Thompson, Warren S. 1956. "The Spiral of Population." In *Man's Role in Changing the Face of the Earth*, edited by William L. Thomas Jr., 970–86. Chicago: Univ. of Chicago Press.

Thornthwaite, C. Warren. 1956. "Modification of Rural Microclimates." In *Man's Role in Changing the Face of the Earth*, edited by William L. Thomas Jr., 567–83. Chicago: Univ. of Chicago Press.

Tolzmann, Don Heinrich. 2000. *The German-American Experience*. Amherst, NY: Humanity Books.

Trimble, Stanley W. 1974. *Man-Induced Soil Erosion on the Southern Piedmont: 1700–1970*. Ankeny, IA: Soil Conservation Society of America.

———. 1985. "Perspectives on the History of Soil Erosion Control in the Eastern United States." *Agricultural History* 59:162–80.

Turner, B. L., II, William C. Clark, Robert W. Kates, John F. Richards, Jessica T. Mathews, and William B. Meyer, eds. 1990. *The Earth as Transformed by Human Action: Global and Regional Changes in the Biosphere over the Past 300 Years.* Cambridge: Cambridge Univ. Press.

Turney, Omar A. 1929. *Prehistoric Irrigation.* Phoenix: Arizona State Historian.

Van Cleef, Eugene. 1931. Review of *Süddeutschland*, by Robert Gradmann. *Geographical Review* 21:691–92.

Van Hise, Charles R. 1910. *The Conservation of Natural Resources in the United States.* New York: Macmillan.

Visher, Stephen S. 1953. "Rollin D. Salisbury and Geography." *Annals of the Association of American Geographers* 43:4–11.

Vogt, William. 1948. *Road to Survival.* New York: Slone.

Vonnegut, Kurt. 1952. *Player Piano.* New York: Scribner's.

Wanklyn, Harriet. 1961. *Friedrich Ratzel: A Biographical Memoir and Bibliography.* Cambridge: Cambridge Univ. Press.

Webb, Walter Prescott. 1930. "The Great Plains and the Industrial Revolution." In *The Trans-Mississippi West: Papers Read at a Conference Held at the University of Colorado, June 18–June 21, 1929*, edited by James F. Willard and Colin B. Goodykoontz, 309–39. Boulder: Univ. of Colorado.

———. 1931. *The Great Plains: A Study in Institutions and Environment.* Boston: Ginn.

———. 1951. *The Great Frontier.* Boston: Houghton Mifflin.

Weidermann, Volker. 2009. *Das Buch der verbrannten Bücher.* Cologne: Kiepenheuer and Witsch.

West, Robert C. 1979. *Carl Sauer's Fieldwork in Latin America.* Ann Arbor, MI: University Microfilms International.

———, ed. 1982. *Andean Reflections: Letters from Carl O. Sauer While on a South American Trip.* Dellplain Latin American Studies, no. 11. Boulder, CO: Westview Press.

Whitaker, J. Russell. 1940. "World View of Destruction and Conservation of Natural Resources." *Annals of the Association of American Geographers* 30:143–62.

White, Lynn T., Jr., ed. 1956. *Frontiers of Knowledge in the Study of Man.* New York: Harper.

Whittlesey, Derwent. 1945. "The Horizon of Geography." *Annals of the Association of American Geographers* 35:1–36.

Williams, Michael. 1970. *The Draining of the Somerset Levels.* Cambridge: Cambridge Univ. Press.

———. 1974. *The Making of the South Australian Landscape.* London: Academic Press.

———. 1983. " 'The Apple of My Eye': Carl Sauer and Historical Geography." *Journal of Historical Geography* 9:1–28.

———. 1987. "Carl Sauer and Man's Role in Changing the Face of the Earth." *Geographical Review* 77:218–31.

———. 1989. *Americans and Their Forests: A Historical Geography.* Cambridge: Cambridge Univ. Press.

———. 1994. "The Relations of Environmental History and Historical Geography." *Journal of Historical Geography* 20:3–21.

———. 2001. "Sauer, Carl Ortwin (1889–1975)." In *International Encyclopedia of the Social & Behavioral Sciences,* edited by Neil J. Smelser and Paul B. Baltes, 5:13490–92. Amsterdam: Elsevier.

———. 2002. "Carl Sauer." In *Encyclopedia of Global Change: Environmental Change and Human Society,* edited by Andrew S. Goudie, 2:351–52. Oxford: Oxford Univ. Press.

———. 2003. "Carl O. Sauer and the Legacy of Man's Role." In *Culture, Land, and Legacy: Perspectives on Carl O. Sauer and Berkeley School Geography,* edited by Kent Mathewson and Martin S. Kenzer, 217–30. Baton Rouge: Louisiana State Univ. Geoscience Publications.

———. 2003. *Deforesting the Earth: From Prehistory to Global Crisis.* Chicago: Univ. of Chicago Press.

———. 2009. Foreword to *Carl Sauer on Culture and Landscape: Readings and Commentaries,* edited by William M. Denevan and Kent Mathewson, xi–xv. Baton Rouge: Louisiana State Univ. Press.

———. 2011. "Conservation and Environmental Concern." In *The SAGE Handbook of Geographical Knowledge,* edited by John A. Agnew and David N. Livingston, 581–95. London: SAGE.

Wilson, Leonard S. 1948. "Geographical Training for the Postwar World: A Proposal." *Geographical Review* 38:575–89.

Wilson, Robert M. 2005. "Retrospective Review of *Man's Role in Changing the Face of the Earth,*" edited by William L. Thomas Jr. *Environmental History* 10:564–66.

Wittke, Carl Frederick. 1936. *German-Americans and the World War.* Ohio Historical Collections, vol. 5. Columbus.

Woeikof, Alexander J. 1901. "De l'influence de l'homme sur la terre." *Annales de Géographie* 10:97–114, 193–215.

Wolf, Eric R. 1957. "General and Theoretical: *Man's Role in Changing the Face of the Earth.*" *American Anthropologist* 59 (6): 1089–91.

Wolff, Theodore H. 1957. "History of Central Wesleyan College." Central Wesleyan College Archive, Truman Univ., Kirksville, MO. (Epilogue by Herbert V. Hake added in 1974.)

Wordsworth, William. [1807] 1973. "The World Is Too Much with Us." In *The Oxford Anthology of English Literature,* edited by Frank Kermode and John Hollander, 2:174–75. New York: Oxford Univ. Press.

Wright, Harold Bell. 1907. *The Shepherd of the Hills.* New York: A. L. Burt Company.

Zelinsky, Wilbur. 1973. "Women in Geography: A Brief Factual Account." *Professional Geographer* 25:151–65.

92–93, 125, 130; women in, 67, 195n51.
See also students
Geography of the Ozark Highland (Sauer),
43, 45–46, 54
"Geography of the Ozark Highland of
Missouri, The" (Ph.D. diss., Sauer),
9, 32–36
Geography of the Pennyroyal (Sauer), 46,
59, 94
Geography of the Upper Illinois Valley
(Sauer), 43, 44, 93–94, 189n32
geology: geography distinguished from,
59; "greatest living teacher" (Salisbury), 21–22; historical processes,
62–63, 143; at Northwestern, 18–19;
Sauer's fieldwork, 19, 25–26, 189n32;
Sauer's view of, 19–20
geomorphology: address, 61; Berkeley
faculty, 62, 130; Sauer's field work
and essays criticized, 62–64; Sauer's
southern Piedmont work, 104–7.
See also Davis, William Morris; "The
Morphology of Landscape"
Georgia: soil erosion, 105
German Americans. See anti-German
and German-American prejudices;
and specific individuals
Germany: intellectual heritage, 9–10,
19, 31, 68, 70, 72; land classification
scheme, 192n36; Nazis, 68–71;
nineteenth-century migrants from,
6–7; retirement travel to, 166; revolution of 1848, 6; Sauer's schooling in
(Calw), 9–10; territorial aggression,
41, 70–71; totalitarianism, 97. See also
World War I; World War II
Gerry, Elbridge, 46
gerrymander, 43, 46–47
Ginsberg, Allen, 151
glaciation, 21, 121, 123, 125–26

Glacken, Clarence J., 162; Traces on the
Rhodian Shore, 131
Goethe, Johann Wolfgang von, 59, 71,
99
Goldthwaite, James Warren, 25
Goode, John Paul, 20, 22–23, 35–36, 137,
193n15
Goode's School Atlas, 23
"Good Neighbors" (U.S. foreign policy),
110
Gradmann, Robert, Süddeutschland, 60
Graham, Edward H., 162
Graham, Michael, 162
Grant, Ulysses Sherman, 19, 27
grasslands and prairies, 106, 122, 167,
171, 173
"Grasslands symposium, 1972," 171, 178
Gratius, Ortwin, 187n11
Graz Institute of Geography, 70
Green Revolution (1960s), 116
Gropius, Walter, 150
Guadalajara (Mexico): archival re-
search, 83–85, 87–89; plant studies,
91, 120–21
Guatemala: maize cultivation, 118
Guggenheim Fellowship: Latin Amer-
ican research interests, 117, 201n35;
Sauer's fellowship, 83, 178; Sauer's on
selection board, 101–2, 107–8, 109,
117, 141, 165, 166, 200n2
Gutkind, Erwin A., 162
Guzmán, Nuño Beltrán de, 87
gypsy moth infestation, 31

Hacker, Walter, 70
Hahn, Eduard, 74, 80, 91, 92, 116, 130
Hamilton, Earl, 90
Hammond, Edwin H., 124
Handbook for Geomorphologists (Sauer),
106

International Geographical Congress, 95

Jacks, Graham V., 161
Jackson, John Brinkerhoff, 169–70
Jenny, Hans, ix, 130
Jesuits, 84, 110, 139, 174, 197n29
Jillson, Willard R., 39
Johns, Jasper, 150
Johns Hopkins University, 70, 132
Johnson, Francis, 103
Joliet, Louis, 174
Jones, Clarence F., 205–6n35
Jones, Stanley, 130
Jones, Wellington D. (Duke): mentioned, 20, 26, 42; Sauer's relationship with, 43, 51, 101, 140–41

Kaiser, Henry J., 158
Kansas: Sauer family property, 34
Kelly, Isabel T.: Guggenheim Fellowship, 108; maize collection study, 117; mentioned, 76, 120, 121; metallurgy evidence, 91; Sauer's collaboration with, 67
Kentucky: geographical diversity, 38–40; gerrymander, 47; soil erosion, 104. See also Mill Springs Field Station
Kentucky Geological Survey, 39
Kenzer, Martin S., 199n33
Kerouac, Jack, 151
Kesseli, John E., 129, 130, 131
Kimble, George H. T., 126, 204n54
Klimm, Lester E., 162, 205–6n35
Kniffen, Fred B., 68, 205–6n35
Knight, Frank H., 159
Knight, M. M., 130
knowledge: frontiers of, 90–100; social science trends and, 142–44. See also curiosity as spur to research

Krebs, Norbert, 192n36
Kriege, Otto E., 30
Kroeber, Alfred Lewis: disputes Sauer's population numbers, 88–89; festschrift, 104; research, 79, 80–81, 83; Sauer's relationship with, 56, 64, 109, 116, 130
Kulturkreis Austrian anthropological school, 79

La Follette, Robert M., Sr., 57
Land Classification Board (Dept. of the Interior), 51
"Land Forms in the Peninsular Range of California" (Sauer), 63, 104
Landscape (journal), 169–70
landscapes. See environmental degradation; human modification of landscapes; "The Morphology of Landscape"
land use and development: changing attitudes toward, 156; cutover (logged) land, 42–43, 47–51, 192n47; public policy development, 102. See also agricultural practices; soils
Lange, Dorothea, 199n31
La Salle, Nicolas de, 174
Lasker, Bruno, 199n38
Latin America: hopes for fieldwork in, 55, 58; interests in agricultural development, 110–11, 118, 119–20, 144–45; proposed institute, 102, 108–12. See also specific countries
Lawson, A. C., 62, 63
Lee, Hermione, xviii
Leighly, John B.: fieldwork, 46, 50–51; mentioned, x, 55, 64, 68, 129, 130–31; on Sauer, 177; Sauer's reliance on, 205–6n35
Leopold, Aldo, 112

soils: conservation efforts, 162; erosion processes and questions, 62–63, 93, 102–7; land classification scheme, 51, 192n36; mapping of, 49; overgrazed, 94–95. *See also* agricultural practices; land use and development

"Soil Wastage" (Chamberlin), 93

Solnick, Bruce B., 172

Sonora (Mexico), 78, 80–81, 86, 116, 123, 196n24

Sotomayor, Antonio, 139

South America: Andean survey for Rockefeller Foundation, 112–13; maize cultivation and study, 116–19

South Carolina: soil erosion, 104–5

Southwest (U.S.): cultural corridor with Aztec Mexico, 80–81, 87, 91; erosion history of, 103; settlement sites and dry lake beds in, 123. *See also specific states*

Spain: catastrophic impact of conquistadors, 78, 83, 85, 87, 88–89; New World expansion, 171–72, 173; retirement travel in, 166

Spencer, Joseph Earle, 65, 76, 137–38, 140, 167

Spengler, Oswald, 108

Spinden, Herbert J., 88

Sproul, Robert Gordon, 112–14, 178

squash (*Cucurbita*), 115–16

Stanford University, Food Research Institute, 70, 92

Star (college newspaper), 14

Starrs, Paul F., 172

Starved Rock State Park (Illinois), 25, 45

Starved Rock State Park (Sauer, Cady, and Cowles), 43, 45, 54, 66

"Status and Change in the Rural Midwest—a Retrospect" (Sauer), 6

Stebbins, George Ledyard, Jr., 117–18

Ste. Genevieve, Missouri, 33, 34

Steward, Julian H., 88, 120

Steward, Walter W., 113

Stewart, George R., 130

Stirton, Reuben A., 124

"St. Scholastic" and "St. Bureaucraticus," 100, 181

Stuart, Gilbert, 47

students: academic appointments for Sauer's graduates, 68; anthropology classes required, 79; fieldwork experience, 38–40, 124; post-WWII influx, 131–32; Sauer's expectations of, ix–x, 135–36, 174, 183–84, 208n20; Sauer's relationship with, ix–x, 65–67, 183–84; text for elementary schools, 138–39

Suhl, Alvena Storm, 67

Swedish Society for Anthropology and Geography, Vega Medal, 166

Syracuse University, 178

Tarr, Ralph S., 137

Taylor, Eva G. R., 74

Taylor, Fred, 159

Taylor, Paul S., 79, 109, 130, 199n31, 201n36

Taylor, T. Griffith, 108

Teilhard de Chardin, Pierre, 158

temporal change: current attention to, 183; in distant past, 169; Sauer's revision of early human timeline, 121–23, 124–26; social science's abandonment of, 142–43. *See also* historical geography

Tennessee: soil erosion, 104

Tennessee Valley Authority (TVA), 40

Thomas, William L., Jr., 154, 155,

Epic life   Life ? Work

Movement
family
time
commitments

→ p 107

search for
cultural
corridor
btwn Mexico
& Sw USA

PAGE 101 (great god)

E 0 sim 106 pim

Shady underbelly

women —

Rivera on 85 (to his mom!)

Michael Williams

Lowenthal

Denevan